Our Towns

North Dakotans tell the story of their communities in words and pictures.

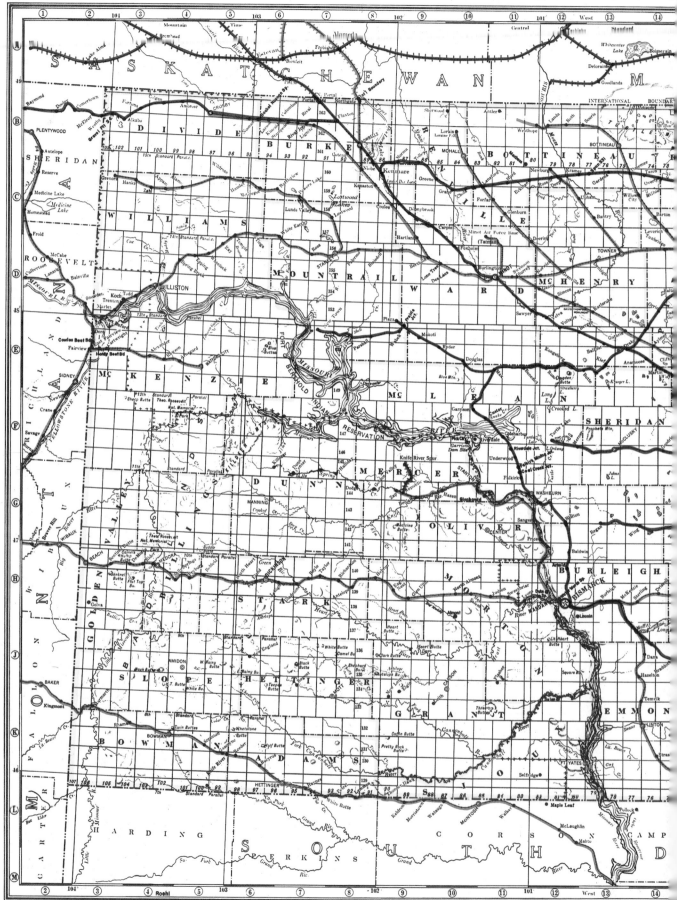

NNIAL RAILROAD MAP

Published by the
**North Dakota
Public Service Commission**
January 1989
Commissioners
Dale V. Sandstrom
Bruce Hagen   Leo M. Reinbold

Burlington Northern RR ....
Soo Line RR ....
Red River Valley & Western RR ...
Canadian National RR ....
Canadian Pacific RR ....
Misc. & Short Line RR ....
Time Zone Boundary

Our Towns

North Dakotans tell the story of their communities in words and pictures.

Five years in the making, *Our Towns* came about after all communities in
the state — past and present — were invited to submit a short history.
The 125 communities featured are here because of the effort of
133 individual North Dakotans, one family, and four groups
interested in the heritage of towns in North Dakota.
The editor and coordinator looked through over 1000 photographs
submitted with the histories and found elsewhere before
selecting the some 400 featured in *Our Towns*.

In the following pages, there are answers to such questions as
When and why was the town founded?
How did the town get its name?
What ethnic groups settled the community?
What are the major milestones in the town's history?
How did major events in the nation's history affect the town?
What makes the town different from others in North Dakota?
What occasions does the town celebrate?

Our Towns tells the story of North Dakota communities from
the perspective of those who lived in and love the
communities they call home.

Our Towns
North Dakota Communities - Our Story

God made the country, and man made the town.
William Cowper, 1785

Warren A. Henke, Ph.D.
General Editor

Rose Marie Henke
Our Town Project Coordinator

Karla K. Whittey
Production & Design

Published & Distributed by
Sweetgrass Communications
PO Box 3221
Bismarck, North Dakota
58502-3221

Our Towns
North Dakota Communities - Our Story

North Dakotans from 125 towns tell the story of their communities in words and photographs they selected.
Made possible in part with a major grant from The North Dakota Humanities Council, Inc.,
an affiliate of the National Endowment for the Humanities.

Photographs submitted by the individual authors listed with the exception of those
acknowledged with the credit SHSND for the State Historical Society of North Dakota
and DPDP for the Dakota Photo Documentary Project.

First Printing 1992

Copyright 1992
by
Sweetgrass Communications

ISBN 0-9632837-1-5

Published & Distributed by
Sweetgrass Communications
PO Box 3221
Bismarck, North Dakota
58502-3221

Contents

Our Towns

Preface

by Everett C. Albers

For better or worse, most people who call a community in North Dakota their hometown live elsewhere. They have left the town, but the town is still part of how they think of themselves. Some of the towns chronicled in the following pages no longer exist; many are much smaller in number of buildings and people who live there than they once were. Yet these too live, in the spirit of people who call these places home.

The history of most of the places described so lovingly by people who know the towns well is short — in time as measured in comparison to most places in the rest of the world. Most were founded about 100 years ago. Not many measure up to the expectation of the founders, who hoped for more people.

Yet the sense of pride in a particular place, the home town, continues. The reader will find many different answers to why the hometown should be fondly remembered in the following pages of history written by townspeople and illustrated with their precious photographs.

As an interested observer of the process of editing contributions by so many different authors with literally hundreds of different styles — authors who were given the opportunity to comment on the changes — I came to appreciate once more the pride North Dakotans have in their heritage. Satisfying the authors was no easy task. Warren and Rose Marie Henke did so — because they share the pride of the authors in their own hometowns.

Our Towns does not pretend to offer an exhaustive history of North Dakota communities. There are 125 towns because people from those places rose to the challenge of writing a short history. It is no hard task to write a fifty-page history. Try telling the story of your town in two pages!

This book is neither a critical history nor a scholarly tome — although historian Warren Henke worked tirelessly for years to check the accuracy of facts and offers an excellent introduction.

Our Towns is an album of snapshots in words and photographs of 125 North Dakota communities taken by people who love these towns. It will be as treasured as the family albums from which many of the photographs came.

First house built in Monango, North Dakota - 1887

Introduction

by Warren A. Henke, Ph.D.

There were few European settlers in what was to become North Dakota when the Civil War ended. In 1870 the population of northern Dakota Territory was only 2,405. During the next several years, however, settlers began to move into the region in ever increasing numbers and in the twelve years from 1878 to 1890 the population increased dramatically, from an estimated 16,000 to 191,000.

There were many reasons why European settlers flooded into what they considered the empty grasslands of what is now North Dakota during two periods of enthusiastic settlement activities. The first period known as the Great Dakota Boom lasted from 1878 to 1886. A second boom which began in 1898 lasted until the coming of World War I and it completed the settlement of the state.[1]

During the latter part of the 19th Century the nation's increasing population caused land values to rise "back east." Land was cheap in Dakota Territory. Moreover, Bonanza farms were established in the Red River Valley of western Minnesota and eastern Dakota in the late 1870s and early 1880s. These huge wheat farms, there were 91 over 3,000 acres and many ranged from 15,000 to 50,000 acres, fixed the country's attention on northern Dakota. Their operators used state-of-the-art farm machinery on treeless, stone-free, level, rich land in the Red River Valley and "proved" that during periods of good rainfall producing hard spring wheat could be profitable. Furthermore, grasshoppers which plagued the farmers in the area, especially in 1872 and 1874, were gone. And large numbers of Norwegian immigrants flocked to America's shores.[2]

Two other factors, however, were primarily responsible for the first boom: improved milling technology made Minneapolis, Minnesota the flour-milling capital of the country and created a huge market for hard spring wheat; and railroad construction made the Red River Valley the chief supplier of that market.[3]

One historian has concluded that it was indeed "the railroads which really opened North Dakota to the outside world, overcame its remoteness, and made it a hinterland of St. Paul and Minneapolis."[4]

The first rail carrier to build within the state was the Northern Pacific which began train service in what is now North Dakota on June 6, 1872 when a steam locomotive rolled westbound across the newly constructed bridge over the Red River between Moorhead, Minnesota and Fargo. It reached Bismarck in June 1873. Other early carriers were the Chicago & Northwestern, the Chicago, Milwaukee & St. Paul, the St. Paul, Minneapolis and Manitoba, and the Minneapolis, St. Paul & Sault Ste Marie.[5]

North Dakota's railroad network expanded significantly from 1878 to the early 1920s. Only 200 miles of track, the Northern Pacific's main line between Fargo and Bismarck, had been laid when the first boom began in 1878.[6] Several months before statehood it was reported that the new state would have 2,006 miles of railroad.[7] From 1898 to 1915 some 250,000 newcomers arrived in the state and during that same period the state's railroad mileage almost doubled, increasing from 2,662 to 5,226.[8] During one three year period alone, 1905-1907, some 945 miles of track were laid, much of it the result of what one geographer calls "North Dakota's Railway War of 1905."[9] The "war" was precipitated when the Soo Line challenged the Great Northern for control of the traffic in northern North Dakota, by invading that region and building its "Wheat Line" from Kenmare to Thief River Falls, Minnesota.[10] The state's rail system peaked at about 5,370 miles of track in the early 1920s. During the late 1920s and the 1930s it shrunk to about 5,300 miles of track and during the next three decades it remained fairly stable at between 5,150 and 5,300 miles of track. During the 1970s and 1980s corporate financial stress and bankruptcy led to track abandonment and by January 1989 there were about 4,320 miles of railroad in North Dakota.[11]

Bird's-eye view of Ryder, North Dakota

In their quest for profits three railroads were primarily responsible for expanding the state's railway network, for luring thousands of immigrants to the state, and for establishing scores of towns throughout what was to become North Dakota.

The Northern Pacific was chartered by Congress in 1864 and given a fifty-million-acre land grant to build a line from Duluth, Minnesota to Puget Sound, Washington. Approximately 10,700,000 acres of its grant were located in what was to become North Dakota, or about 24 percent of the state.[12] In 1970 it merged with the Great Northern and the Chicago, Burlington & Quincy to form the Burlington Northern.

In May 1879 the St. Paul, Minneapolis and Manitoba Railroad (commonly known as the Manitoba) was organized by James J. Hill and his associates. During the 1880s it provided railway transportation for settlers on the Dakota side of the Red River Valley, bridging the river at Grand Forks during the winter of 1880. During the next several years it spread over the valley, building two lines running north and south and two running west. By 1883, the line which became the Manitoba's main line, stretched from Grand Forks to Devils Lake. Six years later Hill and his associates organized the Great Northern Railroad, leasing all the properties of the old St. Paul, Minneapolis and Manitoba. Four years later the Great Northern reached Everett, Washington.[13]

The third railroad which played a major role in developing the state was the Minneapolis, St. Paul and Sault Ste Marie. It was organized in 1888. One of its predecessor lines, the Minneapolis and Pacific had laid almost a hundred miles of track in the southeastern part of the state during 1886-1887.[14] Popularly known as the "Soo Line" it officially adopted its nickname in 1961.

Although the territorial government of Dakota promoted settlement before the Great Dakota Boom by establishing a bureau of immigration in January 1871 and by distributing literature in English, German, and Norwegian for several years, little of the material focused on northern Dakota and its success was extremely limited.[15] It was the railroads which really stimulated the first boom.

In their quest for profit all the lines needed to attract settlers and to increase and to try to control traffic. Furthermore, the Northern Pacific had thousands of acres of land to sell. To accomplish these goals the lines turned to promotion, publicity, advertising, and in many cases to town-building.

For example, the determined effort made by the Northern Pacific during the first boom included various approaches. The land and immigration departments which it set up in 1871 located an agency in London. In one year alone, 1882, over 800 local agents fanned through the British Isles seeking emigrants and in Germany, Switzerland, the Scandinavian countries, and Holland some 124 general agents were seeking prospective emigrants, as many as possible to be organized into colonies. Thousands of pieces of promotional literature were also distributed in the eastern United States and in Europe.

Attractive installment plans to purchase railroad lands were devised and those who were willing to buy land were offered free transportation. Land seekers were also housed temporarily in large reception houses built by the line at various points in Minnesota.[16]

During the second boom the state was also involved in attempting to lure immigrants to the state. Through its agriculture and labor department it sent agents into surrounding states, published the *North Dakota Magazine*, a promotional venture, gave out thousands of folder-type maps of the state, and distributed nearly 400,000 promotional folders and circulars.[17]

The Great Northern used similar techniques during the second boom. Workers, willing to come to the state during harvest time, and while there, look at the country were offered special rates. The railroad also distributed thousands of pieces of promotional literature, and after 1909 brought 64,000 new settlers into North Dakota.[18]

In addition to those kinds of activities

A Symetric Town
Figure 1 (*Benson County Atlas*, Geo. A. Ogle & Co., Chicago, Illinois, 1912, p. 20)

railroads were actively engaged in establishing towns during the two boom periods. Like most of the towns in the northern Great Plains those in North Dakota were established for commercial reasons, to provide goods and services for the surrounding agricultural community. "Plains country towns," according to one geographer, however, "evolved in place, through three phases of regional development: the frontier era of trading posts and military forts, a subsequent phase of inland towns (a regional term referring to settlements not served by a railroad), and a third,

In laying out the streets and blocks of a railroad town planners developed various concepts about street patterns, where the business district should be placed, and where the railroad should be located.

Many towns platted by the Northern Pacific in the northern Great Plains are called symmetric plats *(fig. 1)*. In this arrangement towns were cut in half. Two business streets separated by a 300-foot railway right of way, designed to provide sites for commercial activities needing direct access to the carrier, faced each other. In small towns the two business streets sel-

A third configuration was the "T-shaped" town and its variation the "crossed T." In the former the railroad tracks formed the bar of the T with the Main Street beginning at the tracks *(fig. 2)*. In 1905 the Soo Line modified the "T-shaped" plan when they surveyed the town of Kramer. The "crossed-T" version located the business district several blocks up the cross street from the main intersection *(fig. 3)*. Both the Soo Line and the Great Northern used the design in platting their towns in 1905.[23]

Several towns in North Dakota were laid out in yet another form, around a center square. The concept was promoted mainly by the Soo Line. One of David N. Tallman's many branch banks was located on an 80-foot central green in Antler *(fig. 4)*. Plaza and Ryder were platted around 200-foot-square city parks, with commercial lots facing them on two sides only. And in Kenmare business lots faced its square on three sides. The square was a standard city block in size. Maxbass and Columbus were other Soo Line towns built around central squares[24] *(fig. 5)*.

Early on the Northern Pacific's Land Department managed its townsite efforts. On one occasion it sent its agents into Illinois, Ohio, and Wisconsin to organize settlers into a colonization society and in May 1883 several hundred of them were brought in emigrant cars to a siding where they unloaded their possessions. Glen Ullin sprang up overnight.[25] It also developed several plans to interest local capital in sites platted on its land: it retained an undivided one-half interest in all lots at some sites; at others it simply retained title to half the lots in alternate arrangement with a group that owned the rest; and at others it simply owned land in various blocks.[26] Little effort was made by the carrier to sell its lots and on several occasions it became embroiled in local politics. After a while the carrier decided that its early approach to townsite development resulted in generally unfavorable results and that it produced too much local antagonism. Consequently, it adopted the same strategy

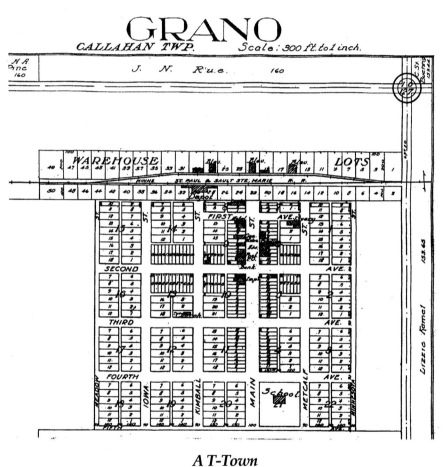

A T-Town

Figure 2 (*Renville County Atlas*, Geo. A. Ogle & Co., Chicago, Illinois, 1914, p. 12)

that of railroad towns, which became the dominant form thereafter."[19]

Railroad town-building strategies varied during the two boom periods. Carriers laid their track where and when they wanted and when they located their stations they established townsites. The site was chosen first, then it was platted, streets and blocks were laid out, and only then were entrepreneurs permitted to locate there.[20]

dom developed evenly and in many cases one street became "the other side of the tracks." The plan was used very rarely after the 1890s.[21]

A more common arrangement used by the railroads was the orthogonal plat where various enterprises were located on both sides of the same street which was at right angles to the track, with the train depot located near the Main Street crossing.[22]

used by the Great Northern and the Soo: an independent company was chosen as townsite agent; it brokered information and it was given the locations of all future stations and charged with platting and selling the townsites. The first company chosen by the Northern Pacific was the McLean County Townsite Company, organized by Charles K. Wing who had business interests in Carrington and J. Austin Regan who was active in the business community in Fessenden. They were successful in promoting such towns as Turtle Lake, Mercer, and Regan.[27]

In the northern part of Dakota Territory the most successful townsite company was the Northwest Land Company, organized in 1883 by Solomon G. Comstock and Almond A. White of Moorhead, Minnesota. The company sold Great Northern townsites during the 1880s. After successfully selling towns in the first few years of its operation it was dissolved in 1886, only to be reorganized a short time later with another stockholder, James J. Hill, who then owned half of the company. The company platted more than two dozen towns for the Great Northern during the 1880s.[28]

In 1905 David N. Tallman, a banker from Willmar, Minnesota organized the Dakota Development Company which eventually was responsible for developing forty-five towns for the same carrier. In one year alone, during the "Wheat Line" war in 1905 with the Soo, the company established twenty-one towns. A little later another of Tallman's companies, the Northern Town & Land Company established six towns and during 1910-1912 when the Great Northern was building the "Surrey cutoff" from Fargo to Minot, Tallman himself, in joint ventures with other risk takers established another thirteen towns.[29]

In 1906 the Great Northern organized the Dakota & Great Northern Townsite Company to manage its townsite endeavors.[30]

Another Minnesota firm, the Minnesota Loan & Trust Company of Minneapolis which was organized in 1883, directed the townsite activities of the Soo Line when it built across

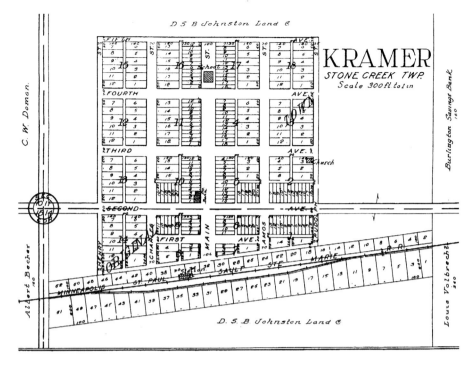

A Crossed T-Town
Figure 3 (*Bottineau County Atlas*, Brock & Co., Chicago, Illinois, 1929, p. 62)

North Dakota in 1893. It was successful in platting and promoting towns like Kenmare, Kramer, Coleharbor, Fessenden, Harvey, and Sawyer. During the railroad war with the Great Northern in 1905 the twenty-five Soo Line townsites on the Thief River Falls-Kenmare Wheat Line were platted by the Minneapolis company. It continued to plat the carrier's North Dakota towns until 1906 when the Soo Line organized the Tri-State Land Company.[31]

Many independent operators were also responsible for establishing numerous towns in the state. For example, W. E. Cooke, a retail lumber merchant, platted two towns, Anamoose and Balfour, on the Soo Line in 1899. He also benefited from his townsite activities by opening lumberyards in each town.[32]

And Frederick H. Stoltze, active in the lumber and coal business in St. Paul became the beneficiary of the Great Northern's decision to resume branch line construction in 1901. Stoltze, who operated coal and lumberyards in a dozen Great Northern towns, agreed to purchase land for the carrier's ten planned stations and to plat the townsites. A shrewd businessman, he took advantage of the

Northern Pacific's failure to select land within its land grant and was able to purchase land outside the original grant area for that carrier's asking price, $10 per acre. Accordingly, the Great Northern towns of Westhope, Glenburn, Lansford, and Mohall developed on land bought from one of its chief competitors, the Northern Pacific.[33]

No one really knew how fast or how large a place would grow. Many townsite agents believed that a site which might become a seat of authority provided excellent opportunities; consequently, they concentrated a great deal of effort on locations that might become county seats. To become a successful town, according to one town promoter, David N. Tallman, the place would include "three to five lumberyards, one or two banks, two to three general stores, one or two hardware stores and farm machinery dealers, plus as many more individual tradespeople as could be attracted—usually a single drugstore, hotel, newspaper, butcher, restaurant, and livery stable."[34] Tallman adjusted the "recipe" based on his estimate of a town's future growth.

The German Evangelical Colonization Association of Chicago, organized in 1884, also had concerns about ensuring the initial success of Hebron, the colony they established the next year. To ensure that the same kinds of trades were not overcrowded during the settlement's first year the leaders of the association asked that those settlers intending to open businesses declare their intentions. For the first year they suggested that the following commercial establishments would be adequate to fulfill the colony's needs: several carpenters, a saddler, a shoemaker, a blacksmith and a wagon maker, one lumberyard and one hardware store, one hotel, and one or two general country stores. The association also warned probable settlers that if they didn't intend to go into farming exclusively there were no other opportunities that would guarantee assured income.[35]

There were opportunities for entrepreneurs in North Dakota and recently platted towns quickly acquired a variety of business and professional enterprises; not in the kind and

quantity, however, as Tallman and the colonization society envisioned. To their list can be added photographers, doctors, veterinarians, maybe a dentist, and a lawyer. Schools and churches were built, newspapers in many cases were published, grain elevators were built and post offices were established.

Besides chains of coal and lumberyards branch banking was commonplace in various parts of North Dakota. Thomas L. Beiseker, an Indiana German who grew up in Minnesota and moved to Sykeston in the early 1890s, opened a bank there in 1893. By 1910 he owned nineteen banks and loan companies in North Dakota, several in Montana and Minnesota, and had a corner on farm loans in Sheridan and Wells counties.[36]

Another branch banker, David N. Tallman, who was also a townsite promoter for the Great Northern, opened forty-two banks in North Dakota and Montana towns along that carrier's lines. As a result of the agri-

cultural depression following World War I, however, his banking empire collapsed and by the mid-1920s his banks were in the hands of receivers.[37] At the end of the Great Dakota Boom in 1890 there were 125 banks operating in the state; 25 had national charters. Thirty years later there were 898. In June 1990 there were 152, of that number 29 were national and 123 were state-chartered.[38] Many towns which had one or two, or perhaps three banks, are without those services today.

One of the most ubiquitous and also one of the most important artifacts which dotted North Dakota's landscape during the settlement period was the grain elevator. It was also the most prominent feature of many a town's skyline, and it was needed if the farmer were going to make a profit. In the 1880s and 1890s farmers spent a day making a round trip to an elevator, if it were no more than eight miles distant. Consequently, in an effort to improve efficiency and increase profits farmers as well as inland town promoters wrote letters and petitioned railroads and the state's railroad commissioners for branch lines, spurs, and sidings. In one year alone, 1893, the number of loading platforms increased from 38 to 147. Farmers who were dissatisfied with prices offered by a local elevator now had an opportunity to sell to a track buyer at a higher price. During the railroad war between the Great Northern and the Soo, 179 elevators were built.[39]

Elevators were unlike most other town commercial enterprises. Although there were independent and cooperatives, many, if not most, of them were "line" elevators owned by outside interests, in many cases by Minneapolis and Duluth firms. The St. Anthony and Dakota Elevator Company of Minneapolis, for example, had 150 country elevators along Great Northern tracks in 1904. And instead of being built on the townsite itself they were located along the tracks. There were 206 elevators and 54 warehouses operating in Dakota Territory in 1884; by 1915 the state had 2,015 elevators, 264 of which were cooperatives. By 1990 that

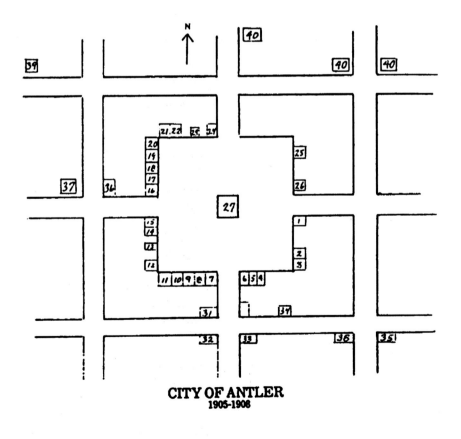

CITY OF ANTLER
1905-1906

A Center Square Town

Figure 4 (*Historical Highlights of Bottineau County*, The Bottineau County Historical Society, 1977, p. 51)

number had shrunk to 575; storage capacity, however, did not decrease.[40]

Towns were also centers for diversion and entertainment. Many towns eventually organized a band and a baseball team and in many places the building which housed the bar, saloon or "blind pig," was among the first to be built, even though prohibition went into effect July 1, 1890 and wouldn't be repealed until 1932. One village, Omemee, now a Bottineau County ghost town, boasted of seven

church auxiliaries provided social and religious fellowship.

Many towns like Donnybrook boasted of a number of secret and fraternal organizations. The American Woodmen of America organized there in 1901; the Ancient Order of United Workmen formed the next year; and the Odd Fellows organized in 1905. Two years later they platted the town's first cemetery and by 1908 they had built a meeting hall. The Royal Neighbors became part of the town's social fabric in 1907 and the American Legion in 1920. Most of the organizations had their women affiliates, also very active in civic affairs.[42]

Of all the diversions and entertainment offered to satisfy their social needs people seemed to prefer such activities as "visiting, dances, parties (house gatherings), card playing, church socials, picnics, and lodge meetings."[43]

No one as yet has counted the exact number of towns that have dotted the plains of North Dakota. One researcher has found 3,200 names of "places which were at some point (at least) intended to represent a place of habitation."[44] By the end of the Great Dakota Boom, 1890, the state could boast of only 50 incorporated towns and villages; ten years later the number stood at 75. In the first decade of the 20th century 137 new ones were incorporated. In one

year alone, the Great Northern and the Soo, during their railroad war of 1905, established 50 towns.

For almost 200 years, since Alexander Henry made a permanent settlement at Pembina in 1801, residents of what is now North Dakota lived in a rural environment. In 1990 the state became officially more urban than rural when the federal census found 53.3 percent of North Dakotans living in urban areas, places with a population of 2,500 or more. Of 364 incorporated cities in the state, there are just 17 such places, only 12 have over 5,000 people, 181 or 49.7 percent have fewer than 200 persons, and 111 have a population under 100.[45] Many of these places, however, have been loosing population for decades and their future is uncertain. The 1990 census revealed that 90 percent of the towns described in this volume lost population during the decade of the 1980s. Belfield lost 32 percent of its people; Zap lost 54 percent. A few small communities, however, did gain population. Burlington, near Minot, saw its population increase from 762 in 1980 to 993 in 1990, a gain of 30 percent. And Hazen, benefiting from energy-producing activities in Mercer County, saw its population increase from 2,365 to 2,879, a gain of over 20 percent.

None of the towns established in North Dakota ever grew into a great metropolis. In fact chambers of commerce herald the day when their city reaches a population of 50,000.

Various scholars have attempted to explain why North Dakota lacks urban centers like Minneapolis, Denver, or Winnipeg, Manitoba. Two think that factors like "the state's location, the nature of its land, the pattern of western settlement, and the presence of Indians"[46] are valid explanations. Furthermore, they suggest that urban development within the Great Plains was discouraged by the growth of cities outside the Great Plains. They also believe that the state's dependency on agricultural production, the marketing of which was controlled by outside forces, was also a contributing factor. Lastly, they say that the state's "unique po-

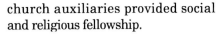
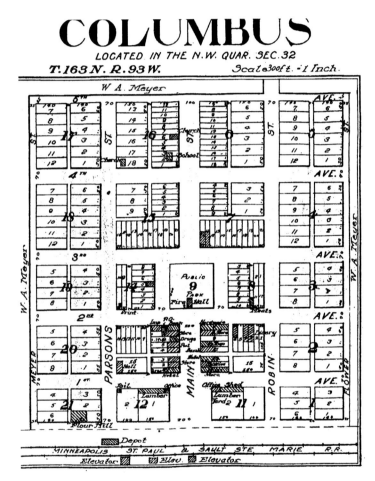

Center Square Town
Figure 5 (*Burke County Atlas*, Geo. A. Ogle & Co., Chicago, Illinois, 1914, p. 2)

"blind pigs" and an equal number of grain elevators in 1905. Baseball games and band concerts along with Fourth of July Celebrations were among town activities which helped Americanize many immigrants. And sponsoring a baseball team was also one way local merchants could "boost" their town.[41] Some towns built theaters, or opera houses, and sponsored chautauqua programs. Literary societies were organized and

litical development after it achieved statehood served to discourage investment and business confidence."[47] The Nonpartisan League, did in fact, establish several state-owned enterprises which are still operating today.

Another scholar concludes that while railroads made country town growth possible they were also effective in limiting their growth and retarding Middle West urbanization. Once rail networks were established trains ran in two directions. It was easy to export wheat from Kenmare and import flour from Minneapolis.[48] One more researcher believes that "the cities took over, almost bodily, the forest man's concepts. Only in isolated instances did urbanization make adjustments which harmonized with grassland-desert regionalism."[49]

The decline of the country town in North Dakota is an excellent example of one of the themes of North Dakota history, what historian Elwyn Robinson calls the Too-Much Mistake, his name for "too many farms, too many miles of railroads and roads, too many towns, banks,

schools, colleges, churches, and governmental institutions, and more people than opportunities—numbers of all that history shows have been far beyond the ability of the state to maintain."[50] Furthermore, the effects of the Too Much Mistake have been intensified by other factors: the coming of the automobile, better roads, the agricultural depression following World War I, the Great Depression, the lure of economic opportunity on the west coast during World War II, school consolidation, farm modernization, and fiscal crises which have plagued the state's agricultural sector for decades.

During the 1990s North Dakotans will be caught up in another of Robinson's themes of North Dakota history, that of Adjustment, his name for "both the painful cutting back of the oversupply of the Too-Much Mistake and the slow forging of more suitable ways of living in a subhumid grassland."[51]

According to one scholar North Dakota's declining country towns are not all hopelessly headed for extinction. Adjustment is possible. He be-

lieves that a community can survive without involving itself in economic activity; people can live in a place and just enjoy the social interaction. On the other hand senior citizens and rural retirees might retain their businesses or land and lease them, while remaining in the community and participating in its activities. Active local development corporations with vision and flexibility, however, seem to be the key to survival, and perhaps growth. Such groups could respond to what some agricultural experts consider to be coming, a transition from mechanical to biological agriculture, controlling disease and insects naturally, for example. That change with its potential for research and development facilities and support personnel housed in a rural community could provide major opportunities for rural areas.[52]

Technological, economic, and social change seems inevitable. The future of the state's declining country towns depends on how North Dakotans respond to Robinson's theme of Adjustment.

Leith Cornet Band - 1911

Endnotes

1. Elwyn B. Robinson, *History of North Dakota* (Lincoln: University of Nebraska Press, 1966), pp. 129, 134.

2. *Ibid.*, p. 134.

3. *Ibid.*

4. *Ibid.*, pp. 122-123.

5. North Dakota, Public Service Commission, *North Dakota Railroads: The Centennial Story*, January, 1989.

6. Robinson, p. 143.

7. North Dakota, Public Service Commission.

8. Robinson, p. 236.

9. John C. Hudson, "North Dakota's Railway War of 1905," *North Dakota History*, 48 (Winter, 1981, No. 1), pp. 4-19.

10. *Ibid.*

11. North Dakota, Public Service Commission.

12. Robert S. Henry, "The Railroad Land Grant Legend in American History Texts," *Mississippi Valley Historical Review*, XXXIII (Sept., 1954), p. 194.

13. Robinson, pp. 141-142, 227-228.

14. *Ibid.*, p. 143.

15. *Ibid.*, p. 132.

16. *Ibid.*, pp. 131, 144.

17. *Ibid.*, p. 242.

18. *Ibid.*

19. John C. Hudson, *Plains Country Towns* (Minneapolis: University of Minnesota Press,1985), pp. 12-13.

20. *Ibid.*, p. 71.

21. *Ibid.*, p. 88-89.

22. *Ibid.*, p. 89.

23. *Ibid.*, pp. 90, 162, note 6.

24. *Ibid.*, pp. 90-93, 162, note 7.

25. Robinson, p. 195.

26. Hudson, *Plain Country Towns*, p. 71.

27. *Ibid.*, pp. 72-77.

28. *Ibid.*, p. 77.

29. *Ibid.*, pp. 84, 133.

30. *Ibid.*, pp. 101, 163, note 18.

31. *Ibid.*, pp. 80, 161, note 27.

32. *Ibid.*, p. 81.

33. *Ibid.*, pp. 83, 133.

34. *Ibid.*, pp. 100-101.

35. Warren A. Henke, "Reichsdeutsche: Germans," in *Plains Folk: North Dakota's Ethnic History* ed. by William C. Sherman and Playford V. Thorson (Fargo: North Dakota Institute for Regional Studies, 1988), pp. 81-82.

36. Hudson, *Plains Country Towns*, p. 114.

37. *Ibid.*, pp. 114, 145.

38. Robinson, "The Themes of North Dakota History," a revision of an address read on November 6, 1958, at the Seventy-Fifth Anniversary conference of the University of North Dakota, p. 13. (Typewritten.) Robinson, *History of North Dakota*, p. 155. North Dakota, Department of Banking and Financial Institutions, interview with information officer, October 23, 1990.

39. Hudson, *Plains Country Towns*, p. 63. Robinson, *History of North Dakota*, p. 222.

40. Hudson, *Plains Country Towns*, p. 63. Robinson, *History of North Dakota*, pp. 154, 275. North Dakota, Public Service Commission, interview with information officer, October 23, 1990.

41. Robinson, *History of North Dakota*, p. 164. Hudson, *Plains Country Towns*, p. 124-125.

42. Hudson, *Plains Country Towns*, p. 166, note 12.

43. *Ibid.*, pp. 165-166, note 11.

44. Warren A. Henke, "The State of The State: 1889-1989," *North Dakota History*, 56 (Winter, 1989), p. 6. Douglas W. Wick, *North Dakota Place Names*, (Bismarck: Hedemarken Collectibles, 1988).

45. Robinson, *History of North Dakota*, pp. 164, 242. Hudson, "North Dakota's Railway War of 1905," pp. 8-9. North Dakota League of Cities, interview with information officer, October 25, 1990.

46. Lawrence H. Larsen and Roger T. Johnson, "A Story That Never Was: North Dakota's Urban Development," *North Dakota History*, 47 (Fall, 1980), p. 7.

47. *Ibid.*

48. Hudson, *Plains Country Towns*, p. 120. See Jeffery G. Williamson, *Late Nineteenth Century American Development: A General Equilibrium History* (Cambridge: Cambridge University Press, 1974).

49. Hudson, *Plain Country Towns*, p. 153, note 5.

50. Robinson, "The Themes of North Dakota History," p. 2.

51. *Ibid.*

52. J. Patrick Smith, "North Dakota's Prairie Communities: The Journey From Twilight to a Dawn," *North Dakota History*, 56 (Winter, 1989), pp. 51-54.

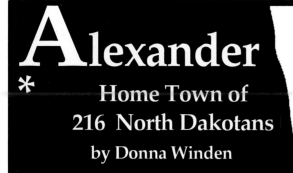

Alexander

Home Town of 216 North Dakotans

by Donna Winden

The town Alexander, twenty-six miles directly south of Williston on US 85, nestles among buttes. Bell's Butte — to the south — was named for Judge Alexander F. Bell who was the first barber in Alexander. He had the first shop outside his tent on his homestead where he filed claim in 1906. Foreman's Butte, to the west, was named for John W. Foreman, a Civil War veteran who also filed claim in 1906 as well. To the northwest is Barrager Butte, named for its owner and to the north is a chain of buttes called Ragged Butte. To the east is Tub Butte which resembles a giant wash tub.

Prior to organization of McKenzie County, the Bird Head Cattle Company established a line camp near the spring at the head of Lonesome Creek. On April 10, 1905 Governor Elmore Y. Sarles issued a proclamation creating the county and providing for a temporary county seat to be located on Sec. 5, T150N, R101W, the place where the cattle company had located its line camp. The county commissioners met there for the first time on May 31, 1905. The town was named after Alexander McKenzie of Bismarck, "the Boss of North Dakota." The county bears his last name.

The Alexander townsite, covering eleven city blocks, was platted on July 24, 1905. Frank B. Chapman served as trustee for the actual owners — Alexander McKenzie, Wilson L. Richards, and Felicia A. Harris. Lots opened for sale immediately. The "Log Shack" became McKenzie County's first courthouse. A rental note of one dollar per month covered the cost of the meeting place for as long as the county commissioners saw fit to use it.

The town's first business was the Dakota Trading Company Store which opened for business in 1905 soon after the county was organized and the town platted. Construction of the Alexander State Bank building was begun on July 1, 1905; it opened for business in August of that year with a capital of $15,000. The Alexander post office (Herbert W. Moore, postmaster) was established on August 14, 1905. A regular star route was served by mail carrier George W. Nohle.

Arthur Maderson and his wife, Selma, came to Alexander in 1905. They built and operated the Alexander Hotel — the town's first. That same year on December 31, E.N. Disney and E.C. Carney of Williston began publishing the *McKenzie County Chronicle*, which operated out of the bank building.

In 1913 the Great Northern Railroad Company built a branch line past the south edge of the town and established the Alexander station. In March of that same year the Alexander Townsite Company platted a nine-block townsite called Alex between the station grounds and the original townsite. It was eventually vacated. Today, the railroad is no

No. 4 MAIN St. ALEXANDER N.D.

Alexander in 1908

Aerial view of Alexander in 1987

longer in operation.

On June 25, 1918 the town suffered a disastrous fire which wiped out twenty-two buildings, sheds and outbuildings — including fourteen businesses and four homes.

The pioneers who settled the area in the early 1900s represented many religious denominations. Seven members organized the Methodist Episcopal Church on July 29, 1906 in the home of O.A. Olives. The congregation later built a church (which stands abandoned today). On March 17, 1907 Reverend M.L. Holey organized Trinity Lutheran Congregation. Its present structure was built in 1913 and has been remodeled several times since. Old timers recall that mass was offered in the Maderson Hotel to Roman Catholics as early as January 1908 by Father Arsenault. Father Dougherty arrived in the spring of 1913 to assume duties as the first resident priest. Our Lady of Consolation Catholic Church was built in 1914. Not until September 15, 1944 was the Church of the Nazarene built. Catholic, Lutheran, and Nazarene congregations still hold regular Sunday services today.

With the 1970s "oil boom" Alexander developed into a little hub-bub town because of the surge of activity in the outlying oil fields. The population increased dramatically in a short time and a good deal of construction followed. A motel and cafe were built and two trailer courts were developed to take care of the rapid influx of residents. Today, this activity has slowed and the town is rather quiet once again.

Since 1946 Alexander has hosted an annual "Old Settler Day" on the first Saturday in September in a celebration which includes a parade and a free noon barbecue beef feed which is donated by early settlers. Baked beans and coffee are also provided. This celebration draws young and old from miles around.

Today, Alexander has three main attractions. First, it has a spring which has been flowing free for many, many years. Second, in the center of town is a City Park where hamburgers are served by the Lions Club every Saturday evening during the summer months. Third, the community sustains the Lewis and Clark Trail Museum which is open from Memorial Day to Labor Day. It is housed in the old, red brick school which was built in 1914 (a new school building was erected in 1967).

Alexander before the Fire of 1918

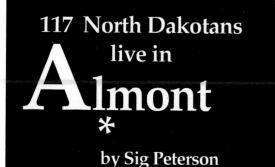
Almont was founded July 4, 1906. Eber W. Hyde of Rauville, South Dakota and Morton County surveyor H.H. Harmon surveyed nine blocks for the future town. Hyde chose the spot as a suitable location to build a lumberyard and grain elevator for C.H. Chase and Company — the side track named Almont, just around the bend of the sharp "Rattlesnake Curve" on the Northern Pacific Railway's new line. A telephone was already in place at the siding.

The word Almont derives from the Spanish word *alta*, meaning "highland," and the French word *mont*, meaning "hill" or "mountain." Almont is surrounded by hills.

The new town held its first celebration when it was only thirty-nine days old. About 300 people attended the non-denominational church service in the new lumber shed. The twenty-four piece Bohemian band put on a concert, and also played during the baseball game between Sims and Almont.

Almont became a melting pot of many nationalities. English, Norwegian, German, Danish, Swedish, German-Russian, Bohemian, Irish, and Scottish cultures were part of the community.

Almont boasted twenty-five businesses after only thirteen months in existence. They included two banks, two elevators, three lumberyards, three general merchandise stores, two hotels, two meat markets, a dray and delivery line, a confectionery, a weekly newspaper, and a post office.

During Almont's first ten years, church services were held in the town hall and in the school. The Evangelical Lutheran, Wesleyan Methodist, and Roman Catholic congregations organized and later built churches. The three congregations still serve the community. Every year an ecumenical service is held, which further unites Almont.

Fires were difficult to control in the early years. The only equipment Almont had was a two-wheeled fire cart, pulled by hand. Fire destroyed both elevators, the Chase lumberyard, and a barn on June 1, 1910. On February 25, 1915 a general store, drug store, barbershop, and hardware store were burned. Fire destroyed another store in 1923. Almont now has a Rural Fire District

Almont in the mid - 1910s

with a volunteer squad and a well-equipped fire truck. The first fire truck was purchased in 1963.

In its early years Almont had flooding problems. The first flood occurred July 3, 1914. The second flood didn't happen until April 17, 1950. A fast snow thaw caused the Muddy Creek to overflow its banks, inundating the entire town. A ten-inch rain on June 15, 1966 in the Hebron-Glen Ullin area caused a three-foot wall of water to rush down the valley to Almont where every building in town was damaged. Flood waters filled several basements again on May 10, 1970. In 1971 three agencies, the Soil Conservation Service, Morton County Water Management Board, and the Resource, Conservation and Development entity, arranged to rechannel Muddy Creek and build a dike around the city. This project has prevented further flooding.

All east and west-bound traffic on rail and highway went through Almont until 1928. In that year US 10 was rerouted directly west from New Salem to Glen Ullin, bypassing Almont. In 1948 Almont experienced another setback when the Northern Pacific Railway rerouted its line the same way. The last train went through Almont December 6, 1947.

Sims School District No. 8 has provided schooling for Almont and the surrounding area. The first senior class graduated in 1920. The Sims School District reorganized on June 28, 1958 to include more of the Almont trade area. The twelve-year school operated until 1988, when high school students became a part of the New Salem school system.

A city water system became a reality in 1958. The sewage disposal system was a 1967 project.

Almont has two annual events which draw people from far and near. The Labor Day Reunion, featuring steam threshing, has been held for the past twenty-nine years. It draws between 2,000 to 3,000 people. The lutefisk, lefse and meatball supper held each November draws an average crowd of 900.

Almont's business district now includes: Marshall Lumber Co., Alm-

Big parade in Almont in 1981 Almont Diamond Jubilee

Hobein Bar at Almont, about 1940
Adults from left to right: Red Olson, Donald Olson, Ted Hobein, Fritz Hoeger, Judy Zemple, Carl Fallgren; Two Hobein Children

ont Service and Feeds, Tavis Cafe, Lantern Lounge and Teen Center, Farmers Supply (automotive supplies and repair), Don's Bar, Country Cut and Curl, Recreation and Fitness Center, Security State Bank, Country Arts and Crafts, and the Post Office. Other services are Livestock Weighing Assn., Ambulance Service, Fire Dept., Senior Citizens Nutritional Program (Meals On Wheels),

City Park, Heritage Park and Museum. Almont has been without a grocery store for several years.

Almont's 1991 population is about 117. The gradual decline in population is due to smaller families, fewer farms, fewer business opportunities for the younger generation, and the ease of traveling to nearby towns and cities for shopping and recreation.

The town wanted to be first and foremost of those in present-day Golden Valley County. Alpha, twenty miles south of Sentinel Butte, was founded in 1906 in the NE1/4 sec. 32, T137N, R104W on land owned by Benjamin G. Odiorne, a druggist from Minneapolis who came west with five other men. During the summer of 1906 he filed a homestead claim in the Alpha area as did Oscar Odman, Ed Eide, Joe and Martin Toft, and Odiorne's brother-in-law, Louis Ferney. Eide and one of the Tofts were barbers, Odman was a streetcar conductor, and Ferney was a druggist.

The men hauled lumber to the site from Beach, and brought poles and wood for fuel from the badlands. They erected a house where the five men, three wives, a grandmother, and a baby all lived that winter. Odiorne's wife, Catherine, had the job of keeping the group supplied with water, hauling it in a barrel on a stone boat for eight miles.

During the spring of 1906, Jake Irons and Odiorne were traveling to Burkey to secure a permit for a post office at Alpha. It is claimed that he chose the name Alpha for the community. It is the first letter of the Greek alphabet and that suggested that their community was the first in the area and was expected to become the area's chief or leading town. Some claim Odiorne's wife suggested the name. The post office was established on May 3, 1907 with Odiorne as postmaster. He also operated a store at his farm.

Alpha's fate was sealed when the Northern Pacific Railroad established Golva on its branch line some miles to the west. Throughout most of its history it consisted of just a few buildings. A Catholic church was built as was a Farmers' Cooperative Store. A Woodmen of the World Community Hall was also built where dances, singing, speaking, debates, home-talent plays and basketball games were enjoyed. The post office closed in 1946.

In 1906 Jacob Irons with his wife and stepson, Ebb West, came to Alpha from Iowa in a covered wagon. Irons was a carpenter who helped build many of the first schoolhouses from Alpha to Sentinel Butte. He also helped build the Protestant church in Alpha. In 1909 the Alpha school was built three-fourths of a mile south of Odiornes.

Albert Irons, his wife and their two children came to Alpha by immigrant railroad car in 1907. He spent his first Sunday in the community fighting a prairie fire which swept through the area from about two miles west of his father's homestead to the Little Missouri River, six miles away. He came from a musical family. His mother traded twelve bushels of corn for a snare drum and he began playing the drum at age twelve. He started the Alpha Band in 1913, as well as several other area bands.

Charles and Mary (Jendro) Otremba and Eddie Jendro came to Alpha from Little Falls, Minnesota. Otremba's wife and their children, Frances (Hagen); Gertrude (Thomas); Mamie (Scherman); and Helen (Sonnek), a baby of three months, travelled by passenger train to Sentinel Butte, standing a great part of the way. Otremba had worked for Charles Lindbergh, Sr. in a hardware store in Little Falls. Their first

The Alpha Store and Hall
(SHSND)

winter here they lived with a friend, Louis Weisgram, while they built a sod house and a barn. For the first three years the two older girls, Frances and Gertrude, were taught by Orpha E. Blue in the Herr School, a sod building.

Alfred (Fritz) Fasching helped build the Catholic Church in Alpha. The church was completed in 1917. In August 1919 Fasching and his wife Violet (Leuenberger) were the first couple married there.

Jens Gronning and his wife were both immigrants from Norway. Gronning had been a streetcar conductor in Minneapolis, but left and moved to Alpha because of health reasons. In addition to farming Gronning carried mail from Alpha to Sentinel Butte three times a week. Later he sold Rawleigh products. Gronning's wife served as clerk for the Woodmen Circle Lodge. Their

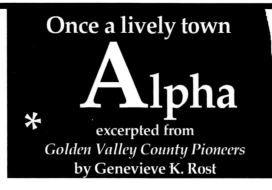

Once a lively town
Alpha
excerpted from
Golden Valley County Pioneers
by Genevieve K. Rost

land was later reclaimed by the government as submarginal and designated for grazing purposes.

Enoch Johnson became postmaster in 1917; he was succeeded by Robert L. Johnston in 1928. Mrs. Robert (Helen) Sonnek assumed the position in 1937 and served until 1946 when the office was closed.

Neil Hogoboom hauled mail from Sentinel Butte to Alpha from 1919 until his retirement in 1963. Neil, his brothers Byron and Maurice, and sister, Dorothy (Johnstone), grew up on

their father's homestead in T136N, R104W, Williams Township. Milo B. Hogoboom was the proud owner of a steam engine and threshing machine. He directed home-talent plays, served on the local school board, and was a member of the state legislature for six years.

Maurice Hogoboom also farmed and traveled extensively. He made five trips to Hawaii and traveled to the Philippines, Hong Kong, the Fiji Islands, and Australia.

"Yes, there was an Alpha, a community founded by early pioneers." "They suffered all the hardships. Many are still here, having successfully run the gauntlet of hardships to remain and prosper."

**Evelyn Cook, Herman Dietz,
Paul C. Popiel, Alma Waldahl,
Muriel Waldahl**

At worship in the United Brethren Church in Alpha
(SHSND)

For any American who had the great and priceless privilege of being raised in a small town there always remains with him nostalgic memories of those days. And the older he grows the more he senses what he owed to the simple honesty and neighborliness, the integrity that he saw all around him in those days.

**Dwight David Eisenhower
Address to National Editorial Association, June 22, 1954**

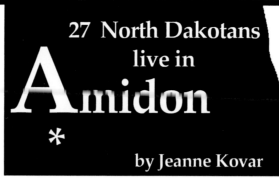

The origin of Amidon can be traced to 1911 when the Chicago, Milwaukee & St. Paul Railroad began surveying a planned extension of its branch line westward from New England into southern Billings County. In May 1911 the Amidon post office (James E. Dinsmore, postmaster) was established at a point on this survey. The new town was named in honor of Charles Fremont Amidon, a United States district judge for North Dakota whose chambers were in Fargo. Although the railroad extension was never built, the Farm Land and Coal Company platted a thirteen-block townsite on land they owned in 1913; four years later the Milwaukee Land Company platted its First Addition to Amidon.

Separated from Billings County by vote of the people, Slope County's first commissioners organized its county government in Amidon in January 1915 and selected Amidon as the temporary county seat. The selection was ratified by vote the next year, but litigation prevented its being officially declared until April 6, 1917. The county-seat community was incorporated as a village in 1918 and obtained a city charter in 1967.

The present courthouse was constructed in 1917; the previous one houses senior citizen activities. In its earlier days Amidon supported various businesses: two banks, a hotel that was later moved to Dickinson, grocery stores, newspapers, blacksmith shop, lumberyard, theater, restaurant, barbershop, livery stable, and service station.

Few original buildings remain. The east side of main street was destroyed in the 1930s and never rebuilt. The Fixit Shop in earlier days housed a restaurant, funeral parlor, and a bar. Part of the Horse Around Bar and Gas is also an original structure. The present post office is located in the Agriculture Stabilization and Conservation Service (ASCS) office building.

The first Slope County fair was held on August 27-28, 1920. To raise money for the event 108 people paid an association membership fee of twenty-five cents.

Today, the community supports two churches: St. Peter and Paul Catholic Church which was built in the winter of 1917 and spring of 1918 and the First Lebanon Lutheran Church, organized in June 1913.

Amidon's first school was constructed in 1914; overcrowding forced the community to build a larger one in 1919. It burned down in the fall of 1939 and a school building was moved in from south of Bowman.

Northwest Ward of Amidon in 1918

Today, Amidon is still thriving and strong. It has an active volunteer rural fire department, a new fire hall which was built in 1984, and it claims to be one of the smallest seats of county government in the country.

We are quite proud of our little town.

Horses and automobiles could both be serviced
(SHSND)

Moonlight in Amidon in 1918
(SHSND)

North business district in Amidon in 1918
(SHSND)

Page 17

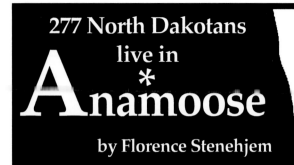

The biggest little city on the Minneapolis, St. Paul and Sault Ste Marie Railroad (Soo Line) originated when a group of Rumanians from Regina, Canada settled in the area in 1893. Curious to know how the town of Anamoose got its name, Albert Glotzbach who arrived in May 1904 directed an inquiry to the Soo Line depot agent. He was told that the grading and rail-laying crews who were pushing the railroad through the area in the late 1890s were composed of men of various nationalities, including Indians. It seems that there was a mongrel dog that joined the crew every day as they ate lunch. Rail workers threw their crusts and leftovers to the hound but couldn't seem to fill him up. The Indians named him *Anamoose*, a corruption of the Chippewa Indian word *uh-nemoosh*, which means Hungry Dog.

The section house was the first building to serve as a home for section foreman William McNamara and his family; it also served as a "whistle stop" for the railway. The townsite owned by W.E. Cooke was platted in the winter of 1899. The first mercantile store built on the original townsite was owned by Albrecht Bros., who provided space for the first post office.

Surrounded by fertile farmlands and being four hundred twelve miles from Minneapolis, the town became an important shipping point for potatoes, cattle, and grain. It was also a distribution center for farm machinery and other merchandise. Prosperity and progress marked its early years; it was incorporated in 1905.

In 1901 Anamoose had the largest primary flax market in the United States. In 1912 the wheat crop marketed was one million bushels, affirming that this section of the state was well adapted to diversified farming.

A 1911 census set the town's population at 669. It was the county's third largest village; a significant majority of its population was of German ancestry.

Business enterprises included four general stores, three hardware stores, three banks, seven elevators, two lumberyards, two pool and billiard halls, four implement dealers, two drug stores, two doctors, two hotels, three restaurants, two livery

Main Street Anamoose in the past

stables, two drag lines, two black-smith and wagon shops, one cement block factory, one photographer, one newspaper, one millinery store, two barbershops, one harness shop, one hospital, two land and loan companies, three lawyers, two dressmaking establishments, one opera house, one telephone exchange with seven connecting farm lines, four rural mail routes, and two meat markets.

The Commercial Club and the Fire Department which organized in the early 1900s are still active. A former Literary Club expanded to a Federated Women's Club and Homemakers' Clubs still exist as does the VFW and Ladies Auxiliary. These organizations continue to cooperate and support school and community improvements. A new Senior Center provided activities for the elderly.

Religion was a dominating force in the early beginning as Baptist, Catholic, Lutheran, Evangelical, and Congregational churches were established. Prior to churches being built, services were conducted in homes and the school.

Education was important to the town's early settlers. In October 1899 citizens met with the county superintendent to organize Anamoose School District No. 14. The first school term was held in an area of the hotel until a wooden school was completed.

Anamoose had one of the oldest and largest consolidated schools in the state. In 1905 a three-story, red brick school building was erected at a cost of $15,000; in 1911 exercises for the town's first two high school graduates were held. A large brick auditorium was built in 1928 on Main Street; it provided a large gymnasium and stage for school and community affairs.

In later years rural students were bussed in and enrollment increased because of annexation of five areas to the district. The school system expanded to three units in one block. The red brick building housed the elementary grades; additional buildings were added in 1952 and 1963.

The expanded facilities included a new gymnasium, a music room, and a kitchen for a lunch program. In 1979 the red brick building was destroyed by fire; elementary students were cared for by building an addition and remodeling other buildings.

A severe thunderstorm in 1907 destroyed four businesses, and in 1915 a disastrous fire destroyed an entire block. The fire department, organized in 1910, fought that blaze with assistance from neighboring departments. The early settlers also endured threatening prairie fires, tornadoes, a scarlet fever epidemic, and drought in the 1930s.

Joyous times were experienced by early settlers at the Emil Splitzstor homestead and the Moorhead ranches where amusements, diversions, and entertainments of various sorts were engaged in by all. Residents recall that Sundays in the summer "were like the Fourth of July." The "Opera House" provided excellent entertainment and in later years a movie theater served the community.

Anamoose village was incorporated as City of Anamoose during the summer of 1922. Like many rural cities Anamoose has suffered a decline in population in recent years but it continues to be a significant shipping center on the Soo Line Railway. An enormous amount of grain is handled by the Cargill Elevator, the town's only one. In recent years it has increased its storage capacity from 165,000 bushels to 651,000 bushels and has added a bulk fertilizer plant and a grain dryer. Total grain shipped from the area has increased to some 3,000,000 bushels per year.

Some of the city's businesses still occupy their original buildings which have been partially remodeled. An eight-plex, low income housing unit was erected in 1978. The most recent project completed by the city was the replacement of the old water lines throughout the city and the addition of a new water treatment plant.

Anamoose School, built in 1905 for $15,000

Main Street Anamoose in the late 1980s

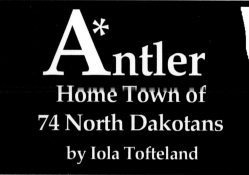

A*ntler
Home Town of 74 North Dakotans
by Iola Tofteland

The "Gateway to the United States," Antler lies a mile and one-half south of the Canadian border and fifty miles north of Minot.

On June 21, 1898 Duncan McLean became postmaster of the country post office to serve settlers who had staked their claims west of the Mouse River. Named after Antler Creek, mainly a Canadian stream which swings below the border in this area, the post office moved five miles southwest in 1902 and moved again in 1905 when the Antler town-site was plotted in June by the Dakota Development Company of Willmar, Minnesota. Great Northern railway construction crews, working on the Westhope branch, reached the newly designated terminal town of Antler in August 1905. The following year Antler was incorporated as a city. Some eight decades later, in 1984, tracks between Westhope and Antler and the Antler and Kuroki stations were abandoned.

Antler Creek is one of two tributaries that branch from the Mouse River in this region (called the Moose by local Indians, the two tributaries together became the Antlers of the Moose). The abundance of deer and antelope along the river also contributed to the name.

The first Antler school was held a mile south of where the town now stands. When the town was built school was held in the Presbyterian Church and various vacant buildings. A new school was built in 1906-1907 and a new high school was constructed in 1964. At the present time the old school is used for a museum.

The town's economy is based on farming, principally raising wheat, but also growing flax, rye, oats, and barley on a smaller scale. Some settlers took to ranching.

At one time six elevators were in operation. Four burned down, one was rebuilt, it is still in operation. Since the boom days, many buildings have been moved out or destroyed by fire. Few new buildings replaced them.

The old hotel was torn down and replaced with a large building which houses the post office, a large auditorium for the use of various clubs, lodges, and community gatherings, and the fire department with its trucks and equipment.

Presbyterian Church, Fire Hall, and Odd Fellows Hall
(The church is gone, but the two buildings on the right survive)

Business block of Antler in 1916
Edgar Fraser throws a ball across the square in front of Yarrows Drug Store
Other buildings include Haugh's Butcher Shop (now Fox residence), Hawley Barber Shop, and State Bank of Antler

The last devastating fire occurred in 1984 when two bars on Main Street burned to the ground. A newly constructed large log cabin now houses a Steak Pit and the town's only bar. Along with those businesses the town presently boasts of a grocery store, garage, and a post office, far less than the twenty-four businesses which operated in 1905.

Entertainment in historic Antler consisted of church affairs, ball games, berry picking, and just plain picnics held at the Antler Park near the creek.

A huge pavilion was built where for many years dances were held every Friday night.

For many years Presbyterians and Roman Catholics were able to maintain active fellowships. In time, however, the Presbyterians concluded that it was no longer feasible to continue. In 1952 a Community Church was founded. It is still very active. Local Roman Catholics attend church in Westhope or Sherwood.

Antler achieved national prominence in 1989 when Leona Tennyson took on the making of the largest quilt in the world for the North Dakota Centennial.

The Antler Squire (Armed Thorpe, owner), 1980
The Post Office and Telephone Exchange

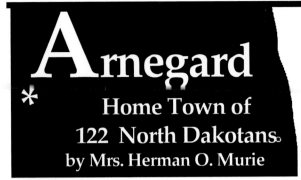

Arnegard
Home Town of 122 North Dakotans
by Mrs. Herman O. Murie

This area of western North Dakota was part of the Fort Berthold Indian Reservation until it was opened for homesteading in June 1902. By 1906 several homesteaders had filed on their quarter sections of land and in July of that year the federal government established a post office named Arnegard in postmaster Gerhard A. Stenehjem's homestead shack, an eight by ten tarpapered cabin half a mile southwest of the current townsite. The station was named Arnegard, after early pioneer homesteaders.

As more settlers moved into the area the need for a store soon became apparent. In 1908 Albert O. Arnegard Sr. built a two-story building for a general merchandising business on his land near a lone tree, one-half mile west of the present townsite. Several other businesses located at the Lone Tree site and at the Hill site during the next few years. A townsite named Arnegard was platted in November 1910.

When the Great Northern Railroad built its first line into McKenzie County in 1913, it established a station named Arnegard a half mile east of the original settlement and platted a new townsite in June. The store and other buildings at the two original locations were then moved to the present townsite by tractor and steam engine. New businesses sprang up shortly. Advertising by the Great Northern Railway Company and the Arnegard Commercial Club described Arnegard as the "Garden Spot" of McKenzie County and encouraged business and professional men to locate here. An example of such a business was the drug store built in 1914. It was operated by its original owner, Charles E. Fleck, until fire destroyed the store in 1959.

The Lutheran Church was the first and only church in Arnegard. It was organized in January 1907 in the P.A. Stenehjem homestead shack. Services were held in homes until a log church, McKenzie County's first church, was built one mile east and one half mile north of the current townsite. This building was used until 1914 when the basement for the present church was built in the newly platted townsite. The sanctuary was built in 1928, following several good crops in the area.

Throughout the years the church and school have worked together closely. Both have played an important and

Bird's-eye view of Arnegard in 1921

Arnegard Choir and Orchestra performing in City Hall
(Located above Arnegard Mercantile Store)

band, the annual Fourth of July celebration, the annual Play Day for all McKenzie County schools, and for its certified seed potatoes.

Early organizations in the area were the Civic League, the Degree of Honor, AOUW, 4-H, Boy Scouts, Homemakers, and home talent plays.

Currently our centers of community activity include an active Lions Club. It has over sixty members, and sponsors a hamburger feed each Friday evening in the city park during the summer. The Lioness Club has over twenty members and holds a health clinic each year. The clubs jointly sponsor a Santa Claus each Christmas.

The city sponsors an athletic program in the park each summer, a town Christmas tree and Christmas tree lighting, and the annual Fourth of July celebration consisting of a parade, barbecue, baseball game, races and roller skating for the young, bingo, an evening dance, and fireworks at dark.

outstanding role in the development and life of the community. The first school in the area was in the homestead shacks until the log church was finished in 1909. School was held there until the Arnegard school was built in 1914. The first high school class graduated in 1926. The little gym was added in 1936 and the big gym was built by locally donated labor in 1953 to meet state standards for a basketball court. It must have helped since the boys' basketball team took first place in the State Class C Tournament in 1961. Other school-sponsored activities included band, programs, plays, speech and music festivals, spelling contest, and operettas. The high school also published a newspaper, *The Spud*, and the yearbook, *The Arnegardian*.

The Great Depression in the 1930s forced many farmers, ranchers, and dairymen to leave the community. Many businesses also closed. The first fire to destroy businesses in Arnegard occurred in 1927 when the Farmers' Elevator was burned. In the late 1940s a blaze destroyed the potato warehouse and in 1959 fire

destroyed the pool hall, butcher shop, the Knotty Pine Bar, the drug store, and the hotel.

Arnegard has long been remembered as having the first church in McKenzie County, the first community

Arnegard's first post office in 1906
Hill Site southwest of present Arnegard

33 North Dakotans live in

B*alfour

by Del Rae Hedstrom

When the construction crews with their cook and bunk cars moved on after the railroad was built and the station was established by the Minneapolis, St. Paul & Sault Ste Marie Railroad Company in 1893, there remained a section house which was to be an informal hotel in the beginning, section foreman Ole Helseth and his family, and a name — Balfour, chosen by the railroad in honor of British author and statesman Lord Arthur Balfour.

The townsite grew when local promoter William E. Cooke divided up the area and sold lots in 1899-1900. The Balfour post office began when Ador A. Jevnager assumed postmaster duties in 1899; he built the first family home that same year. The first elevator was built in 1902.

In 1903 Pat O'Hara opened an addition to the north of the original townsite and donated lots to all the churches in town. The German EVA built the first church, followed by the Lutherans and Methodists. The first school was held in 1901 in Jevnager's machine shed. The first official schoolhouse was built in 1903 and the first paper, the *Balfour Statesman*, was organized in 1901.

Other early Balfourites were Dr. J.R. Pence, Henry Bergman, George Bonine, Frank Maxwell, John Kohler, Kulaas Spurzem, Jim Manning, Pete C. Connelly, William Riebe, John Melhouse, and Linus Peterson.

In April 1904 Balfour held an incorporation meeting. By 1920 Balfour had a population of 322.

The townspeople were left devastated after the fires that wiped out the greater part of main street in 1921. The first fire which started in Lindeman's Garage at about 9:15 pm on September 8 consumed Lindeman's and Frank Swanson's Garages, the J.B. Pendroy Opera House, Henry Peterson's Pool Hall, and a building owned by Dr. Stone.

Then on October 6, just 30 days later, another fire broke out in the rear of Diebold's Hardware and eventually destroyed all of the buildings on the west side of main street, including Diebold's, O.P. Helseth's Hardware Store, the W.P. Campbell Building, Bille's Meat Market, Dr. Stone's office and hospital, and a vacant building. The only buildings left standing were the drug store and hotel.

Balfour Public School closed its doors in 1978; students now attend the Drake schools.

Since its incorporation in 1921, population of Balfour has dropped to 33 people who govern themselves with a

Celebrating the Fourth of July in Balfour
(SHSND)

mayor, two alderman, and a city auditor. Only five businesses remain: Pete's Standard Service and Cafe, Balfour Body Shop, Thompson's Small Engine Repair, Mike's Refrigeration, and the post office with 23 active boxes.

Main Street in Balfour's heyday
(SHSND)

Main Street of Balfour in 1976
(DPDP - Todd Strand)

The country town is one of the great American institutions; perhaps the greatest, in the sense that it has had a greater part than any other in shaping public sentiment and giving character to American culture.

Thorstein Veblen
The Country Town, 1923

When the Northern Pacific Railroad built a branch line west from Wahpeton to Milnor in Sargent County in 1883 it established a station named Barney on Sec. 7, T132N, R50W. The station was named after Ashbel H. Barney of Vermont, one of the original investors in the railroad who was also a long-time director and president for several months in 1881.

In 1899 Frederick Henkel built a house on adjacent property, opened a general store, and was appointed as Barney's postmaster with an annual salary of $26.00. Over the years many postmasters have held the position: J. E. Little, Rose Gagelin Halvorson, Madelyn Moulsoff Haberman, and J. B. Williams. It is presently a contract station. There also were several mail carriers over the years including Carl Haberman who held the position for over thirty years.

A schoolhouse was built in 1904 by Lou Colwill, the local carpenter. School had been held in the upstairs of Henkel's store the previous four years. A two-year high school was started about 1933 and operated until 1942. In 1958 the Barney and Wyndmere school districts consolidated and the Barney School was closed in 1964. The grounds became a public park in 1969 and the school building was razed in 1974. The old school bell was set up in the park as a memorial to Elizabeth Veit, a long-time teacher.

The congregation of the Lutheran Church was organized in 1899 and a church was built that same year. This building was sold to Guido Rudolph in 1902 and another church was built and dedicated on November 23, 1902. This building served the congregation until a new church was erected and dedicated November 1949. A new parsonage was built in 1956.

A Lutheran Parish School was built in 1903 and continued until 1931. Over the years many pastors have served the Lutheran Church. The present pastor is Richard Hallman who also serves as the city mayor.

Guido Rudolph and his wife came to Barney in 1901. He operated a blacksmith shop and helped organize the Farmers Elevator Company, the Potato Warehouse, and the Farmers Co-op Mercantile Association. The Mercantile Association later became privately owned. Among the owners were Oscar Jensen and Raymond Olson. It is no longer in operation.

A creamery operated by Albert Kressin was built in 1902. His son, Everett, born in December 1901, was the first child born in Barney.

The *Barney Champion*, a weekly newspaper began publication in 1902. In that same year a jewelry store and feed mill were operated by Phineas McLaughlin and J. L. Rehmet and his family came to town and managed the Wm. H. White Lumber Company. The next year saw the arrival of the Albert Mathias family. They operated a general merchandise store, a meat market, and they cut and stored ice. The John Thiel family arrived in Barney in 1905 and started an implement business. It was operated by several owners and was discontinued in the mid 40s.

Emil Rieman became the town's first depot agent in 1908. In 1959, while Merle Greenheck was agent, the Northern Pacific ran its last passenger and mail train from Oakes to Staples. The city presently receives freight service from the Burlington Northern Railroad, operating on a completely rebuilt track.

At one time Barney had a hotel, built by Albert Kressin. Various tenants owned the building including Arnold Kressin and Carl Thiel. They con-

Bird's-eye view of Barney, North Dakota - 1907

Aerial view of Barney, North Dakota - 1983

verted it to a liquor store which served the community from 1940 to 1959.

The Moyer Brothers built a livery stable and had a regular freight route from Barney to Wyndmere. Ray Raypheal was a drayman during the early years, delivering coal and freight to business places and residences.

In 1905 Herb Moyer built and operated a pool hall. It is still in operation as Al's Tavern; it is owned by Alvin Leshovsky.

The N. H. Berg family reached Barney in 1908. Berg was the cashier for the Bank of Barney which closed its doors in 1932.

The Barney Auto Service was started by Fremont Faust in 1919 and was sold to Henry Kurtz in 1935. Kurtz retired in 1968 and sold the building to Gutzmer Construction Company which still serves the community.

Frank Pelzl owned and operated a service station until 1964 when his son, Morris, acquired the business. It is now closed. The Albert Gagelin family arrived in Barney in 1924. He purchased the old blacksmith shop from Guido Rudolph. Gagelin retired in 1949 and his son, Walter, assumed responsibility for the business. He is

known to have pounded out 154 plow shares in one day at the age of twenty-five.

The Farmers Elevator was purchased in the early 40s by Cecil McDonald and was operated as the McDonald Seed and Grain Company. Later it was sold to the Schuler Grain Company and is now known as Minn-Kota Ag Products.

Halvor Berg and his wife were the parents of the first set of twins born in Barney. He was employed at Rehmets.

Max Fuestel started the Fuestel Hatchery in Barney in the late 1930s. It operated as a hatchery for about ten years and was then sold and made into a cafe. It was later moved by Floyd Hammond to a site one-half mile south of town and made into a Truck Stop and Cafe.

Barney was established as a village in 1952.

The first fire department was organized in 1947 with Ralph Dunbar acting as the first firechief. In 1975, while Merle Greenheck served as chief, fire districts were established.

In 1968 Barney was incorporated as a city. Also in 1968, a new fire hall and community center was built

next to the Veterans of Foreign Wars Hall and the two buildings were connected.

The Barney Hall has been the center of community activities throughout the years. It was built in 1916 by Art Brosowske and his crew. Labor and materials came to less than $1,000. Brosowske and his son, Vernon, were responsible for constructing many houses in the community.

Barney has had three major fires: in 1948 the old east elevator burned to the ground; in June 1954 the old mainhouse of McDonald Seed and Grain burned; and in December 1956 a new elevator that replaced it was believed to have been hit by lightning and burned to the ground, destroying two cement silos with it. It was rebuilt the following year.

Barney's most recent project was to install a new sewer and water system in 1972. New businesses established in recent years are the Midwest Bean Company, an edible bean plant; Cenex Fertilizer Plant; and an automated fertilizer plant now owned by Minn-Kota Ag Products.

At present Barney City is in the 27th Legislative District. Its population is seventy-nine.

Benedict began as a squatters' village three-fourths of a mile northwest of the present site. In 1906 a station named Benedict was located on Sec. 7, T150N, R81W along a Soo Line Railroad branch line constructed between Drake and Max, North Dakota. In October that same year the post office was established with Alexander Munns as postmaster. In August two years later the townsite itself was platted by a subsidiary of the railroad company, the Tri-State Land Company of Minneapolis, Minnesota.

52 North Dakotans live in

B*enedict

by Marian Gullickson

As with many smaller towns founded at that time, there are several stories about how the town got its name. Some say it was named after a town in Minnesota. Others say it was named after a team of horses, Ben and Dick. The most widely accepted story is that the name was suggested by the Postmaster General at that time, George Von Meyer. He suggested the name because of the large number of newly-wed men, called benedicts in some cultures, who signed the petition for the establishment of a post office.

E. E. Simmons played a prominent role in the development of the city. He and Alvin Lillahaugen were instrumental in persuading the Soo Line to recognize Benedict. A sidetrack was extended to Benedict and a boxcar was dropped to be used as a depot. Soon a grocery store and two businesses started by Simmons stood near the post office at the present site.

Benedict continued to prosper. The west side of main street soon included the First State Bank, a pool hall, post office, meat market, restaurant-hotel, hardware store, barbershop, land office, drug store, co-op store, blacksmith shop, and an elevator. Behind the bank was the town well, the jail, lumberyard, livery stable, Standard bulk station, and another blacksmith shop was located further west.

The east side of main street consisted of a depot, two elevators — the O & M and the Farmer's, stock yards, hotel, grocery store, the Security State Bank, the Bishop building, gas and cream station, meat market, implement dealer, and the town hall. Behind the implement building to the east was the *Benedict Banner* printing office, and another lumberyard and garage stood farther north. Only the bar and elevator remain in business; however, many of the buildings still stand, including the original jail.

Churches were not built in the early years. Itinerant preachers served the community, preaching in the homes. In May 1906 the Union Banner Sunday School opened its doors. Later, a number of churches were built: Concordia Lutheran Church; Concordia Evangeliske Lutherske Menighed of McLean County, January 1908; Congregational Church, 1908; Church of God, 1912; Methodist Church, 1912; Swedish Church, Bethenia Congregation, 1917; Nazarene Church, 1927. Initially, most of the church groups held services and meetings in private homes. The churches that were built later were built by the congregations themselves. Today, Concordia Lutheran Church is the only active church remaining in Benedict.

The first school in the district was built in 1906; the Benedict school was built in 1912. In 1934 one large

North view of Main Street- 1988

room was added on for two years of high school. In 1960, Benedict school consolidated the seventh and eighth grades with the Max school. Grades 1-6 continued to be taught in Benedict until the 1966 consolidation with the Max school, after which students were bussed to Max. The school building was torn down in 1979. A softball park now stands in its place.

Over the years, fire claimed much of Benedict. In the early 1930s four businesses on the west side and an elevator owned by Alex Harchenko burned down. In 1934 another elevator owned by local farmers was lost to fire. In 1985 the Farmer's Elevator went up in flames, but it was rebuilt and remains in business today.

The local fire department was organized in 1965. An old Sweetheart Bakery truck was converted into Benedict's first fire truck. The truck and volunteer manpower served the community until a 1976 merger with the Max Rural Fire Department. A fire truck, which serves the entire district, is maintained by the Rural Fire Department in Benedict.

Among the community events each year is a large fireworks display each 4th of July. The Gullickson-Erlien Legion Post, perhaps the most active of community organizations, maintains the softball park and sponsors various activities throughout the year.

The community has made recent improvements: city water in 1968 and a city sewer system in 1988. Benedict remains a small but pleasant community.

Benedict City Hall - 1988

Original jailhouse - 1988

A Small Town
LaVerne P. Larson

Oh, give me just a small town
  Away from the city's roar,
  Where I can have a little home
  With roses around my door.

A garden filled with flowers,
  And a shade tree on the lawn,
  Plus a vast expanse of view
  Where I can see the dawn.

Then from out my shining windows,
  When the sun sinks in the west,
  I can sit and look and wonder,
  And think of how I'm blessed.

Oh, give me just a small town
  Where each neighbor is a friend,
  And the birds sing cheerful melodies
  Until each fine day's end;

With a church tucked in the valley,
  Down a winding country lane,
  And all of nature's wonders
  Kissed by sun and rain.

Fertile fields and woodlands
  And stars so big and bright;
  The moon in all its splendor
  Lighting up the night.

The four seasons with their glories,
  Each one a magic gem,
  And my heart and mind so thankful
  For every one of them.

Oh, give me just a small town
  With a lovely village store,
  And all the simple pleasures
  I have been looking for.

It seems within the city
  We lose so much of life,
  Worrying and hurrying,
  Under stress and strain and strife.

Old-fashioned are the small towns
  But they are best indeed . . .
  Because you'll truly find there
  The joy and peace you need.

Diamond Jubilee Book Committee,
Arnegard Diamond Jubilee: **1913-1988**
(Williston: Basin Printers Inc., 1988), p. 9

BuchananisSplitlocated thirteen miles northwest of Jamestown. It is one of the "newest" cities in the state, although it has been in existence since 1879. In 1983 it became an incorporated city with its own mayor and council members. Previously, it was governed by the township board.

The city was named for James and John Buchanan, early settlers who came to the area from Rio, Wisconsin in 1879 and who operated a large bonanza farm in the locality. The village was first called Rio, but was renamed on September 6, 1894, when a post office in Emmons County named Buchanan was closed. The townsite was plotted in May 1903 by Augustus Roberts with streets 80-feet wide and trees planted on either side. A grove 70-feet wide was planted on the west edge of town. Buchanan's slogan was, "This shall be a town of many trees—no shanty or shack."

In 1880 the first cheese factory in North Dakota was started in Buchanan. The venture proved unsatisfactory and it was closed in 1891.

The Northern Pacific Railroad began construction from Jamestown to Car-

40 North Dakotans live in Buchanan*

by Hazel Holzwarth

rington in 1881. In 1905 a depot was built in Buchanan, and served the area for many years. With the coming of the railroad, a grain elevator soon appeared. In 1886 the Sawyer Brothers of Minneapolis built the first elevator. In 1901 the Buchanan Brothers built an elevator which is now the only elevator in Buchanan, and is known as the Farmers Elevator. In the early 1900s three other elevators were established.

The Buchanan School District was organized in 1881. The first school had only a summer session with Martha Buchanan as the first teacher. In 1884 the first school building was constructed in Buchanan. In 1908 a larger grade school was built but it wasn't until 1916 that the first high school graduating

class appeared. The building, built in 1908, is still used for band, special classes, and kindergarten. A new grade school and gym were added in 1963. Since 1982 the towns of Buchanan and Pingree consolidated their school systems with K-6 in Buchanan and 7-12 in the Pingree School.

The first church was the Congregational Church, organized in 1887. A building was erected in 1903. This building was moved from town in 1967 when the church was closed; its congregation joined the Jamestown church. The Roman Catholic church was built in 1924. It is the only church in Buchanan at the present time.

In 1903 Drawz and Neilson opened a general store. Other early businesses were: a bank, a hotel, pool hall, dressmaking shop, a blacksmith, the Price Company Store, Issac's Store, Leverenz Store, Eastman Store, Lutz Lumber Company, a barbershop, a light plant, two shipping companies, a stockyard, two implement dealers,

The Buchanan Bank served as Buchanan Post Office until 1988

Old Buchanan schoolhouse

a cream station, a livery barn, and a telephone exchange.

Socially townspeople kept busy with two lodges, a chamber of commerce, a federated club, a cornet band, and two churches.

At the present time there are approximately forty people living in Buchanan, most of whom are either employed in Jamestown or are retired. The only businesses left are the elevator, a beauty shop, a school, one church, a new post office built in 1988, and a bar. Buchanan, like many small towns is a victim of modern times: good roads, automobiles, and competition from larger businesses. Many people, however, still choose to live in the smaller rural environment.

Buchanan Catholic Church

North Dakotans
once lived here

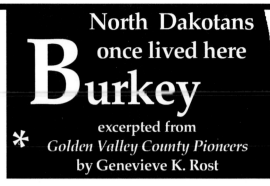

Burkey

excerpted from
Golden Valley County Pioneers
by Genevieve K. Rost

Burkey began in 1903-1904 when Joseph, John, and Zelma Bosserman homesteaded in Sec. 10, T137N, R105W. The Bosserman's came from Ohio and Missouri and had lived in Carrington, North Dakota for seven years. Another early resident was Ira Burkey after whom the town was named.

In 1906 the German Catholic Golden Valley Land Company of St. Cloud, Minnesota promoted homesteading and ran excursion trains for land seekers to the area. Many families from that area settled in and near Burkey.

William H. Hunck from Foley, Minnesota erected the first building, a two-level store in the settlement. Hunck lived in the upstairs and stocked the first floor with merchandise, groceries, and some dry goods. The post office was established September 9, 1905 with Ira Burkey as postmaster. William Hunck became postmaster in 1906; he was succeeded by Leon Kremers who served until the office was closed in 1916.

In 1906 (1907?) a small Catholic Church was built, but because of faulty construction and failure to use enough nails it was severely damaged by a windstorm in 1908. A loan of $1,500 from The Farmers and Merchants Bank of Sleepy Eye, Minnesota was made to rebuild it. Father John Dignam came to Burkey from Dickinson to serve the parish. In 1910 the parish decided to erect a Rectory at a cost of $1,600. It was poorly built and sold nine years later. A new parsonage was built in Golva.

The first resident priest was Father Mathias Minixhofer who served from 1912 to 1916. He was followed briefly by Father Carl Hierlmeier. Father Michael Lack served from October 1916 until 1920.

A school was built in 1907. It became quite a large school. The first teacher was Lyman Page. The first graduation ceremony of the Lone Tree School District was held in Burkey Hall April 30, 1915. According to the *Beach Advance* 10 schools participated, 16 students graduated, and 150 pupils and 350 spectators were in attendance.

Lewis Tungsvik, a carpenter from Story County, Iowa, constructed a blacksmith building in 1908. His blacksmith, Earl Kenney, was kept busy shoeing horses and sharpening lays for breaker plows.

Martin Zinsli, father of former sheriff Ray Zinsli, started a second general merchandise store. It was later owned by Hubert Maus, then one Lemke.

Hunck sold his general merchandise store to Leon Kremers in 1910. Kremers also operated a livery barn, providing a place for people who came to church to keep their horses. For twelve dollars a year residents could rent a stall for two horses. Chris Bares bought the store from Kremers in 1912 or 1914.

A cheese factory, financed by stockholders, was built in 1912. It made big, round cheeses, but was a short-lived venture. When it ceased operation, Martin Gass began an International Harvester Implement dealership in the facility. He owned the first high-wheel truck. It had solid tires and went fifteen miles per hour.

The first elected school board members were B. Rogers, Joe Vetsch, and John Nistler. Frank Noll, who also sold farm implements, was clerk.

The first funeral services held in the Catholic Church were for Gerhardt Wehrman and his oldest son, Norbert. Both were killed in May 1907 while digging coal on Bullion Creek. A bank caved in on them. The Wehrmans came to the area in March 1906. After the tragedy Gerhardt's widow, Mary, was left with four children. In 1908 she married Lorenz Schulte, a widower with eight children. Together they had eight children. In all they raised twenty children.

A community hall was built in 1912, again with donated labor. It was one of the major social centers in the community. Anyone in the community who could play a violin did. Tonie Barthel often played his guitar, Matt Krause his violin, and Jim Thill was the caller for many square dances. The hall was moved to Golva in 1917.

The "Burkey Musicians" on a Saturday night
(Tom Finneman, Charlie Doubles, Herb Finneman) (SHSND)

The First State Bank opened its doors in July 1914. Charles Bohart was cashier. It was moved to Golva in 1916.

When the Northern Pacific Railroad built its branch line south from Beach to Ollie, Montana, in 1915 many of the townspeople from Burkey and many of the buildings were moved to the new townsite of Golva.

In February 1921 the decision was made to move the Catholic Church to Golva. Alois G. Nistler who did a great deal of carpentry in the area was put in charge of the operation. First the roof was removed; then the sides and ends were laid down and moved on horse-drawn wagons to the new location. It was then reassembled just as it had been taken down. Nistler also moved most of the graves from the Burkey cemetery to Golva.

Gerald and Rick Noll now live where Burkey once was.

**Evelyn Cook, Herman Dietz,
Paul C. Popiel, Alma Waldahl,
Muriel Waldahl**

St. Mary's Church after moving to Golva, North Dakota - 1921
(SHSND)

Burkey Community Hall being moved to Golva - 1917
(Herb Finneman's steam engine) (SHSND)

B*urlington

by Billie Haider

Home Town of 995 North Dakotans

Burlington was established in 1883, the first town in all of "Imperial" Ward County. Here, Joseph L. Colton and James Johnson accompanied by J. J. Rogers arrived at the Forks on April 30, 1883. Through their efforts this place became the site of many "firsts" in what is now Burlington. Building a fire on their campsite led to the discovery of lignite coal and the town became the first center for lignite coal mining in the county. In the summer of 1883 the first hotel and store in this region was built. Johnson became the first postmaster when he obtained approval in August 1883 for a post office.

On February 28, 1884 the name Burlington became official and in that same year Colton started the first newspaper in Ward County. The *Burlington Reporter* later became the *Minot Daily News*. A courthouse, the symbol of authority and administration, was built in November 1885.

That same year the first law enforcement organization, The Burlington Regulators, was organized to protect the settlers.

In the spring of 1906 Johnson invited members of the Ward County Old Settlers to camp on a tract of land known as "No Man's Land"; the site became known as "Old Settlers Park."

The Soo Line Railroad pushed into the area in 1891-1892 and helped to promote the coal industry, Black Gold, and provided a means to ship bricks manufactured by a near-by brickyard, an enterprise which lasted some sixty years.

A $25,000 fire in 1929 destroyed four business places.

During the Great Depression the federal government funded a $100,000 homestead project for the local miners. The first of its kind in the state it completed 35 homes by 1939.

Burlington was incorporated on May 22, 1957 and elected a village board. In 1968 it elected its first mayor.

The first school in Ward County was managed by Colton in 1884. It also served as a church and county courthouse. In 1909, using locally made bricks, a new schoolhouse was constructed. The present, new elementary school was built in 1962.

A City Hall and Fire Hall were constructed in 1979. The Fire Department, organized in 1958, has grown until today it has 25 firemen and 6 pieces of fire equipment. The Burlington Firemen's Auxiliary was established in January 1987 with twelve members. Its main purpose is to promote family and social interaction among the firefighters and to support the various activities of the fire department. Burlington, being the oldest settlement in Ward County, held its centennial in 1983 with a four-day celebration.

Community Action of Burlington, C.A.B., was organized in January 1987 by Burlington citizens. As a non-profit organization it has several goals: establishment of a senior citizens' organization, establishment of a youth group, printing and distributing a Burlington "newspaper" and promoting the general growth and betterment of the community. A senior citizens club called the "Friendly Seniors Club" has been organized and it dreams of having its own center in the future. C.A.B. also publishes the *Burlington Press* twice a month; it contains all present day news, events, ads, sports events, schedules for the community's four churches, and other material of local interest.

Main Street, Burlington, ND - 1904
(SHSND)

In February 1982 the Burlington Recreation Program was organized. It has sponsored basketball tournaments for students each year; the number of participants has increased from 80 to over 125 in 1987. Its summer program has served over 325 children interested in playing ball. The program's long range goal is to build a sports complex with two softball diamonds, a park-picnic area, and a swimming pool.

In the early sixties the city modernized with the installation of both a water and a sewage system; in 1984 an additional reservoir was built. By August 1987 the town anticipated the completion of a curb and gutter and street paving project.

The community supports sixty-two business enterprises in Burlington and adjoining areas. With the acquisition of Johnson Additions 1 and 11; Burlington Heights Additions 1 and 11; Clementich Addition; and Ask, Steen's, Trailer Court, Hacienda Acres, Jost, Parkway First, Schoenwald, and Hillside Additions the town population now stands at 995.

Burlington's first annual 4th of July celebration was held in 1987. Other annual events are the Firemen's Muster and the Old Settlers Picnic.

Burlington Lignite Coal Company
(SHSND)

Geo Tiller's Confectionery - 1920
(SHSND)

Carson, county seat of Grant County, is a thriving and progressive city of some 380 citizens.

Just prior to 1900 settlers began moving into the region south of the Heart River and shortly thereafter they met to request the federal government to establish a post office. They proposed to call the facility Carson, a name made up from the names of three men present at the meeting, Frank C. Carter and two brothers, Simon and David Pederson. David Pederson was appointed the first postmaster and the office was located on his homestead in August 1902. Two years later, in October 1904, Frank Carter became postmaster and it was moved to his farm. Carter also managed a coal mine and general store.

2,500 lbs. of butter ready for shipment

383 North Dakotans live in Carson
by Karen Stevenson & Mildred Ochoxner

Several years later, in 1907, another community known as "North Carson" developed several miles north. In a short time it grew to include a meat market, a general store, and it boasted of a weekly newspaper, the *Carson Press*.

The two communities merged as a result of the construction in 1909 of a new Northern Pacific branch line. The new Carson townsite was platted by a subsidiary of the railroad, the Northwestern Improvement Company, in December 1909. The new town began to develop the next year when track-laying crews finished their job, the Carson railway station was established, and the Carson post office was moved to the new town.

After the new county of Grant was organized in November 1916 Carson was selected as the temporary county seat. After a bitterly fought campaign in the general election of November 1918 Carson was chosen as the permanent Grant County seat.

The community was incorporated as a village in May 1917 and was granted a city charter in July 1967.

Carson has an outstanding high school and elementary school, a bank that has been well established since 1910, several churches, and some lively men and womens' civic organizations.

The Grant County Fair is a yearly event held at the modern fair grounds on the outskirts of the city. The acreage includes new rodeo grounds built in 1983 that have no equal in North Dakota. A yearly rodeo is held there. Brenda Lee Bonogofsky, Miss Rodeo America, 1983, calls Carson her home.

Several government offices bring many people to the city to conduct business. The Quain and Ramstad Clinic of Bismarck operates a satellite branch in the city and modern hospital facilities are available in Elgin, some fifteen miles distant. The community also supports an ambulance service.

A modern structure was completed in 1980, following the destruction by fire of the old court house in 1978.

Today Carson supports the following businesses: a modern grocery store, recreation parlor and bowling alley, hardware store, three service stations, a ceramics shop, clothing store, cafe, ice cream parlor, two bars, a machine shop, cement plant, welding and metal work shop, a repair shop, feed store, locker plant, shoe repair shop, and grain elevators. Recreational facilities include: a community center, horseshoe court, tennis courts, and a softball diamond. The community also includes three low-income houses, two four-plex housing units, and a ten-unit housing complex.

The Carson Pioneers, a senior citizen's group was organized in 1970 and is very active.

Bohn Enterprises was responsible for "westernizing" the Main Street in 1984.

Carson boasts of some of the best drinking water in the state and the "western hospitality" shown by Carson citizens makes it one of the finest little towns in the "Banana Belt of North Dakota."

Cashier Herb Hallenberg at Carson's First State Bank

A community where no one knows a rich policeman. A place where everybody knows whose check is good. Where the folks know all the news before the paper comes out, but merely take it to see whether the editor got the stories the way they heard them.

C. H. Spurgeon

Carson's present bank - Grant County State Bank

O n May 11, 1875 John Bechtel's dream to build an empire in this vast, beautiful country took form when his wagon train of 13 covered wagons, 7 families, 365 head of cattle, and 100 head of horses left Enterprise, Missouri for virgin land in the Red River Valley of the North. Cavalier is the result of that dream.

The Bechtel Party included John, his wife Elizabeth, six teenage children; their daughter Catherine with her husband Noah Johnson and their three small children, John Well, Sr., a widower with two small children, and Hank Green.

The party arrived on July 31, 1875 and John chose his virgin soil homestead which he later platted into the original townsite of Cavalier. Other

County Courthouse was dedicated Nov. 7, 1913
Placed on National Register of Historic Places - 1971

Cavalier *
by Dr. Frances Branchaud, Gertrude Bechtel, Lorraine Schroeder
Home Town of 1,508 North Dakotans

pioneer families came later: George Douglas, Thomas Mahew, Joseph Gregoire, and Mose Heller came in 1876; Narcisse Hebert appeared in 1877; William Shahane turned up in 1878; John Cranley and J. McHolland reached the area in 1879; and the O'Brien family arrived in 1880. Only traveling bands of Chippewa and Sioux Indians were passing through when the Bechtel Wagon Train arrived.

Many firsts originated in Bechtel's home: first church services, day school, post office and pony express, grocery store, way station for Indians and pioneers, Mrs. John Bechtel was the first mid-wife, and Catherine Bechtel Johnson was the first school teacher.

The first business established in town was a flour and saw mill built by Bechtel, a miller by trade, and his partner, David Ellenbaum. The second enterprise established was McHolland's blacksmith shop which was followed by the *Cavalier Chronicle,* founded in 1886 and edited by Mr. Frawley.

An outbreak of diphtheria in 1879 and whooping cough in 1886 plagued the early settlers and caused the death of many children.

Cavalier was incorporated as a village in 1890 and as a city in 1903. It was named for Charles T. Cavileer, a pioneer resident of Pembina who acquired 160 acres of land adjoining Bechtel's claim. Cavileer was the only federally-appointed postmaster in the territory. The petition for a post office for the town specified the name Cavileer, but the spelling was changed to Cavalier.

Two important events contributed to Cavalier's early growth: the Great Northern Railroad reached the town in 1890 and the county seat was moved from Pembina. In the general election of November 1910 the change had been approved by 2,269 of the 3,084 votes cast but the removal was contested in the courts and it was not until October 1911 that the State Supreme Court held

for Cavalier. The county courthouse was dedicated on November 7, 1913.

The town suffered damaging floods until the Renwick Dam was constructed on the Tongue River. On Thanksgiving Day evening fire destroyed the General Store and the Jennings Hotel on Main Street. In 1986 the Kids-On-Up Store, housed in the old Pico Furniture Store building, constructed in 1891, was destroyed by fire.

The last passenger train went through Cavalier in 1963. Today, the town relies on freight trains and large transport trucks to carry the area's produce.

The town supports nine churches: Trinity United Methodist, St. Bridget's Catholic, United Presbyterian, Baptist, First United Methodist, Assembly of God, Evangelical Free, Our Saviour's Lutheran, United Lutheran, and the Baha'i Faith.

The town enjoys all the modern means of communication: United States Mail, a weekly newspaper, telephone service, and television and radio programming.

Services for the elderly include a 60-bed nursing home, a 20 unit retirement facility, low-rent housing, and a Senior Citizen Center.

The town also supports various entertainment facilities: ball park and track, bowling alleys, city park with playground equipment, a heated swimming pool, golf course and country club, movie theater, pubs, restaurants and drive-ins, skating arena, a curling rink, a hockey rink, tennis courts, and dance bands.

Citizens have a choice of various financial institutions: banks, credit union, and a savings and loan.

Cavalier has an industrial park, a bean plant, fertilizer plant, grain elevators, potato warehouses and is blessed with adequate medical services including ambulance service, a clinic, a C.A.T. Unit, a 53-bed hospital, 2 drug stores, a dentist, optometrist, and medical specialists, hearing aid technicians, ophthalmologist, and a chiropractor come on schedule from Fargo, Grand Forks, Devils Lake, and Hallock.

Area citizens may join many organizations: arts and crafts, historical society, literary clubs, lodges, service clubs, and a theatrical society.

Both a historical museum and a library benefit the surrounding community.

In 1991-1992 the community supported a modern school system with 695 students and 52 professional staff members. Rural students are bussed in and the district sponsors a summer school for migrants.

Today, the following services are available: abstract, artist, agronomist, architect, auctioneer, barber, construction, crop spraying, pilot instruction, ferrying, day care, dry cleaning, electrician, farm services, funeral home, heating, house painters, insurance, lawyers, meals-on-

Cavalier High School - 1936

wheels, mechanics, motels, trailer courts, apartments, music teachers, photographer, piano tuner, plumber, real estate dealers, roofers, upholsterers, and wheel alignment.

The following trades are also in place in Cavalier: appliances (gas and electric), bakery, beauty-massage, electrolysis studios, catalog house, car dealers, craft, drapery center, farm machinery, furniture, general merchandise, hardware, house decorating, jewelry, lumberyards, food markets, music, oil stations-parts supplies-repairs, shops for men, women, children, and a Variety Store.

Transportation services include local airplanes, railroad, senior citizen bus, and trucking firms.

There is also a military presence in the community. The 957th Engineering Company, AFB, RIB of the National Guard is located in Cavalier and the community is in the proximity of a billion-dollar anti-ballistic missile site.

Beautiful homes are surrounded by fertile farms raising wheat, small grains, corn, flax, potatoes, sugar beets, beans, sunflowers, and livestock.

With river, trees, paved streets, water and sewer, located six miles from Icelandic State Park with beautiful Lake Renwick and Gunlogson Arboretum, Cavalier is indeed a great place to live.

Public School in present day Cavalier

Page 41

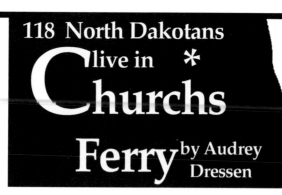

Coming to Larimore from Northfield, Minnesota in 1882 Irvine Church purchased an interest in a general store. That same year three other men, H. D. Orvis, a surveyor, and Henry and August Noltimier arrived in the area. All apparently were attracted by Devil's Lake, several smaller lakes in the area, their connecting waterways, and the possibility of a land rush into the region. Orvis, after studying an area map anticipated that a town would eventually be located on the west bank of the Mauvais Coulee which drained south into the lake.

In Larimore the men organized the Dakota Farming Company for the purpose of locating settlers who they thought would be pushing into the area shortly and building for them temporary shacks for sixty dollars each. The company's first load of lumber left Larimore in November 1882, after the Coulee had been solidly frozen over. Twenty shacks were quickly built and were purchased at once by land-hungry settlers.

When the ice went out of the Coulee in April 1883 it was found that it was shallow but difficult to ford; consequently, a flat-bottomed ferry boat, 12 by 24 feet, was constructed to facilitate crossing. The venture proved to be very profitable. Built at a cost of $188.37 it was put to use in late April 1883; total receipts for the first year amounted to $708.60. For the next three years the ferry, manned by Frank Gove, the captain, Irvine Church, the mate, and Archie Bullock, the pilot, carried scores of travelers and tons of supplies across the raging Mauvais.

The settlement on the west bank began to grow. Church built the first structure to house the ferry crew; Orvis erected a hotel; and a general store operated by Barnhart and Bollman of St. Paul opened for business in a tent. A saloon and a few other buildings were soon erected and the Church post office was established on December 12, 1883 with Irvine Church as postmaster.

In 1886 the St. Paul, Minneapolis and Manitoba Railroad (Great Northern) laid track northwest from Devils Lake and located a station called Churchs Ferry a short distance northwest of the ferry crossing. The ferry business failed as a result of the coming of the railroad.

Charles M. Fisher platted the Churchs Ferry townsite there in August 1886. The Church post office was moved to the new townsite and it was renamed Churchs Ferry in November 1886. A number of the other first buildings were also moved to the new location and new structures were quickly built.

A Methodist Church was constructed in 1886; ten years later a Lutheran Church was built. The first school building was erected in 1887.

Area farmers were blessed with good crops in the mid-1880s. In 1885 fields yielded 26 bushels of wheat per acre;

Greeting card from Churchs Ferry - 1907
(SHSND)

Public School in Churchs Ferry
(SHSND)

two years later some 15,000 bushels of wheat were marketed locally.

By the end of World War I Churchs Ferry had three hotels, three banks, medical and dental doctors, two department stores with groceries, furniture store, millinery shop, photographer, drug store, dray lines and livery stables, three grain elevators, flour mill, bakery, meat market, creamery, blacksmith shops, garage, mortuary, theater hall, newspaper, and lumberyard, but no lawyer. The town also boasted of saloons before the state adopted prohibition.

Churchs Ferry maintained its position during the 1920s, but the Great Depression took its toll, although a City Hall was built in 1936-1937 as a result of a Works Project Administration (WPA) project. It is used at the present time. During World War II many homes were moved to larger towns because building materials and labor were scarce; some homes were vacated because people moved elsewhere to support the war effort.

Incorporated as a village in March 1897 Churchs Ferry became a city in 1967 and observed its centennial in

July 1983. A replica of the ferry that was used to cross the Mauvais Coulee in the early days was a major feature of the centennial parade.

The town's population, 118 in 1991, has remained relatively stable for several years even though business continues to decline. The region continues to produce an abundance of farm produce and supports a prosperous grain terminal.

The residents are proud to have Churchs Ferry as their home.

Main Street, Churchs Ferry - 1976

The origin of Colfax dates back to the period when railroads were expanding their lines into what was to become North Dakota. During 1880 the St. Paul, Minneapolis and Manitoba Railroad (Great Northern) laid track northwest from Wahpeton toward Casselton. It located a station called Colfax on Sec. 32, T135N, R49W, land upon which Horace Crandall had homesteaded. The eighty-acre Colfax townsite was platted by him in March 1881; he had been appointed Colfax postmaster the previous month.

The town was named for Schuyler Colfax who served as vice-president under Ulysses S. Grant, 1869-73. He had purchased land adjacent to town and while visiting the area he platted

Anfin Wollan's Blacksmith Shop - 1911
(SHSND)

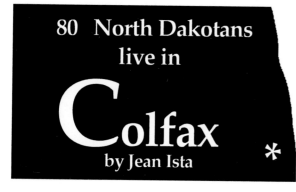

80 North Dakotans live in

Colfax

by Jean Ista

*

its first addition.

Colfax incorporated as a village in 1954 and changed to a city government in 1967.

Before the last few years, the town's population remained at about 100. Before the turn of the century the town boasted of a hotel, two stores, a lumberyard, a blacksmith shop, livery service, a flour mill, bank, grain elevator, tavern, land office, and other establishments. At the present time only a few businesses remain.

Colfax is reputed to be the smallest city in the United States with a swimming school. Operating for twenty-six years with good attendance the pool features Red Cross swimming lessons. The town also has a tennis court and two soft-ball diamonds. All these projects were built with donations.

A Junior-Senior High School is located in town, an older building having been remodeled extensively and a large, new addition completed in 1975.

The only church in town is Our Savior's Lutheran Church.

At 4:05 P.M. on August 6, 1980 a devastating storm with tornado-like winds and golf-ball sized hail struck the town without warning. Most of the trees in town were up-rooted, many buildings were completely blown away, and every home suffered damage. Crops in the surrounding area were totally destroyed.

While residents were still in shock the Salvation Army canteen arrived with food and water and stayed for ten days. The National Guard, the Mennonites, the Richland County Highway employees, and hundreds of other volunteers also came to help. Rebuilding began immediately and every home and business was restored in time for the two-day Centennial Celebration the following summer.

What the small town may have contributed in the past is one side of the coin; the other side is urbanism and the greatest opportunity in the history of man for him to reach his full potential. Where the small town kept him prisoner, urbanism gives him freedom of choice—choice of education, choice of profession, choice of marriage. If the small town is passing, we can't bemoan it.

Philip Hauser, sociologist
Newsweek, **July 8, 1963**

Colfax Stockyards and Loading Chute - 1918
(SHSND)

Main Street Colfax, North Dakota - 1976
(DPDP - Fred Schumacher)

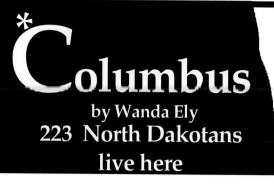

Columbus

by Wanda Ely

223 North Dakotans live here

Columbus M. Larson from St. James, Minnesota filed on a claim in Forthun Township in 1901 and founded a town, "Old Columbus," by building a store there. It was located about three-fourths of a mile west of the present Pleasant Prairie Church. Soon there was a huddle of shacks and an inland town was born. Legend has it that Ole Forthun, another early settler, got together with his friend Larson and named the township Forthun and the shack town Columbus. Other businesses that sprang up were Bannister Drug Store, Frank Fiegel Cafe and Pool Hall, Wenzell Hierath Blacksmith Shop, and the Thorkild Thorildson Grocery Store. Thorildson also ran a coach and locater bus from Portal. The bus, driven by Tony McKay, carried mail and passengers. A post office named Columbus was established in Larson's store in February 1903.

The prosperous little shack town also included a "blind pig" which upset many of the ladies in town because the men folks spent a lot of time in there. One night they raided the place, took all the bottles, emptied them, and threw them along the dirt streets. The next morning a group of young boys saw a chance to make a

few cents. They picked up the bottles that weren't broken and sold them back to the "pig" owner.

In 1906 the Soo Line Railroad began building a branch line west from its main line at Flaxton; the extension ran some six miles southeast of "Old Columbus." In 1906 the railroad finished its track-laying, established a station named Columbus, and had its subsidiary, the Tri-State Land Company plat the new Columbus townsite. One Bert Helgeson is said to have stepped out the plat. The settlers in "Old Columbus" were now faced with the choice remaining or moving to the new townsite. The post office was moved to the new townsite and the "town moving" was completed in the late summer and early fall of 1906.

The first known church service was a Roman Catholic Mass, held in 1907, in a pool hall with planks laid over

malt barrels to make the altar. The first church was the Swain Memorial Methodist, built in 1907. Today, the community supports three churches: St. Michael's Catholic, Trinity Lutheran, and Faith Lutheran.

The first train ran through town on July 4, 1906. The following year the railroad was given a contract to carry the mail. A local story recounts that when the railroad dropped off the first bags of mail a homesteader by the name of William Graham picked them up and took it upon himself to be the first postmaster. About 1960 the railroad removed their track and a spur line was built from Kincaid into town.

The *Columbus Reporter* went to press in 1906; it was first published by L. E. Woods and I. P. Neale. It was sold over the years to various people, the last sale being in 1950. Today, the community is without a local paper.

Coal mining was the big industry in the era of the 1920s and 1930s. Columbus was a "boom-town" with the Whittier-Crocket Coal Company and the Truax-Traer Coal Company being responsible for employing more

Main Street, Columbus, North Dakota 1914

Main Street, Columbus, North Dakota - 1949

than a hundred men in their mines. Montana-Dakota Utilities used the mines to their advantage and built a power plant near the sites. In addition to these two large mines more than twenty privately owned mines were operating in the area. Today, all the mines have been closed and the Montana-Dakota Utilities power plant has been shut down.

The Short Creek School District was organized in 1906. The first high school class registered in 1915 and graduated in 1919. In 1951 a new gymnasium was built and in 1960-1961 a new elementary school was constructed. The new Columbus School District No. 34 resulted from reorganization efforts in the northwestern part of Burke County in 1949. A high school reunion was held in 1969 to commemorate the 50th anniversary of the school's first graduation class.

Active community organizations today include: the American Legion and its Auxiliary, a Lions Club, a Senior Citizens group, the Friendship Club, Columbus Community Men, Columbus Community Women, an Art Club, a Sportsmen Club, a Columbus Recreation Club, and various church sponsored organizations.

The community also supports a volunteer fire department and a local ambulance service. A new commu-

nity building was constructed in 1984; the project was paid for by individual donations from the community, by contributions from various organizations, and by township funds. The newest community projects include the development of a mini-park on main street, sponsored by the Lions Club in 1987, and a centennial project which would line both sides of main street with trees, begun in the spring of 1988.

Shortcreek Dam, located seven miles north of Columbus, attracts many campers and fishermen. The Sportsmen Club provides much of the up-

keep for the area and they also sponsor an annual fishing derby. In 1986 they established a playground and equipped it with swings, slides, and sandboxes.

The city park is used for many family gatherings and group picnics. Other recreational facilities include: a golf course and club house, a baseball diamond and grandstand, and the American Veteran's Memorial Park. Playground equipment was donated by the Columbus Jaceettes and a tennis court and arena was donated by the Columbus Jaycees. The arena is used for ice skating in the winter and dances or picnics in the summer. Burke-Divide Electric holds their annual picnic in the park. The Park District hires a custodian to care for the grounds each summer.

Drought and grasshoppers caused major problems for our farmers in the 1980s. The population has declined and the community suffers from unemployment.

Present businesses include: the First National Bank, Wally's Grocery, Ken's Cafe, the Columbus Clinic, Dan's Standard, Montana-Dakota Utilities, Burke-Divide Electric, the Post Office, Ken's Bar & Motel, Maxine's Beauty Shop, Great Plains Supply, Melgaard Sand and Gravel, Buerkly Heavy Equipment, Oas Implement, and Continental Grain Company at Stampede.

Main Street, Columbus, North Dakota - 1988

Home Town of 70 North Dakotans

Courtenay*

by Betty Larson

The earliest settlers came by covered wagon, horseback, and even by walking. They were met by endless, treeless miles of billowing grass. For the first few years small sod houses or tar-paper shacks were the shelter from summer storms, winter's icy blasts, and devastating prairie fires. Later many came by rail boxcar with all possessions, animals, and family crowded for many days into cramped quarters. But they saw the beauty and the promise of the land, and they stayed.

Located in the northeastern corner of Stutsman County on the Soo Line Railroad, Courtenay was built on land owned by John Reid. The railroad reached the town in 1892. Prior to this time, grain produced in this area had to be hauled a distance of 30 miles, the nearest elevators being in Dazey or Jamestown. With horses hitched to a wagon the trip took a full day, the return trip being made the following day with the wagon loaded with supplies for the months ahead.

In 1892 H. N. Tucker began buying grain for the Osborne McMillan Elevator and Ole Fosholdt with John Syvertson as his partner, started a general store, thereby giving farmers and ranchers a closer source of supplies. This general store, later known as Fosholdt Bros., continued in business for 84 years. Howard Fosholdt, after his father's death, became manager until 1976, when because of ill health an auction was held and Courtenay lost a landmark business, well-known throughout the region.

Among other first business ventures were Smith & Roger Lumber Company and Royal Lumber. Courtenay soon became a shipping center for a large area, embracing portions of Griggs and Barnes counties as well as Stutsman. In a few years more businesses began including Courtenay State Bank, Stutsman County Bank, Flax and Tow Mill, L. H. Larson Hardware, Tucker Farm Machinery, Larson & Cooper Furniture and Undertaking, and Hotel Courtenay. Dr. McDonald also began practice. By 1915 Courtenay had grown to a village with a population of over 1,000.

Churches played an important part in the lives of early settlers. After holding services in Corinne Township since 1888, the First Presbyterian Church was erected in 1896 to serve the area until it was closed in 1984. St. Mary's Roman Catholic Church in Durham Township burned in 1928, after which a brick structure was erected in town; it is still an active congregation. Zion Lutheran Church in Ashland Township, built in 1892 by mostly German immigrants, burned after lightning struck it in 1941. The congregation merged with the Lutheran church in town, which in turn merged with St. Paul's Lutheran Church in Wimbledon in 1971.

In the very early years, mail was brought by team from Jamestown to a farm in Corinne township with D. A. Langworthy as postmaster. It was also delivered to the Horn farm in Courtenay Township with E. F. Horn as postmaster. In 1893 a post office was established in town. At the present time the post office occupies the former National Bank building with M. Sabinash serving as postmaster.

Realizing the need to educate their children the pioneers in 1883 organized the New Washington School District which included the townships of Courtenay, Corinne, and two congressional townships west of town, namely Nogosek and New Washington, later known as Durham. A small building was erected in Courtenay Township and relocated several times until in 1899 when a four-room school was built in town for elemen-

Courtenay Mercantile - 1915

Aerial view of Courtenay, North Dakota - 1984

tary grades. A four-year high school was added in 1906. In 1916 a larger brick building was completed and served until 1980 when declining enrollment and increasing costs made it necessary to merge with the neighboring town of Wimbledon.

Over the years the town has experienced many tragedies. In 1895 a devastating fire destroyed a great portion of the buildings. Evidencing great faith in their community, the people rebuilt with better buildings. Other businesses destroyed by flames were Ernies Garage in 1920 and a mercantile store a few years later. In the early 1930s the Opera House and a hardware store burned and Courtenay Motors was destroyed in 1958. Another tragedy was the robbery of the National Bank which resulted in the death of a bank employee, Elmer Bunkowski. An unwelcome visitor in 1968 was a tornado

which totally or partially destroyed many homes, an elevator, and a portion of the school. The townspeople were thankful that no lives were lost.

Early social life centered around the churches and the school. One active organization was the commercial club. Local Ladies Aid societies, study clubs, 4-H clubs, scouts, drama club, and band organizations kept young and old busy.

The devastating economic conditions of the Great Depression, World War II, the growth of larger, but fewer farms, smaller families, and better roads giving easier access to larger shopping areas all had their effect on small towns in the state, Courtenay included.

Although Courtenay's population has dwindled to 70 people, the community is proud of: its new fire station with a well-staffed fire department, its newly refurbished community

center, an excellent cafe and bar, a well-equipped garage, employing an experienced and capable mechanic, and a grocery and gift store. A thriving enterprise, Agri-Cover, is operating in the former school building and Harvest States Elevator serves area farmers. A custom gunsmith looks after the interests of area-wide sportsmen and the local Senior Citizen's Center is used by many for meetings and social gatherings. A tree-moving service and a trenching service are also available.

With the same spirit as its early pioneers Courtenay held its Centennial celebration in June 1987 by looking undauntedly forward to the next 100 years. A more complete and detailed history of the community may be found in the *Courtenay Centennial History Book*.

Interested homesteaders saw Divide County prairie land for the first time shortly after the turn of the century and were very favorably impressed with it. Seth O. Crosby, a general store partner in Portal, a town some 42 miles to the east, had faith in this part of the country and assured new arrivals that he would follow them with a store and post office to supply the needs of early settlers. In 1903, under his leadership and with other Portal businessmen, land scrip was used to acquire title to some forty acres in the SE1/4 SW1/4 sec. 30, T163N, R97W. It is reported that Crosby drove a stake into the fertile soil and posted a notice that the tract was to be used as the townsite for Crosby. Samuel S. Nelson was appointed postmaster of an office that was located there on June 25, 1904.

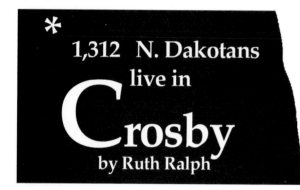

1,312 N. Dakotans live in Crosby
by Ruth Ralph

S. S. Nelson bought Crosby's site and opened a general business called The Crosby Store in the spring of 1904 in "old" Crosby. This was the beginning of Crosby.

"Old" Crosby grew to be quite a town before competing railroads pronounced its death sentence. Two newspapers were published in the little settlement: the *Crosby Eagle* and the *Crosby Review*. The former became the present *Crosby Journal* and the latter became the *Farmer's Press* which survived until 1946. Both papers moved later, along with the rest of the town to the new settlement.

"Old" Crosby had grown into a thriving little community by 1906 when it drew the attention of two competing railroads: the Minneapolis, St. Paul & Sault Ste. Marie (Soo Line), and the Great Northern. Both railroads planned to extend their lines into the region and both planned to establish stations called Crosby.

An early advantage was gained by the Soo Line when they by-passed "old" Crosby and laid tracks west from Flaxton to the new town of Ambrose. They planned to locate their station in the eastern part of Sec. 27, T163N, R97W. In July 1906, their subsidiary, the Tri-State Land Company, platted their "new" Crosby townsite alongside it; but, a month later, plans changed and a Crosby City townsite was platted in the northwestern part of Sec. 27.

Meanwhile, the Great Northern sent paid agents into the area to persuade residents to wait for their line which they planned to build northwest of Berthold and which would also terminate in their town of Crosby. It was going to be located on Sec. 29, a mile east of "old" Crosby.

For whatever reasons, most of the "old" community favored the Great Northern site and in September 1906 the Crosby post office was moved there. Confronted with this situation the Soo Line's station on Sec. 27 was named Imperial. Even though a post office was established there in February 1907 the Soo Line town failed to grow and the post office was discontinued several months later. The Soo Line then decided to move its station from Imperial and establish its own Crosby station. This was done in 1908.

Businesses which flourished in early Crosby included the following: the State Bank of Williams County, First State Bank of Crosby, Crosby Meat Market, the office of Blake Lancaster, a medical doctor, John D. Clark, Attorney, Crosby-Portal Stage Coach Line, Pioneer Hotel and Restaurant, Nelson Brothers Hardware, Gustafson's Drug Store, The Headquarters, a confectionery and pool room, Crosby Livery Stable, Crosby Hotel

Main Street Crosby, North Dakota - 1976
(DPDP - Todd Strand)

and Restaurant, Feeney Tonsorial Parlor, Hopkins Credit Business, Rud Anderson Tree Planter and Seller, and J. E. Johnson Real Estate.

Crosby's selection as county seat in December 1910, after the creation of Divide County, was undoubtedly the greatest thing that every happened to the city. The first county commissioners found it difficult to select the county seat, each having committed himself to support a specific town, Ambrose, Crosby, and Noonan. After much arguing Crosby was finally chosen as the temporary county seat. That decision was made permanent in 1912.

The city made great strides in the five year period which followed. Population increased steadily: 1,011 in 1915, in 1920 it stood at 1,147, by 1930 it reached 1,270, in 1960 it had grown to 1,759. Since the 1960s the population has declined and the 1990 population was about 1,300.

One of Crosby's biggest business building boom years was 1917. Besides the construction of the Divide County Court House new structures were built for the J. C. Penney Company, the Citizen's National Bank, and Saint Luke's Hospital.

Crosby was incorporated as a village in May 1907 and by vote of its citizens in 1911 adopted a city form of government. On August 8, 1911 J. C. Rousseau became the city's first mayor. He was followed by D. W. Madden, E. O. Halvorson, John K. Jensen, C. J. Clark, Anton Otheim, A. Ingwalson, William Homestead, C. B. Gardner, Dr. R. M. Bergem, E. A Tuftedal, Orville Tryhus, Kenneth Engberg, George Larsen, Herbert Engberg, and Oscar Svangstu.

Today, Crosby is a thriving community in the northwest corner of the state, boasting about 110 business places.

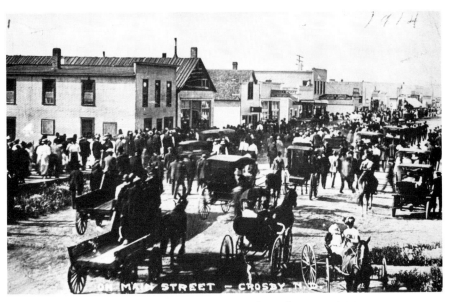

Main Street Crosby, North Dakota - 1914
(SHSND)

What are American institutions? Everything is an institution. Having iced water to drink in every room of the house is an institution. Having hospitals in every town is an institution. Travelling altogether in one class of railway cars is an institution. Saying sir is an institution. Plenty of food is an institution. Getting drunk is an institution in a great many towns. Lecturing is an institution.

Anthony Trollope
He Knew He Was Right, XLVI, 1869

Kjorlein Hardware Store - early 1900s
(SHSND)

Dawson, like so many North Dakota communities, began as a railway siding. When the Northern Pacific Railroad was constructing its main line from Jamestown to Bismarck in 1872 it built a station and siding on Sec. 10, T130N, R72W and named it the Thirteenth Siding, a common practice when railroads built through unsettled territory. The site was the thirteenth siding the railroad built west of Fargo.

In October 1880 an early homesteader and land developer from Pennsylvania, Josuah Dawson Thomson, along with Fred D. Hager and Robert E. Wallace of Jamestown platted the townsite. In 1881 ownership of the townsite was vested in the Dawson City Land and Improvement Company with Thomson as secretary.

Dawson, the first established town in Kidder County, became the hub of the surrounding area. As a rail center it housed a water tower and coal docks for steam engines and settlers were taken to their claims from a land office.

78 North Dakotans live in

Dawson *

by Rosemarie Birrenkott

There are several distinctive facts about the town. Mabel Baldwin the first white child born in Kidder county, was born in Dawson. Tuttle and Pettibone, two towns in the northern part of Kidder County, were named for W. P. Tuttle and Lee Pettibone, prominent citizens and land developers from Dawson. The Sibley House, a community landmark, was a three-story hotel, containing an opera house on its third floor for dances, traveling troupes, and local talent shows.

At one time the town boasted of a creamery, a mill, banks, newspapers, churches, and a fine school.

The school produced outstanding athletic teams; it captured the girls' state basketball championship three times. It consolidated with Steele in 1959, but kindergarten and third and fourth grade classes are still held in town.

The town suffered a decrease in population for various reasons: the Great Depression, the 1940 tornado which devastated the community, causing two deaths and extensive property damage, and the demise of the railroad after World War II.

However, the area remains a mecca for sportsmen, with waterfowl, small game-land birds, and deer in abundance. Hunters fill the area each fall. George Slade, vice-president of the Northern Pacific Railroad, built a hunting lodge near Lake Isabel, to the south of town, in the twenties. The area was later donated to the United States Fish and Wildlife Service as a preserve.

Lake Isabel remains a summer resort for fishing, swimming, and boating enthusiasts. There is a public picnic area with a beach for swimmers and a dock for boaters on the east side of the lake. Cabins surround the north and west sides. Camp Grassick

Main Street Dawson, North Dakota - early 1900s

The Sibley Hotel, Dawson, North Dakota

is located on the south beach of the lake. It began as a camp for tuberculosis patients but was purchased in 1947 by the North Dakota Elks Association as a camp for handicapped children. Handicapped adults and the blind also use the facilities for one-week camps during the summer.

Despite Dawson's present size there remains an enthusiastic spirit. Kemmet's Grocery, Midway Service, and The Yankee Doodle Diner, all owned by Alan Kemmet, serve the community. The Big D, located across from Lake Isabel and owned by Duane and Elsie Draeger; Don's Bar owned by Don and Colene Wick; Wentz Elevator operated by Wayne Lang; and Ritter Repair owned by Marshall Ritter also serve the area. The Dawson post office, first established on October 14, 1881 with Irving E. Philleo as postmaster, remains in operation.

The community supports various activities: summer baseball with youngsters dreaming of championships, an active senior citizens club which meets each month to share lively comradery, active 4-H and homemaker clubs, an annual pancake-sausage supper sponsored by the fire department, the American Legion John Green Post No. 231 which holds a memorial program each spring and sponsors fireworks on the Fourth of July, and the recently-formed theater group, The Dawson Players, who entertain the community with a rousing production each fall.

Bird's-eye view of Dawson - early 1900s

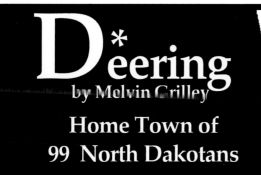

D*eering
by Melvin Grilley

Home Town of 99 North Dakotans

By the end of 1901 all of the Deering area had been homesteaded. The town grew on the site where railroad workers set their tents. The origin of the town's name is questionable; some believe it was named after a Great Northern Railroad official; others believe it was named after William Deering of the Deering Harvester Company which had established its headquarters in Fargo in 1881 and distributed its grain and grass cutting equipment in northern Minnesota and Dakota Territory.

The first school in Thursby Butte District was held in John Hagan's 8 by 10 foot claim shack in 1902; Charlie Holmes taught 13 students. In 1904 the district rented the Congregational Church for six months at $4.00 per month. A wood frame school was built for 27 students near the present location; by the 1920s it was overflowing and a brick building, still in use, was constructed in 1922. Jim Corum, the school's first high school graduate, received his diploma in 1920. The school has been remodeled in recent years.

By the end of 1904 the town's businesses included: A. E. Turner, elevator; Frank Jestrab, hardware dealer; O. C. Haug, shoes and harness; a grocery store, English and Guyton, proprietors; Allen Brothers, butcher shop; the *Deering Enterprise*, edited by Bill Jackman; a restaurant operated by the Southerlands; Dilley's Hardware; and a hotel.

The Congregational Church, the town's first church, was built in 1904 for $185.00. O. C. Haug was its founder; Reverend Severt Olson was its minister. The Catholic Church was the second house of worship to be built; later the Lutherans established a congregation and purchased the Free Methodist Church. It was moved to its present location.

As the town thrived other businesses were established: W. A. Dunlop, J. I. Case Implement; the Opera House included a dance floor and theater on the second floor with a pool hall on the main floor; a drugstore; the Webb elevator; a Doctor's office; a barbershop; mortuary; candy shop; flour mill which sent flour to Europe during World War I; a railroad mail service; and telephone service.

Deering was incorporated as a village on September 17, 1908. At the first election 35 ballots were cast; only men went to the polls.

In the early 1900s the town's business district grew to include: four more elevators, three banks, a photograph studio, a lumberyard, dray line, a blacksmith and a tailor shop.

The first couple to be married in Deering were Fred Allen and Clare Holo who were wed in 1906.

The most devastating fire occurred in 1933 when at least six businesses and some homes were destroyed.

In 1959 a small tornado damaged two businesses and demolished the Standard Oil Station.

Main Street Deering, North Dakota

In 1964 a city water system was constructed; a sewage system was installed in 1974. In 1976 the abandoned Great Northern Railroad depot was moved near the post office and converted into a community center. In 1980 Main Street was paved.

Today's businesses include: Mel's Hardware and Repair, formerly Jestrab's Hardware; Big Red's Saloon, originally built as a bank; S. & L. Market and Cafe; Ray Miller's Bulk Fuel which provides year round delivery; and the Farmers Elevator which accepts year round delivery; and Deering Mobile Estates. Deering's school is now only an elementary school and the town supports only two churches.

All of these enterprises provide a valuable service to the community and surrounding area.

Deering Community Center

Fire destroying Imperial Lumber Co. & Bank - 1917

In the summer of 1893 the Minneapolis, St. Paul & Sault Ste Marie Railroad extended its tracks to Portal, North Dakota and established a station called Donnybrook. Many people believe the station was named by the wife of some unknown official after a town in Ireland.

In November 1894 Martha Jane Power received her appointment as postmaster of Donnybrook; however, the post office, located about a half mile south of the station, wasn't opened until March 20, 1895. In 1897 it closed and moved to Goetz on Sec. 29, T158N, R86W where E.C. Henry had a coal mine. The railroad built a spur to that location; a brick plant and store were also established there. In 1898 the post office was re-established in Donnybrook with Delos Hunnewell as postmaster.

Main Street Donnybrook, North Dakota - 1910

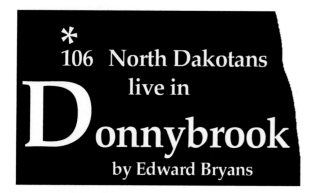

106 North Dakotans live in Donnybrook
by Edward Bryans

In 1900 Donnybrook had two groceries: one run by John Mecklenberg and Fred Barke and another by Frank and Phil Killian. The Killian brothers built on the extreme eastern edge of Donnybrook in an attempt to attract the town to their property, which they called Killianville. They were unsuccessful, although they had at least a barbershop there in addition to the store. The brothers filed a plat known as Donnybrook's original plat on March 22, 1901. In April 1901 John Power filed a plat south of the railroad tracks where he had established a livery stable and rooming house. Crow's plat was located north of the railroad tracks where Fred Barke had established his store in

1900. Mrs. Carlson, wife of the railroad section foreman, had established a rooming house there earlier. It was on this plat that the town originally grew.

In 1902, Clark Hovey established the *Donnybrook Mirror*.

In December 1903 the business district was almost completely destroyed by fire. In March 1904 another fire destroyed more buildings. As a result, most of the village moved to the south side of the tracks to its present location. The village was incorporated in 1904.

Long distance telephone service was begun in 1903; in 1905 the Donnybrook-Aurelia Telephone Company organized. The area is now serviced by the Souris River Telephone Company.

In 1915 M.A. McIntire installed an electrical generator in his home. He provided electrical service to the town until 1927, when Montana-Dakota Utilities Company took over.

The Upper Souris River Water Users began service to the town in 1980. A city sewer system was installed in 1985.

Today, Donnybrook consists of the Methodist and Roman Catholic churches, a meat market and a bar, one service station, a grain elevator, a hardware store, and a convenience store.

The school serves the first six grades (grades 7-12 go to Kenmare).

This Midwest. A dissonance of parts and people, we are a consonance of Towns. Like a man grown fat in everything but heart, we overlabor; our outlook never really urban, never rural either, we enlarge and linger at the same time, as Alice both changed and remained in her story.

William Gass
In the Heart of the Heart of the Country, 1968

Donnybrook, North Dakota - 1907

Donnybrook, North Dakota - 1905

Dunn Center's original site, established in 1913 one and a half miles east of its present location, was chosen because it was believed it would be near a Northern Pacific Railroad branch line then under construction. The railroad arrived in the fall of 1914, passed by the original site, and established a station. Realizing the importance of the railroad, residents "pulled up stakes" and moved to the present location.

A. C. Diehl was the first residential agent. In the mid-1980s the railroad tracks were dismantled, the railroad ties were sold, and the station was abandoned.

The townsite itself was platted by the Tuttle Land Company of Dawson, North Dakota in May 1914 and named for its locus near the center of the county.

Normanna Lutheran Church was built in 1915, but in recent times the parish merged with the rural Vang Lutheran Church and continues to serve the community. The Church of Jesus Christ of Latter-day Saints, Mormon, was built in 1917 and the Congregational Church basement was built in 1922.

The Dunn Center school was constructed in 1916, but declining school enrollments eventually forced the community to dissolve its school district in 1963 and its lands were annexed to the Killdeer district. The last senior class to graduate from

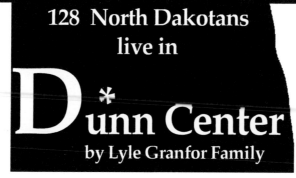

128 North Dakotans live in
Dunn Center*
by Lyle Granfor Family

Dunn Center High School was the class of 1961. High school students thereafter went to Killdeer, but a grade school was maintained for ten years. In 1971, with only grades one through four being taught, Dunn Center school closed its doors.

The families of John Thompson and Bert Nyhagen were among the first settlers in Dunn Center. Mail was first distributed to the early settlers in the area from a rural post office named Melby which had been established in January 1907 on Carl R. Melby's homestead; Melby was appointed postmaster. Seven years later the office was moved to Dunn Center and Gustave B. Nyhagen was postmaster. Early mail carriers in the area were Charles Fuller, C. W. Kempf, and Bill Dehn.

As the town grew a full complement of businesses served the area. Lumber yards were operated by Kilzer, Dunham, and Mandan. The Occident, Powers, and Farmers Elevators purchased grain from surrounding farmers; settlers could deposit money in the First State Bank where Char-

lie Hein acted as cashier or in the Farmers Bank where Thomas Ahern was employed as cashier. A drug store was owned and operated by William Moede and the Skude Brothers sold clothing. Two hotels, Taylor's and Phillips', accommodated travelers and the Hart Restaurant and Bakery operated behind the Taylor Hotel.

At one time the town boasted of two hardware stores: Boyd and Peterson, and Rosendahl and Nyhagen. After the latter was destroyed by fire they purchased the former company. Harness and shoe repair shops were operated by John Pockert and Godfred Bjorge. Blacksmiths M.A. Davis and Oscar Boe served community needs and in later years Sherman McConnell also operated a blacksmith shop.

Thompson and Howe managed a grocery store; Robinson and Mellow ran a department store; Lundeens Dry Good and Hat Shop supplied the community with those specialties; and Genye Grocery and Meat also competed for the settler's business.

Legal problems in the area were resolved by attorneys A. S. Boe, W. A. Carns, Alf O. Nelson, and T. H. Thorson. Theo G. Nelson opened a real estate office and pool halls managed by Dude Holt, Shorty Rasmussen, Simms, and C. P. Rosendahl provided recreation for the residents.

Main Street Dunn Center, North Dakota - 1987

Recreation was also provided the community in the early years by the Dunn Center Band which at one time boasted of about forty members.

Transportation companies were established early in the town's history. Dray lines were operated by Jesse Whitaker, Harry Shepard, and Ole Finholt and livery stables were managed by Lee Paul and David Sands. The Sands Livery Stable was purchased later by Lewis Granfor and converted into a garage, although Oscar Ebeltoft opened the town's first garage.

The barbering business was also established early in Dunn Center. One Chapin was an early practitioner and in 1915 Stanley Beaton opened his shop; it closed sometime in the 1970s. A flour mill built by George Schmidt Sr. also began operations in 1915 and that same year telephone service came to the area, the exchange was owned and operated by Ole Kittilson.

Medical services were first provided by Dr. Linson; then by Drs. Gibson, Barton, and Moreland. Optical services were provided by Edith Thompson and veterinarian services by Dr. Kearnes.

Dunn Center boasted of two newspapers: the *Spring Valley Times*, edited by R. W. Robertson and the *Dunn County Journal* edited by Charles Doherty.

Through the years many enterprises closed their doors for one reason or another: M. A. Olson Mortuary, Anderson Grocery Store, Sword's Grocery Store, Circle Food Store, 200 Cafe, D. & D. Steel & Machine,

Whitaker's Dray Barn - early 1900s

Dvorak's Store, Krieger Cabinet Shop, and numerous other businesses.

Dunn Center remains a thriving little community. Alice Goetz owns and operates Alice's Cafe and Grocery; Dunn Center Grain and Lumber is owned and operated by the Lloyd Nantt family; the post office is managed by Karen Aarvig and rural mail carriers include Sandra Benz, Sally Decker, and Myra Walker; Granfor Chevrolet is owned and operated by Lyle Granfor with Clair Kittilson the mechanic; and for many years Dunn Center Motor was operated by Carl Pedersen and Blaine Fockler. In the early 1980s it was sold to Mark Eckelberg and Ray Bird and was renamed Dunn Center Sales and Service; it is now closed.

An early well-drilling operation was established by A. J. Thompson; his son, Kendall, operated the business

for several years. Today, Thompson Well Drilling remains in the family and is managed by Rodney Thompson.

Other businesses currently operating include: Mead Carpentry, Ilo Bar, Corner Shop, The Craft Cabin, Dunn County Thrift Shop, Dunn Center Cable TV, and Knutson Trailer Court. C & I Jerky Plant was built in 1986 and is owned and operated by Cheryl Knutson and Ileene Nodland.

In 1917 a Community Hall was erected and was a major center of activity until the mid 1970s. It was purchased in the early 1980s and moved to a different location and has now been restored by Laudie and Martha Dvorak. A new city hall which also houses the local fire department was built in the early 1980s.

A few years ago the Dunn Center Park Board was formed. It sponsors card parties and along with other activities is responsible for caring for the local park.

The school was beyond repair and in 1985 demolition work began. In the spring of 1986 a museum was built which included portions of the old school. Treasures which are meaningful to Dunn County residents are on display.

The operation is administered by the Dunn County Historical Society which also sponsors the community's major annual event: the Fourth of July parade and Pot-Luck Picnic.

Main Street Dunn Center, North Dakota - 1917

A particular bend in the Missouri River and the thickly wooded river bottoms at the site was called Elbowoods by the Mandan and Arikara Indians. Elbowoods, a picturesque village nestled in the foothills near the Missouri, was founded in 1891 for the Fort Berthold Agency headquarters. The road, leading into town with its white-clapped buildings and moss green roofs, was an avenue between lofty cottonwoods, a scenic drive.

Here on the outskirts was the Mission School begun by the pioneer missionary, Reverend Charles Hall, in 1876. Commissioned as missionaries, he and his bride, Emma Calhoun, took a 1,000 mile, two-week trip up the Missouri by flat-bottom paddle-wheel boats to the Like-a-Fishook village of the Hidatsas,

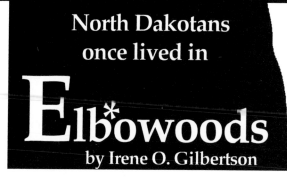

North Dakotans
once lived in

Elbowoods

by Irene O. Gilbertson

Mandans, and Arikara Indians. Here he worked among the tribes until 1922 when Reverend Harold and Eva Case "inherited" the mission, spending 45 years, until 1965, working with, and for, the Indian peoples. A boarding school with a mission farm was begun and continued until the public school with dormitories was put into use in 1939.

The Roman Catholic Mission (The Sacred Heart Indian Mission and the Immaculate Conception Church) was also on the outskirts of the little settlement, and served both the Indian and white populace.

Here Reverend Reinhard Kauffman, from Switzerland, worked with the Indians for twenty-five years, taking charge of the mission, church, and boarding school. Interested in horticulture, an interest he continued after his retirement, he had an orchard of 170 fruit trees and shrubs, in spite of the severe North Dakota winters. He named Mandaree the new segment west of the river by taking the letters *MAN* from Mandan, *DA* from Hidatsa, and *REE*

which was the name often given to the Arikaras. He was honored in 1955 by the Fort Berthold Catholic Indian Congress for twenty-five years of service to the Indians.

Government business pertaining to the tribes was conducted in the Agency Office under the supervision of an appointed superintendent and his staff. Here was handled the leasing of lands to the non-Indian farmers, here was conducted the tribal-United States government legation, here was stationed the government doctor who made house calls both on and off the reservation. Probably best known and remembered was Dr. Mary McKee, an Easterner from Philadelphia who spent many years journeying in buggies, wagons, and Model Ts to the homes where she was needed.

Elbowoods was modernized. In 1934 a brick hospital was built and a high school replaced the public school which served the children of the Agency employees. It was the first public and federal government school in the United States. It was later replaced by the modern edifice, White Shield, the "Jewel of the Prairie," one of the best equipped schools in North Dakota. It accommodated the children of the reservation along with students from several county school districts.

Some of the log cabin homes were replaced by frame homes, although the log cabins were warmer in winter and cooler in summer than the wood ones. Fruit, bull berries (buffalo berries), chokecherries, June berries, wild grapes, and plums grew in abundance along the river banks and were a source of food as well as income. In the early years it is said that wagonloads of wild plums would be taken to the pioneer settlements such as Plaza by the Native Americans and sold by the pailful to those who welcomed such a change of diet.

Most squaws had a small garden. Vari-colored Squaw corn, squash,

Bust of Drags Wolf on Dedication Day

American Legion Post No. 253 at Drags Wolf bust dedication

turnips, and potatoes were cultivated.

A ferry hauled passengers, vehicles, horse-drawn wagons, and riders across the "wide Missouri," dodging sandbars enroute. It was the connecting link for the various segments of the reservation which lay on both sides of the river which could be crossed in bullboats, log canoes, or on the ice during the winter season.

Then came progress. A bridge, appropriately named Four Bears after a prominent Indian chief, was dedicated in 1934. It was the only bridge spanning the Missouri between Williston and Bismarck. A crowd of 25,000 witnessed the event; some suggested it was the largest crowd ever assembled in one place in North Dakota up to that time.

Soon there were rumblings about building the world's largest earth-filled dam some forty or fifty miles below Elbowoods. The dam, a gigantic undertaking which would affect the lives of thousands of people, would back up waters some 200 miles to Williston, forcing the evacuation of the towns of Elbowoods, Van Hook, and Sanish. A multi-purpose project, hydroelectric power, flood control, irrigation, and recreation, the Garrison Dam soon became a reality despite the protests of white and Indian settlers caught in its web.

Elbowoods was dismantled, board by board, brick by brick. A new Agency appropriately named New Town was to be built in Mountrail County. The settlers, nestled in the shelter of the timbered river bottoms, were forced to flee to the treeless plateaus above the 1,850 foot elevation, the proposed height of the dam.

Farmers with their farmsteads within the contoured shorelines were given the option of accepting the offer made by the Corps of Engineers or submitting to arbitration.

Four Bears Bridge, in use less than twenty years, was taken apart, span by span like tinker toys and re-assembled as the midsection of a bridge over forty miles upstream. It remains a monument to a bygone era and a traffic hazard because its two-lane roadbed no longer accommodates today's traffic burden.

Ninety feet of yellow Missouri water cover the former site of Elbowoods. The towering cottonwoods have long since washed up on the shores as grotesque drift wood stumps. The inaccessible Saddle Butte is a blue haze westward in the distance and only scarred memories remain for those who lived in the shadow of Elbowoods during the forties and fifties.

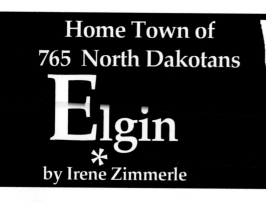

Home Town of 765 North Dakotans

Elgin

*

by Irene Zimmerle

As far back as 1902 immigrants, mostly German-Russian, and a sprinkling of other ethnic groups settled in the area that is now known as Elgin, North Dakota. Before the town was established settlers did their trading in a small inland town called Leipzig, located along the Antelope Creek. Towns without a railroad, however, were at a disadvantage; railroads were necessary for the efficient transportation of livestock, supplies, and passengers. In 1910 the Northern Pacific Railroad Company extended a branch line south and west from Mandan and established a station on Sec. 22, T134N, R89W. Originally, the site was to be named Shanley, for the recently deceased Roman Catholic Bishop of North Dakota, the Right Reverend John Shanley.

Postal officials, however, objected to the name Shanley after the townsite had been platted by the Northwestern Improvement Company in February 1910 because it was too similar to the name Stanley, another North Dakota town. Local legend has it that during a meeting of local residents and after much debate, one Isaadore Gintzler checked the time, noted the name Elgin on the face of his pocket watch, and suggested it as the new name. The Elgin post office was established on August 11, 1910; Julius Heil was named postmaster. When the Northern Pacific Railroad finished laying its tracks through the site it also named its new station Elgin.

Another railroad, the Chicago, Milwaukee & St. Paul and Pacific Railroad Company, was located only a short distance south of Elgin, but the company failed to build a station there. When the area between the two sets of tracks became subdivided and the town began to grow in that direction it finally built a sidetrack

and established its Elgin station on Sec. 27, T134N, R89W in October 1927.

The land on which Shanley was located was owned by homesteader Paul Meintzer who sold it for $55.00 an acre to the Northwestern Improvement Company. The first building constructed on this site was a real estate office with living quarters; it was built by William Heil. Heil's partners, D. J. Barnes and J. T. Nelson of Glen Ullin owned the Antelope Loan Company and a considerable amount of the land in this territory.

According to local residents Elgin's birthdate is May 1, 1910. It cost $100 to get the land platted and the village incorporated in 1911.

By that time several Glen Ullin business men had become established in Elgin. Among them were P. B. Wickham, president and Charles Wachter, vice-president of the First State Bank. The new post office with Julius Heil as postmaster was located near the alley west of the H. S. Koff General Store. Jake and Theobold Martell established a blacksmith shop while Fred Zeller built the J. C. Bender Store. The Davenport Brothers of Almont opened a drugstore and George Zeller built

Main Street Elgin, North Dakota - 1916

and operated the first hardware store. The Mandan Mercantile Company, managed by August Hoffman, and the F. E. Lumberyard, managed by Henry Englehardt, had their beginnings during this time.

The American Congregational Church, the English Congregational Church, and the Zion American Lutheran Church were all established in 1910. In 1911 a wooden two-story schoolhouse with a basement was built. Two years of high school was offered.

Elgin was incorporated as a city in 1918. By then the population had grown to 600 and more businesses began while some changed hands. The city progressed nicely with new dwellings being built and a variety of services being offered to its inhabitants.

In 1919 disaster struck. A fire broke out which almost wiped Main Street off the map. While other fires struck Elgin throughout the years, none were as destructive as the fire of 1919.

Another disaster struck nearly sixty years later. The 1978 tornado killed five people, toppled the water tower, and caused considerable damage and demolition to homes. Elgin recovered with the help of the National Guard, Red Cross, Salvation Army, and people in the community and other areas.

Quite a number of changes took place during the seventies and eighties. West Acres and the senior citizen housing units were built for low income families. The Jacobson Memorial Hospital and Care Center was constructed and the old hospital remodeled for the Dakota Hills Retirement Home. The Elgin School added wings to accommodate the grade and senior high school. An indoor swimming pool became a reality and several new business places made their appearance on Main Street. When the old Legion Hall burned, a new Community Center was built.

Elgin offers its people such recreation as golfing and bowling. The new Family Recreation Center houses the

Aerial view of Elgin, North Dakota - 1985

Tornado damage to Elgin Water Tower - 1978

bowling alley, an arcade, pool tables, and dining facilities. Residents of Elgin are involved in many different organizations and clubs. Every year the city celebrates "Elgin Days." One of the highlights of that event was the celebration of Elgin's Diamond Jubilee in 1985.

North Dakotans once lived in

*Fayette

by Agnes Fisher

Only memories of this townsite remain among those who remember it as it was. It no longer appears on recent highway maps and its post office was discontinued after July 31, 1956 and the mail sent to Manning.

This little community in Dunn County (SE1/4 sec. 26, T144N, R97W) about thirty-five miles northwest of Dickinson, just north of the Knife River, was founded by Frank A. Little in 1896. Little, a factory worker from Augusta, Maine developed a lung ailment and was advised by his doctor to move to North Dakota for his health. He arrived in 1880, being one of the many men with ox teams who formed wagon trains hauling supplies from Bismarck to the Standing Rock Indian Reservation.

After overcoming his illness his greatest desire was to own a ranch in the western part of North Dakota where the first white people were just beginning to settle. With his wife Isabelle and a flock of sheep he arrived at the site of Fayette in 1896. Impressed with the lofty hills for animal shelter, an ample supply of spring water, and wide open spaces not yet settled, he decided to settle and develop a combined ranching-farming operation.

A group of cowboys, at a dance near the Fayette ranch, complained about making the long ride to Dickinson to pick up their mail and wondered if something could be done about it. As a result a petition was drawn and the rural Fayette post office was established on May 5, 1898 in the living room of a dirt-roofed structure built of logs and mud which served both as the Little's residence and also as a country store. Isabelle Little was appointed postmaster by President William McKinley. Twice a week a one-horse, one-seat buggy brought mail from Dickinson. It was the second post office in Dunn County, serving a territory from Watford City to Emerson.

In 1900 Little erected a one-story building and the post office was moved there. Constructed of sod and gumbo with a roof made of tree branches with brush laid across poles and dirt piled on top, the inside walls were smoothed and white-washed. This building looked just as primitive on the inside as it did on the outside. It was the oldest sod post office in the United States.

Anything and everything from a needle to a threshing machine could be bought at this store. Kerosene lanterns, tools, and gloves hung from the ceiling. Harnesses and saddles were displayed on the wall.

In 1940 when Isabelle, then past eighty years, was forced to retire because of postal regulations Anna Fisher became postmaster and remained in charge of both the post office and store for many years. As a young girl she had come to work for the Littles in 1905, spending her lifetime working for them and inheriting the operation when the Littles passed away. The Little's only child, Ruth Estelle, died during a flu epidemic when she was twelve years old.

Mrs. Tony (Clementine) Hartman, now Mrs. Edgar Svetenko was postmaster until the post office was abolished.

The town was named for a friend and financial backer of the Littles. Born in November 1856 in Dryden, Michigan Dr. Fayette Dwight Kendrick practiced medicine in Bismarck for some years, later moving his practice to St. Paul, Minnesota where he retired.

Fayette Stage Coach - early 1900s

Country Sunday School in Fayette, North Dakota - 1900s

Fayette, North Dakota - early 1900s

Fessenden is a small town in central North Dakota, an area blessed with some of the richest top soil in the world.

People who come here to make a living usually end up staying a lifetime. Today's farmers are frequently the third generation cultivating the same land. Others, too, have stayed many years. Fessenden has had only three superintendents of schools in sixty-seven years: John Thornton, 1920-1933; E. S. Killie, 1933-1968; Owen Wallace, 1968-1987. Sherman Sylling was hired in 1987.

An old style country doctor, D. W. Mattaei, served the community before Dr. M. J. Towarnicky arrived in 1957. He retired in 1990. Dr. W. K. Taylor practiced dentistry in the community fifty-two years before re-

655 North Dakotans live in

F*essenden

by Carol Beck

tiring in 1970. Dr. Paul Heese established his dentistry practice in 1965. He continues to live in Fessenden although he has moved his practice to Harvey.

Gerald Johnson, now a retired pharmacist, had owned the local drug store since 1954; his predecessor, Perry Stanton, had been the pharmacist for many years. Otto Neuenschwander, and later his sons, owned the funeral home and hardware store for many years before Mark Nelson purchased the business in 1978.

Fessenden, the county seat of Wells County, was founded in 1893 when the Minneapolis, St. Paul & Sault Ste Marie Railroad (the Soo) established a station called Fessenden along its new branch line.

First called Oshkosh because Welsh settlers Frank H. Beans and R. T. Roberts, on whose homesteads the townsite was platted in 1893, came from Oshkosh, Wisconsin, it was renamed Fessenden after Cortez Fessenden, the Surveyor General of Dakota Territory from 1881 to 1885. One authority suggests that it is difficult to understand how or why the railroad chose the name since Fessenden had no known connection with either the railroad or the state; he returned to his native state of Michigan at the end of his term in 1885.

The town hosts the Wells County Fair each summer. In addition to the exhibits, food stands and carnival, the Fair is the only county fair in the state that has thoroughbred horse racing. In 1991 the Fairgrounds was placed on the National Register of Historic Places.

A nine-hole golf course with grass greens, a swimming pool, and an airport are all big pluses for this small town.

One of the community's landmarks is a beautiful mansion built by banker T. L. Beiseker on "Quality Hill" in 1899-1900. The most stately home in Fessenden, it has been restored and was placed on the National Register of Historic Places. The present owners now offer bed and breakfast.

The Viking Store, later known as Quarve's, was the largest dry goods, hardware, and grocery store in the area. The building is unoccupied at this time.

The Christian community is served by six denominations which have

The Beiseker Mansion

constructed buildings: First Congregational, First Baptist, Church of the Nazarene, St. Augustine's Catholic, First Lutheran, and St. John's Lutheran. Several smaller Christian groups without their own facilities also serve the town.

The completion of the Wells County Courthouse was celebrated with a big New Year's Eve party in 1895. Its exterior was refurbished in 1981; the building remains the most impressive in town and is on the National Register of Historic Places.

Fessenden's story would not be complete without mentioning the support the people give their high school sports events. Many coaches have said that Fessenden has the best fans anywhere. One stated that if Fessenden had a game in Timbuktu, loyal fans would travel there.

Several books have been written about people and life in Fessenden. *The Coffee Train* by novelist Margarethe Erdahl Shank tells the story of a Norwegian family living here in the 1890s. State Senator Bryce Streibel published his autobiography in 1983. In it he discusses his political career and describes the life of a German immigrant family homesteading near Fessenden. In 1986, Richard Critchfield, a noted author, wrote *Those Days* in which several chapters are devoted to his family's life in Fessenden.

The town will celebrate its centennial in 1993 and it is looking forward to the next one hundred years.

Horse Racing at the Wells County Fair

1937 Alfalfa Day Celebration - Main Street Fessenden

The Soo Line Railroad built a water tank and section house and dug a well on a site in Secs. 31 and 32, T163N, R90W in 1893. Six years later a sidetrack was laid and a station named Flaxton was established. Much of the townsite was originally a field of flax, a productive grain crop which was grown in the region.

A mile and a half northwest a small community called Postville had grown to include a grocery store, a blacksmith shop, and a rural post office, established in May 1900, on postmaster William Henry Post's homestead. The Postville post office was moved to a site alongside the Flaxton station in January 1901 and several months later it was renamed Flaxton.

Flaxton grew quickly after its townsite was platted in May 1901 and soon served a large trade area. People came regularly from Westby, Montana to shop before the completion of a branch line from Flaxton to Westby in 1906.

Homes and halls were used for Sunday School and church services before the Presbyterian Church was completed in 1904, the Norwegian Lutheran Church in 1905, and Saint Paul's Evangelical Church in 1920. The Presbyterian Church is no longer in use.

Many Flaxton settlers came from Minnesota, many remained. Bliss

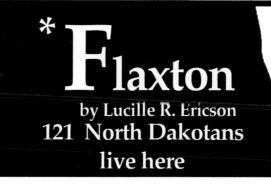

*Flaxton
by Lucille R. Ericson
121 North Dakotans
live here

and Ninow moved their wagon shop here in 1907; later they operated a woodwork shop. John Bliss died and Herman Ninow operated the South Side Garage before opening a Woodwork Shop in 1946. He remained in business until his death in 1957. His expert craftsmanship is known far and wide.

The Seibert Hotel, built in 1909, was known as the finest northwest of Minot. It was of brick construction, well-equipped, and had a large dining room. President William Howard Taft once stayed overnight in the facility. Seibert prepared chicken dinner and invited Flaxton's dignitaries to dine with the president. The old hotel was torn down in 1987.

Other celebrities also visited Flaxton. In the summer of 1948 the Duke and Duchess of Windsor passed through the city. They talked to people from the observation-car platform while the long passenger train made its stopover.

Taking land from two school districts, Richland and Carter, the Ward

County commissioners created Flaxton School District No. 114 in June 1905. The district was reorganized and renumbered in 1911 and again reorganized in 1950. The first schoolhouse was built in 1902 and a second in 1905. A brick high school was built in 1913, a modern grade school was constructed in 1952 and a gymnasium was erected in 1965. The schools were closed in 1986.

Flaxton was incorporated as a village in 1904 and as a city in 1920 and since that time it has boasted of award-winning bands, baseball and basketball teams, singing groups and debate teams. The city can also boast of two female mayors, Louise Fossum elected in 1924 and Irene Hanson elected in 1984.

Yearly Old Settler's Celebrations were held from 1907 to 1936. Flaxton is the home of the Burke County Fair, with a three-day event annually since 1910. A new grandstand was built on the grounds in 1986 after a tornado demolished the original one.

Farmers organized a cooperative in 1927 and erected a building. It was the first of its kind and served a wide area. The World War Memorial Hall was dedicated on November 11, 1931. A Mall was built in 1979 and houses an exchange, the post office, a grocery store, cafe, and bakery. A new fire hall was erected in 1985. Senior citizens organized in 1986 and bought and renovated the old post office building for their center. Guests numbered 125 at the open house which was held September 30, 1987.

Oil was discovered in the area in 1952; the Flaxton Field was one of the largest.

Active in the city today are the Volunteer Fire Department, the American Legion and Auxiliary, the Senior Citizens, the Community Club, the 4-H Club, and the Flaxton Development Association.

Old Settler's Picnic - June 11, 1911

Walter Hingst Service Station - 1941

Inside South Side Garage - 1924-1925

Home Town of 56 North Dakotans

Forbes

by Wilma Flakoll *

An agreement had been made between James J. Hill of the Great Northern Railroad and the Milwaukee Railroad not to extend Great Northern tracks west of Ellendale for twenty years. When this agreement expired in 1905 the Great Northern extended its Ellendale Branch fourteen miles southwest to a terminal site on Sec. 35, T129N, R65W. The station was named after Stanfell F. Forbes who was at one time the railroad's general storekeeper at St. Paul, Minnesota and a local pioneer storekeeper. The townsite was purchased in 1905 at a cost of $3,600 or $22.50 an acre and lots were sold at a sale in Ellendale on September 19th.

With the coming of the railroad a great potential for shipping grain, livestock, freight, and passengers into western Dickey County and across the state line, into McPherson County, South Dakota was realized. The Forbes territory was large and often there would be a dozen or more railroad cars of livestock to go out on a single train. The Forbes terminal was well planned. Forbes was a railway "hub"; Merricourt was 20 miles distant, Ellendale was 18, Frederick was 20, and Leola was 22. The only suburb of Forbes was just across the state line in South Dakota, at the end of its main street in a community called Dunnville. Patt Dunn operated the only business there, a saloon. Selling alcoholic beverages in North Dakota at this time was illegal.

Religion is a very important part of the Forbes community. The first religious services were held in the train depot and later in the Town Hall. The Presbyterian Church was built in 1908; it closed in 1970. Bethlehem Lutheran Church was organized on February 4, 1923. The parsonage was built in 1959 and an educational unit was added in 1966. At the present time Bethlehem's membership is 128.

St. Marks United Methodist Church began as a mission church in 1925. In 1946 a new church structure was completed and dedicated. In 1966 an addition was added and remodeling was done. In 1946 the Evangelical Church and the United Brethren Church were united and in 1968 the Evangelical and United Brethren Church and the Methodist Church united to form St. Marks United Methodist Church.

Three homemakers clubs are active in the community as well as the Girls Scouts, a 4-H Club, and a saddle club.

A Rural Fire Department was organized in 1971 and a new fire hall built in 1984. A new American Legion Hall was constructed in 1982.

Aerial view of Forbes, North Dakota

1980 Jubilee Parade on Main Street, Forbes, North Dakota

The first school in Forbes was attended by twenty-four pupils. Soon, so many people moved into the area that the small schoolhouse could not accommodate all the pupils. Older pupils had to hold classes in the Town Hall until 1910 when a two-story brick building was built. A gymnasium was constructed in 1939 as a Works Progress Administration (WPA) project using lumber from a flour mill in Ellendale which was torn down. The gym was used for many activities: school functions, roller skating, movies, and community functions of various kinds. In 1961 a new one-story brick school was built.

Although school districts in this area were reorganized in July 1959 as Forbes School District No. 42 the Forbes public school was closed in 1987. Children in the area now attend schools in Kulm and Ellendale, North Dakota and in Leola, South Dakota.

For many years the community had the crank type telephone with a central operator in Forbes. The dial telephone was installed in 1954 and one-party lines with direct dialing and underground lines were installed in 1971. Since 1950 the community has been served by the Dickey Rural Telephone Co-operative.

The first train arrived in Forbes in November 1905. The roundhouse had been moved from Ellendale to

Forbes' citizens at the 1980 Jubilee Parade

Forbes and a depot built. The first trains were pulled by steam engine. The last train out of Forbes was on December 22, 1978.

Business places in Forbes at the present time are: The People Store, the post office which was established on December 22, 1905 with George H. Ladd as postmaster, D & B Repair Shop, Long Branch Saloon, Martin Construction, Forbes Equity Exchange, and Ronald Casey Trucking.

The population of Forbes at one time numbered well over 500 people, but at the present time is approximately 56 people.

Forbes celebrated its Golden Anniversary on July 10, 1955 with over 3,000 persons in attendance. In 1980 the Diamond Jubilee was celebrated with over 5,000 people in attendance. The parade had almost 100 floats, with Governor Arthur Link as its honored guest.

West side Main Street, Gascoyne - 1910

Gascoyne is a small community located in the eastern end of Bowman County, twelve miles from the South Dakota border at an altitude of 2,759 feet.

In 1900 the government survey through western North Dakota was completed and the local landowner, The Western Securities Company, opened the region for settlement. Homesteaders of every nationality came to file, first coming in immigrant rail cars with all their possessions to Dickinson, some seventy miles to the north. They then drove by team and buggy or caught the stage going south, fording the Cannonball River, Cedar Creek, and other streams.

One of the major unanswered ques-

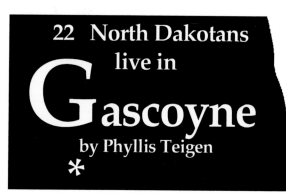

22 North Dakotans live in Gascoyne
by Phyllis Teigen

tions in the area was the exact location of the new main line of the Chicago, Milwaukee & St. Paul Railroad which was being constructed through the region. Max Fischbein, a homesteader, through whose land the road was being built, began a new town and in November 1907 a post office named for him was established there. He was also named the first postmaster. The railroad, however, decided to locate its town a short distance from Fischbein. The new station, established in early 1908, was named Gascoyne, probably after one of the railroad's construction foreman. Another reason given for the name change is that there were too many dots and dashes in the name Fischbein when using Morse Code. The Fischbein post office was moved to the new site and in March 1908 it

was renamed Gascoyne. The new townsite was platted by owners Oscar Nordell and William Sherman in July 1908, both had homesteaded their land.

Many early settlers helped lay steel for the railroad company. The first passenger arrived on November 6, 1907. On one particular Saturday ninety-two passengers stopped off at the station.

The first school was built in 1907 with H. O. Saxvik as its first teacher. Later elected Bowman County Superintendent of Schools, he also served as Superintendent of the Bismarck School System from 1922 to 1942. A four-room schoolhouse was eventually built; it included a high school which graduated its last class in May 1940. The local school district was merged with the Scranton School District in the 1960s.

The Gascoyne Village Hall was built by The Modern Woodmen of America Lodge in 1908. Homesteaders, ranchers, and cowboys came to the grand opening dance. Throughout the years many types of activities were held in the hall: church services, church dinners, funerals, various school functions including high school proms, community-wide banquets, roller skating, basketball games, and silent movies. The building was destroyed in the 1980s.

The village was incorporated on March 20, 1911 and became a city as a result of legislative action in 1967.

Over the years citizens have been community-minded. Homemaker's clubs have been supported, 4-H Clubs have been active, and the Red Cross has been helped. Circuit riders

have been welcomed as well as Congregational and Lutheran church denominations. One of the most unique aspects of the community's history is that at one time a Ladies Aid Society had members from five different religious faiths.

Since its beginning the town has been served by four newspapers: *Gascoyne Advance*, *Gascoyne Gazette*, *Yellowstone Pennant*, and in the 1930s, the *Gascoyne News*. At one time there were almost 20 business places operating in the city, including the First State Bank of Gascoyne.

The region is served by US 12, known in the "old days" as the Yellowstone Trail; it followed Main Street in 1914.

Utilizing mineral deposits is an important economic activity in the area. Knife River Coal Mine, a wholly owned subsidiary of Montana-Dakota Utilities Company is located about two miles east of the city. Coal is shipped from the mine in closed lid-cars, the only ones of this type used today, via a 3.5 mile spur line off the former Milwaukee mainline to the 440-megawatt Big Stone Plant in northeastern South Dakota.

The American Colloid Company, located two miles southeast of Gascoyne processes leonardite and bentonite. Its home office is located in Skokie, Illinois.

Both companies provide employment for people in the surrounding area.

Gone is the hustle and bustle of early days; Gascoyne is now a quiet, residential city, served by a rural route out of Scranton, North Dakota.

Gascoyne citizens in front of the City Hall - 1912

Gascoyne "Boosters" in front of bank building

G* lenburn

by Glenburn Alumni Committee
439 North Dakotans live here

Glenburn's origins can be traced back to the original homesteaders who moved into the area and found a need for a local shopping and trading center, since the nearest large town, Minot, was a long distance to travel at that time. In 1902 Wilson Walter opened a store in the area and in September of that year he was named postmaster of the Walter post office.

The next year the Great Northern Railroad established a station called Glenburn along its Mohall branch line on a site a short distance from that post office which was moved to the railroad town in October 1903. The post office was renamed to reflect its new location.

There are conflicting versions of how the town acquired its name. One story suggests that residents originally named the town Lincoln, but after discovering that there was another Lincoln, North Dakota they renamed it Glenburn. Another anecdote suggests that the town was named for Glenn Colcord, a young homesteader who was a subscription solicitor and news reporter for the *Ward County Reporter* who had a flair for making quick trips on his bi-cycle when there was a story to be covered. On one occasion a local resident, after having observed Colcord riding his bicycle, is said to have exclaimed: "Look at Glenn burn up the road." One authority declares that "the 'Glen-Burn' story was actually concocted in later years as a hoax by fellow Minot newspapermen."

In any case the Glenburn townsite was platted in September 1903. It incorporated as a village in October 1904 and became a city in 1958.

The early settlers were mostly Scandinavian and German, coming to this area from Wisconsin, Michigan, Iowa, Illinois, and Minnesota. Businesses began springing up in the busy railroad town and by 1914 there were: two banks, four general stores, two hardware stores, two drugstores, two lumberyards, seven grain elevators, coal sheds, newspapers, daily mail, one grocery store, one pool room, one barbershop, two meat markets, two blacksmith shops, two restaurants, one furniture store, two doctors, two livery barns, two implement dealers, one auto garage, and 100 miles of rural telephone lines.

On October 4, 1922 seven buildings on the south side of Main Street were destroyed by fire and on September 27, 1926 the north side was leveled by fire.

In 1904 the Methodist, Roman Catholic, and Presbyterian churches were organized. Other churches organized later: the Baptists in 1907, Trinity Lutheran in 1915, and Faith Lutheran (Missouri Synod) in 1948, the latter becoming Hope Lutheran in 1974. The Methodist and Presbyterian congregations dissolved within a few years; the others are still active congregations.

School classes began in 1905 and were held in the Presbyterian and Methodist churches; the first school was built in 1907. The second school building with an auditorium and gymnasium was completed in 1923; the first school was torn down. High

South side Main Street, Glenburn, North Dakota - 1979

Bird's-eye view of Glenburn, North Dakota - early 1900s

school graduation exercises were first conducted in 1922. A new Memorial gymnasium was added to the school plant in 1960, a new classroom addition was built in 1961, and four more classrooms were added in 1970. Later a new school addition was constructed; it was occupied during Christmas vacation of 1982; the old school torn down in the spring of 1983.

School re-organization has taken place in the area through the years. Today, students are bussed in from surrounding rural areas to take part in a curriculum which includes learning centers, music and band instruction, vocational courses, and computer classes. The school plant includes a lighted football field and an asphalt track.

Today, though the town is small, it boasts of several businesses, good school and church facilities, volunteer fire and ambulance services, city utilities, paved streets, two parks, municipal airport, and a clean wholesome atmosphere in which to live.

Main Street Glenburn, North Dakota - Dec. 31, 1903

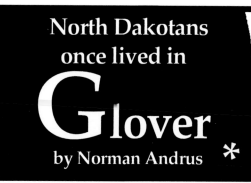

Elling O. Ulness moved west from Kindred, Dakota Territory in 1883 to homestead in Dickey County. On December 19 of that year a rural post office called Ulness was established in a small building he owned and had moved from Kindred to his homestead, the SW1/4 sec. 24 in James River Township. He also operated a small country store there; the place became known as Ulness.

The building continued to be used as a store and post office until it was moved to Sec. 13, T132N, R60W in January 1887 to the new railroad town of Glover. The office was renamed Glover; Ulness became the first Glover postmaster and also the town's first businessman. He traveled to LaMoure by horseback or team and buggy to pick up the mail and get supplies for his store. For many years the store served as a major trading center for the early pioneers in the area.

Glover, Dakota Territory, was established through the efforts of Samuel Glover. Like many other bonanza farmers in North Dakota he had traded his Northern Pacific Railroad stock for railroad land, acquiring some 30,000 acres in LaMoure and Dickey counties. As part of the transaction it was agreed that if Glover would develop and promote the area the railroad would build a line from Independence which was several miles southeast of LaMoure to Oakes, in Dickey County. He established Glover Ranch and in the fall of 1886 the Northern Pacific Railroad Company extended its James River Valley Branch south, grading and laying track to Oakes. That same year the railroad established a station named Glover on Secs. 13 and 24, T132N, R60W and built a depot, Glover's only improvement.

As proprietor Glover had M. E. Severance survey and lay out the townsite on April 13, 1887. The original plot was recorded in LaMoure and Ransom Counties, Dakota Territory on April 20, 1887 and in Dickey County two days later.

Ulness moved his store from what is known as the Phil Kraft farm to Glover on January 20, 1887 and managed it until about 1888 at which time it was sold to O. A. Olson and L. P. Ekern. They continued their partnership until 1893.

In that year Ekern sold his interest to Olson, who in 1897, hired Ed Iverson to build a new store building with an attached house. A small wooden structure, it was located west of where the large Glover Store building was erected in 1910. The Glover Store was operated by Oscar Olson, Edwin Olson, and Clara Olson Grosshans, both as a post office and

Glover, North Dakota - 1902

Glover, North Dakota - 1910

general store until 1943. To make room for that building the original Ulness building was moved once more to its final location, the Boyle place, one mile east of Glover on the SW1/4 sec. 18 Divide Township.

Six people served as Glover's postmaster: Elling O. Ulness held that job until 1888; L. P. Ekern then served for about two years; O. A. Olson was postmaster from 1889 until his death in 1905; he was followed by Oscar Olson, 1905-1920; Gust Buske was appointed to the office in 1920 and served five years; he was followed by Oscar Olson; after his retirement in October 1942 his wife assumed the position and continued in that capacity until the office was discontinued on March 1, 1943.

The Glover Church, affiliated with the Methodist Episcopal Church, was built in 1914 and served the people of the community until 1952 when its parishioners decided to attend services in Oakes. Church services were held first in 1888 in the first schoolhouse which was located on top of the hill east of the Edwin Olson farm, presently occupied by Bob Olson. At first the congregation was served by pastors who came from Verona: Bishop, Ballard, Wyley, Taylor, Jeffery, and Dickensen. Later Pastors Delong, Scarbourough, Smith, Babcock, Gernhardt, and Emprie served the congregation from Oakes.

Many people were buried in the local cemetery prior to it becoming the community's official cemetery. On October 26, 1920, block nine of the Iverson addition was vacated and commissioned as the Glover Cemetery.

Effective January 1, 1922 James River Valley Township was divided into James River Valley Township and Divide Township. After they became separate civil townships, the Glover Cemetery was deeded to both townships on October 6, 1931 and recorded four days later in Dickey County. The cemetery is maintained by both townships.

Glover, North Dakota - 1926

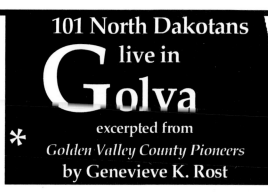

Golva came into existence in 1914 after both land and money, "the balance of $2,500 still needed to make up the amount of the required guarantee," were donated. In the summer of 1915 the Northern Pacific Railroad Company, constructing its Ollie branch south from Beach, established the Golva station on Sec. 30, T138N, R105W. That same year A. L. Martin of Sentinel Butte platted the Golva townsite adjacent to the railroad station. On February 15, 1916 the Golva post office was established with Johanna Christensen as postmaster.

The first homesteaders came to the area during the years 1904-1906. Many came from the St. Cloud, Minnesota area as a result of the promotional efforts of the German Catholic Golden Valley Land Company.

The town's name was derived from that of the county: GOLden VAlley. It soon boasted of a hotel, livery barn, two banks, three grocery stores and meat market, two hardware stores, a drug store, creamery, two garages, an implement dealer, three lumber yards, a blacksmith shop, two barbers, two restaurants, and three grain elevators. The First State Bank which began operation in Burkey in June 1914 moved to Golva two years later. Another bank went "under" in February 1924. The Burkey Hall was moved to Golva in 1917. It is now used as a storage warehouse for the elevator. The Burkey Catholic Church was taken down in four sections and moved to Golva in February 1921. During the flu epidemic of 1918 Father Michael Lack, the local priest for forty-one years, turned the Town Hall into a hospital.

A new Catholic church was dedicated in 1968. In 1928 a natural gas line was laid from Cabin Creek. In 1935 the FAA built an airport 1 1/2 miles east of the town. In 1930 and 1935 Montana-Dakota Utilities was coaxed to bring electricity the 12 miles to Golva, but it wasn't until June 19, 1948 that Golva could rejoice when the rural electric cooperative "turned on the juice."

Surviving in Golva has not been easy. The town has suffered several terrible fires, a major flood in June 1929, many hail storms, and many, many severe winters, including the one in 1949 when army caterpillars plowed snow and air lifts brought groceries, medical assistance, and even hay. During the Great Depression the community suffered dust storms, grasshopper plagues from 1936 to 1940, extreme drought, and no crops.

In 1921 a brick school building, the first consolidated school in the county, was built. Since 1968 several rural school districts have been annexed to Lone Tree School District. In 1971 the district built a new grade school and music room and in 1990 a new addition was made when the old high school was razed. The Lone Tree Township built a new Community Hall and gymnasium in 1949; the latter has been used by the school district. That same year street lighting was introduced and in 1954 the village installed a modern sewage system. In 1970 a city well was drilled and water mains were laid; nine years later a second well was drilled.

Golva incorporated as a Village on July 1, 1947. It was a Village for exactly twenty years, to the minute, because of state legislation. Richard T. Hanson, Joe L. Popiel, and Chester K. Puda were elected to the first Village Board of Trustees in 1947. Genevieve Schrom served as clerk and Bert Covert was elected treasurer. He resigned immediately and recommended that the latter two offices be combined; the clerk then took over the combined office. In 1967 Genevieve Schrom (Rost) became city auditor, she held the office until 1991.

In 1950 the village organized a fire department and acquired equipment and a fire hall. Later a rural fire district was established and a new fire hall was erected. A children's summer recreation program has been sponsored by at least six or more local organizations for many years. The community has cooperated in other ways. In 1968 a Park District was created and a picnic park was developed for the community's annual picnic and parade. Someone suggested a canopy be built to protect the food; however, with volunteer labor and donated material a fully enclosed, heated building was constructed, used by the entire community for wedding receptions, anniversaries, and any and all community get-togethers.

"Although small in population, the City of Golva is large in community spirit and cooperation!"

The axis of the earth sticks out visibly through the center of each and every town or city.
Oliver Wendell Holmes
The Autocrat of the Breakfast Table,
Ch. 6, 1858

Construction of the Golva School - 1971

Main Street Golva, North Dakota - 1920s

Bird's-eye view of Grano, North Dakota - 1976
(DPDP - James R. Dean)

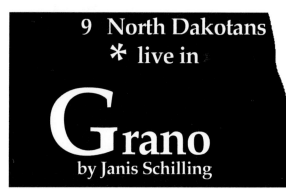

9 North Dakotans * live in Grano
by Janis Schilling

Like many towns in North Dakota Grano had its beginning when the Minneapolis, St. Paul & Sault Ste Marie Railroad (Soo Line) established the Grano station on Sec. 12, T159N, R85W in 1905. Its townsite was platted by the Minnesota Loan & Trust Company of Minneapolis in July of that year and the Overholt post office was also moved to the new town at the same time and renamed Grano.

By 1911 it was a thriving little community consisting of the following businesses: a drug store with an opera house upstairs, three general stores, a hardware store, two pool rooms, a newspaper, two implement shops, two lumber companies, a livery stable, a blacksmith shop, two meat markets, two banks, a post office, two hotels, a medical doctor, two dray lines, two restaurants, three elevators, a barbershop, and a stockyards.

No one is quite sure of the origin of the town's name; several stories survive. It is claimed that one morning while Charles Lano, who was postmaster at Mohall, was eating breakfast he noticed a new cereal, Grain-O, on the shelf and later suggested that as the name of the town. Another version suggests that it might have been coined from the names of Charles Grace and LaNo Robert Ortberg, a newspaperman from Mohall. One more story suggests that it was coined from the names of A. D. Greene and Charles Lano. The town was also called "Grano on the Soo."

Satisfying spiritual and educational needs were a problem in the early days. Grano itself was served only by the Methodist Church, which had been built in Overholt, a rural community along the Mouse River. It was moved into Grano in 1903. The other church in the Grano area was the St. Henry Catholic Church about eight miles south of Grano.

The first school in what became Renville County was built in 1898 on the Ole Person homestead, northwest of Grano. Later when Callahan Township was organized in 1903 additional schools and roads were built. The school offered work through the 10th grade in the early days and employed three teachers. Later, it offered work through the 12th grade. The original building was remodeled before 1920 and continued to be used until Callahan was redistricted in 1958 and the Grano school closed.

Grano competed with Greene and Mohall, a much larger town north of Grano, for the county seat of Renville. In 1910 Mohall was selected as county seat.

With the coming of automobiles, trucks, and better roads Grano lost trade to larger towns. The decline of small towns which were a "must" in pioneer days had begun.

Today, Grano consists of one elevator, the Grano Grain Company, one bar, the Grano Lakeside Lounge, City Hall, and the City Park. The Soo Line continues to make at least one trip a week through Grano on the Wheat Line.

Grano was incorporated in 1911 and is one of the smallest cities in North Dakota. Its post office was closed on January 31, 1956; mail is now distributed from Lansford.

The major recreational attraction in the Grano area is the great fishing at Lake Darling, one mile west of Grano.

Winter lies too long in country towns; hangs on until it is stale and shabby, old and sullen.
Willa Sibert Cather
My Antonia, **Book II, ch. 7, 1918**

Main Street Grano, North Dakota - 1936
(SHSND)

Main Street Grano, North Dakota - 1976
(DPDP - James R. Dean)

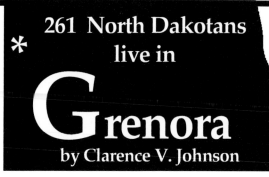

261 North Dakotans live in

Grenora

by Clarence V. Johnson

Perhaps in all the history of the west no city has risen more rapidly from the bare level prairie than has Grenora, founded in 1916 as the end of the line of the westward extension of the Wildrose Branch of the Great Northern Railroad. Its name was coined from that of the Great Northern Railroad and almost overnight the town grew busy as anxious settlers started businesses and built homes.

When the Northern Town and Land Company of Willmar, Minnesota learned of the coming railroad they purchased land in the surrounding area. Much of the townsite was purchased from Ragna Anderson for $5,000. The area was platted and a town lot sale was held on June 20, 1916.

Tents, sod houses, cook cars, and every conceivable means of housing were used by the first settlers until permanent buildings could be erected. Lumber was hauled to the site by wagon, mainly from Wildrose, North Dakota and Westby and Medicine Lake, Montana. As an old timer said, "buildings were going up all at one time."

Enterprising businessmen who didn't know exactly where the town would be located or when the branch line would be completed built their business places on skids and when the townsite was platted they purchased lots and moved their stores to their proper location. They are today basically the same buildings, having now perhaps been insulated, re-roofed, sometimes refaced, and repainted several times.

The Grenora railroad station was not established until tracklayers reached the site. On November 4, 1916, the "Day of the Golden Spike," everyone came from near and far to see the last mile of track laid. The weather was warm and pleasant and in the early forenoon throngs of people poured into town from every direction, by team and auto. Before noon hundreds of people were assembled on the village street or were watching

the track machine, which was then at the lower end of the railroad yards, move rapidly into town.

Haaken Isaacson, the region's pioneer resident, welcomed the town of Grenora on behalf of the old residents. The major address of the day was delivered by States Attorney William B. Owens. The next item on the program was the ceremony of driving the Golden Spike, marking the completion of the branch line to Grenora. The rails had just been laid a few moments before and this part of the program was carried out by Albert Fischer, one of the pioneer residents of northwestern Williams County. After delivering a brief and appropriate address, he proceeded to drive in the spike, after first having held it aloft for all to see. As this big man held it above his head the spike caught the glow of the afternoon sun and sent out a thousand rays from its golden surface.

The history of Grenora Township begins with the ranchers who settled the area in the late 1800s. The story of Haakon and Clara Isaacson presents the most complete record of this area's earliest settlement days, and it is with them that Grenora's earliest history begins. Aside from being one of the first settlers in the northwestern part of North Dakota Clara Isaacson was the first white woman in the area.

Year by year more settlers began homesteading in this area. The need arose for a post office and a school, both of which were housed on the Isaacson ranch. The post office was named Sandlie, after Isaacson's hometown in Norway. Clara Isaacson served as postmaster, distributing mail brought in by stage from

Marmon, a rural post office some twenty miles north of Williston. The Sandlie office served the homesteaders and ranchers for miles around until it was closed in March 1913 when its business was moved to Fertile.

Grenora's post office traces its history to the Howard rural post office, established November 30, 1906. Located on postmaster Howard N. Nelson's homestead it served the community of Howard until 1916 when it was moved in July to Grenora. Shortly thereafter the office was renamed Grenora. During that decade Nelson sold his interests to James E. Huskett and returned to Northwood. With the coming of the railroad to the area Howard businessmen abandoned the community and moved to the new railroad towns.

Since its earliest years Grenora has had numerous businesses. The Grenora Commercial Club, since its establishment in 1917, was and is, the city's most important club. Today, as always, the rural areas together with the city residents have displayed excellent cooperation in promoting many varied community activities.

The Gladys Helping Hand Club, one of the community's older organizations, was organized in 1921 in the Henry Lewis home. The Lewis farm was located near the site of the former pioneer village of Gladys, a rural community bypassed by the railroad, some ten miles southeast of Grenora. Today, just as in the beginning the club extends a helping hand to any one in need.

The history of Grenora's school begins in September 1916. Nellie Ledell taught in a one-room house, presently located in the northeastern corner of town. Fifteen pupils were enrolled and all grades were taught. Coal was kept in a little shed annexed to the school. Today, the school is housed in a new modern facility and continues to grow and serve the community. Students have ranked in the upper 15 percent of the nation's schools and some have won national acclaim.

Several churches serve the community: St. Olaf Lutheran Church, organized in 1908; St. Boniface Catholic Church, organized in 1908; Grenora Methodist Church, organized in 1910; and the Assembly of God Church, organized in 1927, now disbanded.

The city of Grenora, located in the heart of the vast Williston oil basin was chosen as one of the most beautiful cities in the state several years ago. City streets were paved in 1979 and a beautiful Senior Citizen's building was constructed in 1980.

Grenora continues to thrive with a spirit and drive that will carry it into the next century. "Friendliness lives here. You will be a stranger only once." This motto reflects the nature of the townspeople who have lived in the community, past and present, as neighbors and friends.

Grenora celebrated it's Diamond Jubilee on July 5-7, 1991. Some 3,000 people attended the festive occasion.

Flat-out flatness, the hard line of the horizon. I like the little towns with their handfuls of buildings huddled close to the grain elevators, like medieval towns clustered around their cathedrals.

Gordon Webber
on small towns of the Dakota plains
The Great Buffalo Hotel, **Little Brown, 1979**

Aerial view of Grenora, North Dakota - 1950

In April 1883 four families from Neenah and Menasha, Wisconsin arrived on a treeless, unnamed, grassy plain. They had heard much about the cheap, fertile land with luxuriant grass in Dakota Territory's James River Valley and had settled on claims surrounding the crossroads: the Myron H. Puffer family on the quarter to the northeast; the True Thatcher family on the quarter south of Puffers; Carlton Batchelor on the quarter west of Thatchers; and Philip Brown on the other quarter to the north.

Since its founding in 1883 residents of this aspiring frontier community had dreamed, planned, and worked toward the day when the community would be served by a railroad. Their dreams began to be realized when in

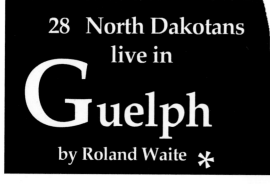

28 North Dakotans live in

Guelph

by Roland Waite ✳

1886 work began on the St. Paul, Minneapolis and Manitoba Railroad's branch line between Rutland and Ellendale. It was no wonder then, that the October 1, 1886 edition of the neighboring town's *Ludden Times* reported:

THATCHERVILLE JUBILANT
"Mr. Morrison, right of way agent for the Manitoba, arrived from the east this morning and closed the bargain for side track room and depot grounds on Mr. Boyce's claim one mile north of Ludden and with Truman Thatcher six miles west. This settles the location of the town on the Manitoba line in as favorable a manner as could be asked. The people of Thatcherville are feeling jubilant over their success and a good little town may be expected at this point."

A railroad brought prosperity and convenience and its presence often

determined which towns flourished, so it was of no small consequence that the Manitoba had chosen a route that would take it through Guelph and incidentally directly over Truman Thatcher's stone-curbed well, the only one in town.

With the rail secured Myron H. Puffer wasted no time selling lots to eager buyers after getting forty acres of his land platted into a twelve-block townsite named Centralia. The residents upon petitioning for a post office in December 1886 found that the postal department would not accept the name Centralia. The issue was finally settled on March 8, 1887 when the department accepted the name Guelph. The name had been suggested by Silas R.. Dales who had emigrated from Guelph, Ontario, Canada, had proved his claim here, and now had built a grocery store building on main street. He became the first postmaster and his store building housed the post office periodically for several years. Thus, a great deal of bickering which almost led to a feud ended. Many in the community were

probably also aware that Guelph, Ontario was the birthplace of James J. Hill, the railroad's president.

The resolution of the name issue led the *Ludden Times* to comment: "Ludden's greeting of welcome to a sister town of Guelph: Guelph alias Thatcherville, alias Coldwater, alias Thatcher, alias Centralia, alias Centropolis, alias Center, and very near alias Church, now goes on record as Guelph, to grow and flourish under that name."

Settlers came from Canada, Michigan, and Wisconsin and were primarily of Scandinavian, Finnish, and German extraction.

With the completion of the railroad in 1887 Guelph became a bustling little village which at its prime had three general stores, three cream stations, a hardware store, barbershop, blacksmith shop, garage, a bank, a lumberyard and implement store, post office, two churches, two grain elevators, two cafes, IOOF Hall, recreation hall, rail depot and stockyards, and a population of over 100. It was never incorporated because it was split down the center by Port Emma and Hudson townships.

Because of the coming of the automobile and the building of better roads people began going to larger towns

Aerial view of Guelph, North Dakota - 1983

fifteen miles away for services not provided in Guelph and one-by-one in the 1940s and 1950s businesses closed and buildings were torn down or moved away.

One of Guelph's oldest organizations, however, spearheaded several local, cooperative community projects. Independent Order of Odd Fellows Lodge No. 48 was organized in 1913 to promote fellowship and to aid widows, orphans, and those who were in distress or who were suffering afflictions. In 1948 money was needed to repair the lodge hall and the brothers decided to put in a crop. Land was secured and on May 10, 1948, using 32 tractors and the necessary other equipment and with the help of a lot of good people of the community, they seeded nearly 160 acres of flax in one day. The fuel cost for the entire operation was $97.85 for gasoline and $5.40 for 23 gallons of diesel fuel. Later four lodge members used their swathers to prepare the flax for combining which was hired for $540.00. The project netted the Lodge $3,731.40. Volunteers were treated to an oyster stew. Instead of repairing the hall it was decided to purchase for $1,000 the former Guelph State Bank, the town's only brick structure, and use it for Lodge activities. The old hall was donated to the Hudson School District.

The Lodge organized a similar project and on May 5, 1951 some 112 acres of barley and 84 acres of flax were seeded. The harvest yielded

Original store and post office - 1906

3,469 bushels of barley and 1,352 bushels of flax. Selling the barley for $1.21 per bushel and the flax for $3.43 per bushel the Lodge received $4,637.36 for its three-fourths share. The Lodge furnished a room at the new Memorial Hospital in Ellendale at a cost of $600.

Another community-wide project raised $3,756.19 for the school gymnasium project in 1954. Fifty-five "outfits" participated in that project.

In 1970 the town's new, modern school was annexed to the Oakes school district. It was used successfully by them for relief of their overcrowded facility by having their fifth and sixth grades bussed out for several years. Eventually the district bonded for expansion at Oakes and the Guelph school became expendable whereupon it reverted to the Guelph Community where it presently is used as a community center

and nucleus for the annual Guelph-Ludden turkey barbecue, held each July since the town's centennial.

The last train was seen in Guelph on November 26, 1984; the railroad company, now the Burlington Northern, had made good its two-decade threat to abandon the road. The Guelph station, along with the entire line from Ludden Junction west to Ellendale, was abandoned in 1985.

Presently the United Methodist Church, the Farmers Elevator, the post office, and eight dwellings remain. It looks as though Guelph will return to its four-corner's beginning, but it did survive to celebrate its 100th birthday in a glowing three-day celebration which saw many of its 204 graduates, now successful citizens, come back home to Guelph to share in the celebration of its finest hour.

Work crew on a farm project - 1948

Gwinner

by Pauline Lee *

Gwinner was established in 1900 as a result of the Northern Pacific Railroad Company's extension of a branch line eastward from Milnor to Oakes. The railroad's president Henry Villard had enticed German investors to invest large amounts of capital in the railroad. The company, however, went bankrupt. The station was named for Arthur von Gwinner, a large stockholder in German and Spanish banks who represented the Deutsche Bank of Berlin and played an important part in the bankrupt railroad's reorganization in the late 1890s. Gwinner's father and grandfather had been mayors of Frankfort, Germany. He never visited the United States.

Because many early settlers had come directly from Sweden and many more of the same ethnic stock had emigrated from Minnesota the town in its early days was known as "Little Sweden." Germans and Norwegians also settled in the area. Gwinner's early settlers included: I. W. Meinhardt, a blacksmith; Albert N. Carlblom, a general store operator who later became a North Dakota state auditor; R. P. Williams, a medical doctor; S. E. Lee, a bank cashier; Frank Youngberg, a merchant; Swan Friberg and Axel Johnson, carpenters; E. J. Hoel, a grain elevator manager; A. Korstad, restaurant owner; and J. Edor Larson, pastor of a Lutheran church. Nicholls and J. P. Bearthune operated drug stores; Gus Sandell opened a meat market; Eric Warn was the town's barber; John Pearson operated a dray line; Fredolf Safstrom managed a hardware store; and Josephine Carlblom became the town's first postmaster when the post office was established in her husband Albert's store in May 1901.

The earliest church in Gwinner was the Congregational Church, but it was dissolved shortly after 1914. The Independent Swedish Lutheran Church of Forsby (a rural post office moved to Gwinner in 1900) which was organized in 1897 later became Gustaf Adolf Lutheran Church. Its first building was constructed about a mile from the future townsite of Gwinner in 1898 and moved there in the winter of 1907-1908. A modern structure was completed in 1964.

Zion Lutheran Church (Missouri Synod) organized about 1900 and in 1909 the Evangelical Lutheran Zion Congregation built about four miles from Gwinner. Its present building was completed in Gwinner in 1956. Both Gustaf Adolf and Zion Lutheran Churches are active and flourishing today. In 1986 a new Roman Catholic Church was built in Gwinner.

Fires have plagued the town throughout its history. The first occurred in 1911 when the Gwinner State Bank, a doctor's office, and a drug-confectionery store were destroyed. A disastrous fire in 1921 wiped out Thompson Lumber Yard, McGrann's Restaurant, Parmeter Hotel, *Prairie Press* Printing Office, Safstrom & Ek's Hardware, Hample-Crete Telephone Central Office, and Frank Edblom's tinner shop. Eight years later the Gwinner Farmers Elevator was completely destroyed. About 1933 fire destroyed Andy Fausett's dry-goods store, a barbershop, and M. O. Satre's confectionery store.

A "most exciting time" occurred in August 1929 when the Gwinner State Bank was burglarized. One night a young man and his girlfriend were resting on the steps of the bank after having strolled around town;

Bird's-eye view of Gwinner, North Dakota - early 1900s

Thought to be the first bank in Gwinner

they spotted the burglars. He went home and alerted his brothers and neighbors. An armed posse was formed. It fired on the burglars as they emerged from the bank. During the ensuing gun battle no one was killed, but there was bloody evidence that the robbers had been hit. Disappearing into the darkness they were captured some time later by law officers and heavily armed citizens, aided by airplanes and bloodhounds brought in from Bismarck. They were found hiding under some hay in a barn and in a ditch along side the railroad tracks. One Gwinner citizen remembers that 165 BB's were removed from the body of one of the bandits.

Gwinner's claim to fame is no doubt the "Melroe Company," North Dakota's largest equipment manufacturer and distributor of specialized farm and industrial equipment. The company was founded in 1947 by E. G. Melroe who began by building a new type of windrow pickup attachment for combines. Today, its workforce has grown to 2,000 employees, located in three places. The ultra modern plant in Gwinner contains 362,000 square feet of space. The company's manufacturing line includes the original combine pickup attachment, a harrow weeder, a self tripping plow, and a trencher. It has become the world's largest producer of skid steer loaders, the Bobcat, and markets its products in the United States, Canada, and some 56 other countries.

Today, Gwinner still has good farm land surrounding the town. Wheat, barley, and sunflowers are major crops.

The largest city in Sargent County, it has 47 businesses, a large modern Farmer's Cooperative Elevator, an airport with 5,000 feet of lighted runway, summer youth programs, many clubs and organizations, and a school system with a new building and a well-rounded and extensive curriculum.

First Melroe building with founder E.G. Melroe - 1948

The people of Halliday take great pride and interest in their early history. In 1900 "Old Halliday," named after its first postmaster, was a country store and post office established two miles north of its present site. In 1914 it was moved south to the site of a proposed Halliday station along the "North Branch" of the Northern Pacific Railroad line being built from Mandan to Killdeer.

The earliest settlers, mostly German and Scandinavian immigrants, came to homestead. They built sod houses and cultivated the wild prairies to raise food for themselves and their livestock. Business people came later to build and develop the town of Halliday.

The railroad was their lifeline, bring-

Aerial view of present day Halliday, North Dakota

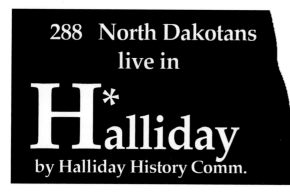

288 North Dakotans live in

H*alliday

by Halliday History Comm.

ing them food, clothing, and medicine and enabling them to ship their grain and livestock. After moving the store, post office, and bank to the new townsite more stores and homes, now wooden frame buildings, were erected to accommodate the growing population. Over the years the country churches were moved into town and the rural children were bussed into the brick school on the south hill.

The stock market crash of 1929 had an important effect on the growing town, closing banks and business places, and devastating farmers and ranchers. It caused many to leave the Halliday area. The Dirty Thirties were plagued by dust storms, drought, and poor crops.

One positive note was the successful efforts of Halliday businessmen to persuade the state legislature to build a bridge across the Missouri

River north of Halliday in 1932-1934. It connected the Fort Berthold Reservation with the Halliday area and brought friendship and commerce with the Indians and ranchers north of the river.

The hardship and unemployment of this period was relieved by Works Progress Administration (WPA) and Public Works Administration (PWA) programs. A bridge was built across Spring Creek just north of Halliday, along with a dam, a swimming house, paved sidewalks on Main Street, a park, and many other projects.

The economy improved in 1940 and there was prosperity until after World War II. In 1970 Halliday was in the middle of the "oil boom" to the west and extensive coal mining to the east. This energy development caused all the towns in the area to expand and prosper. The economy began to suffer with the lowering prices of Mid-East oil and excessive state taxation. Halliday is presently feeling the economic depression; it has fewer business places and its population has decreased.

If a person had gone to sleep like Rip Van Winkle and wakened now after 75 years he would be amazed at the changes in Halliday. Instead of dirt roads he would see paved highways leading into a clean town with paved, well-lighted streets, many trees, and well kept lawns. There is no longer a railroad depot and he could no longer hear the whistle of the "Goose," a local train, in early morning and evening. In its place are huge trucks, vans, and a bus. Grain elevators are on the site of the old stock yards.

He would hear of the fires that demolished the old brick school house and other buildings. Now, he would see a new school, gymnasium, and athletic complex on the south hill. As he wandered up Main Street he could see a new City Hall housing three fire engines and two ambulances, a new post office, a supermarket instead of the four stores, and a meat processing plant instead of farm butchering.

He might taste honey from the honey factory west of town. He would certainly notice the senior housing and see the city sanitation truck rumble by. He couldn't miss the blue water tower instead of the old pumps and wells and he would surely notice cable TV in all the homes. There could be a class reunion in the picturesque park, a tennis or softball game at school, a Bingo game at the new

Legion Hall, or a rodeo at the rodeo grounds.

On Sunday he would see people attending the two Lutheran or one Catholic Church instead of the former six churches. He would not be able to stay at the old hotel on Main Street but could find accommodations at the new motel or three trailer courts. He could eat at the Cafe or Pizza Parlor, where he would probably hear about some of the people who have brought fame to Halliday: Janet Voigt, Miss Rodeo North Dakota, 1985; Brad Gjermundson, national saddle bronc riding champion for four years; and Pete Fredericks and Joe Chase, well-known rodeo riders.

Halliday's public school

Main Street Halliday, North Dakota - mid 1900s

Harvey came into existence in the early spring of 1893 when the Minneapolis, St. Paul and Sault Ste Marie Railroad (Soo Line) completed its trackage to Portal, North Dakota. With the proximity of the Sheyenne River assuring them of an ample supply of water for their engines and shops it was established as a freight and passenger division point. A twelve-stall roundhouse and various shops and facilities were built and in the early days several hundred people in the community were employed by the railroad. Though operations have been reduced the Soo Line still plays a major role in the community with over ninety local people employed.

dozen buildings were quickly moved in the spring of 1895 and the major development of the business district and community developed on the south side.

The Harvey public high school

Harvey was incorporated as a village in April 1903 and as a city in June 1906 with Aloys Wartner serving as its first mayor. Growth of the community was phenomenal. By 1907 the city boasted of a population of over 1,200, a commercial club, 6 churches, 10 large grain elevators handling 1,500,000 bushels of wheat per year, 3 hotels, a flour mill producing 200 barrels of flour per day, 6 general stores, 3 hardware and furniture stores, 3 banks, 2 physicians, a dentist, a jewelry store , and many other business establishments. The commercial club was confidently predicting a population of 5,000 to 6,000 people within the next few years.

Through the years the business district suffered several major fires. In 1927 fire destroyed the north half of the 700 block. In later years the Kirton Building, the Pioneer Building, the Harvey Locker plant, the State Theater, the Sgutt Building, and an 85,000 bushel elevator were all destroyed by fires. Most of these were 2-story or 3-story buildings; fortunately, in most cases, they were rebuilt.

Harvey could easily be termed the melting pot of central North Dakota. Its early settlers were of varied ethnic backgrounds: German-Russian, German, Norwegian, Swedish, English, and Danish. Evidence of this can be seen in the many churches that served the community: Baptist,

Home of 2,263 North Dakotans

H *
Harvey

by Bob Nesbit

Opinions differ over the origin of the town's name; some say it was named after Harvey, Illinois; others hold that it was named after Colonel Harvey, a stockholder and director of the Soo Line.

The original townsite was planned for the south side of the tracks, but Tyrus I. Hurd, a company right-of-way agent, experienced difficulties in obtaining title to the land and the first business was established in a tent on the north side of the tracks by Ben Pearson of Carrington in April 1893. He was soon joined by J. G. Moore, also of Carrington, who opened a livery barn in the same vicinity.

In May 1894 Hurd received title to the land and the following month he surveyed and platted Harvey's original four-block townsite. Since the Soo Line had constructed its depot and shops on the south side of the tracks the existing businesses and about a

Catholic, Lutheran, Mennonite, Seventh-day Adventists, Methodist, Pentecostal, Congregational, and Assembly of God.

Harvey is justifiably proud of its school system which serves an area of 435 square miles. New school buildings were built in 1960 and 1970. The school is known for its excellent music department. The choir toured Europe in 1973. Many of its graduates have achieved prominence in their chosen fields. Among them are: Patrick Haggerty, former president and chairman of the board of Texas Instruments; Levon West (Ivan Dimitri), noted artist and photographer; Douglas Hanson, a vice-president of 3M; and Dr. Merton Utgard, founder of the International Music Camp at the Peace Garden.

Present day Harvey is a prosperous, growing community. Its excellent school system, 55-bed hospital, 120-bed nursing home, medical clinic, and its many churches and business establishments serve an ever-expanding trade territory. Two small manufacturing plants produce specialized farm equipment. Excellent recreational facilities include: an athletic field with 4 softball diamonds, a well-lighted baseball diamond, the North Dakota Softball Hall of Fame, a grass green golf course, a swimming pool, and boating and fishing in the Sheyenne Reservoir.

The Chamber of Commerce employs a full time director. The motto "Growing with Pride" reflects the enthusiasm and progressive spirit which makes Harvey one of the outstanding cities in central North Dakota.

Elevators on the Soo Line Railroad, Harvey, ND - 1909

Soo Line Round House in Harvey, North Dakota - 1909

The Chicago, Milwaukee and St. Paul Railroad established the station Gadsen on Sec. 29, T129N, R94W on its new line in 1907. Because of the similarity to Gladstone, the United States Postal Department rejected the name, which was changed in 1908 to Haynes in honor of George B. Haynes, the railroad's immigration agent at that time. In 1908 the Milwaukee Land Company and the Brown Land Company surveyed the land the same time as the Milwaukee tracks were being laid through the area. Town lots were first sold in May 1907.

Lot sale — 1907 — Haynes

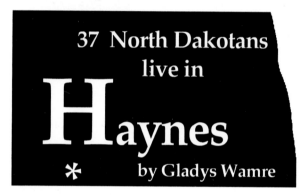

37 North Dakotans live in Haynes
* by Gladys Wamre

The first store, operated by Ganvoort and Settergreen, opened in a shack in 1907. In 1908 it became a larger store known as the Haynes Mercantile Company. Other early businesses opening in 1908 included a livery barn and dray line, the newspapers *Haynes Gazette* and *Haynes Register*, three lumberyards, a hardware store, a blacksmith shop and pool hall, a bakery and short order cafe, a hotel, the First State Bank, a barbershop, a telephone company which provided service from Mott to Haynes, a fire department, a grain elevator with a capacity of 30,000 bushels, and a meat market.

In 1909 new businesses included a confectionery store and the stock yards which shipped out eighty-seven car loads of cattle from the Grand River ranches to the Chicago and St. Paul markets the first year. Haynes's

cultural life was enriched when the Haynes Orchestra formed in 1909.

Congregational church services were first held in 1908 at the schoolhouse. By September 1909, a 28 by 32 foot structure was used for worship by the Norwegian Lutheran congregation. This building burned down in October 1965. A Roman Catholic Church was built in 1908 and served the community until about 1927.

The first elevator, built in 1908, was purchased by the Farmers Equity in 1914. When fire destroyed it in 1916, a larger elevator immediately replaced it. But when the new one burned down in 1977, it was not replaced. The Western Elevator also operated in Haynes at one time.

School was first held in 1908 in a 20 by 34 foot building, one of the schools in the Clermont School District until September 1912, when the Haynes Special School District No. 21 was organized. The district was enlarged in 1917. The second school, built in 1917, was used for both elementary and high school. The school reached its peak enrollment in the 1930s, with about 100 students in elementary school and 60 in high school. With declining enrollment and difficulty in finding teachers the district

was dissolved and the children were bussed to Hettinger in 1970. The school building is one of two that was not destroyed by fire.

The east side of Main Street burned down in 1925 and several years later the west side was destroyed by fire. The only structure left standing on Main Street was a brick building which housed the First Mercantile Company. It now houses the Wild Turkey Saloon, a bar and dance hall.

The post office began in 1908 (Alfred Geurkink, postmaster). Mail was brought by carrier from Hettinger three times a week; later the train which stopped twice a day dropped off the mail. The original two rural routes which distributed mail from Haynes were combined in recent years to one route. The Haynes post office closed in 1988; mail is now delivered by carrier from Hettinger.

Coal mining was the basis for the town's growth; at least six mines were in operation at one time. The state of South Dakota bought a mine three miles north of Haynes and built a railroad spur from the mine to Haynes. Thousands of tons of coal were shipped out to state-owned institutions. This mine closed down in 1933, and the population declined from the high of 250 when the mines were operating.

The pioneers who settled the land around Haynes were mostly German-Russians and Scandinavians.

Store in Haynes — 1909 — Haynes Mercantile Co.

The Haynes area saw one of the last buffalo hunts in 1882 in the valley between Haynes and White Butte. Some 5,000 bison were killed in a three-day hunt. George Custer and the 7th Cavalry camped at Bushy Bank, two miles east of Haynes, on the way from Fort Lincoln to the Black Hills in July 1874. At one time the Yellowstone Trail, an automobile route from Chicago to Seattle, passed through Haynes, but when US 12 was constructed, Haynes was by-passed by two miles.

Today, it is a sleepy, little town consisting of 37 people, a fertilizer plant, a lumber-yard, and the Wild Turkey Saloon. Haynes is part of the Heritage Crossroad Country of Adams County which includes the trail of the last buffalo hunt, the Custer Trail, the Old Yellowstone Trail, and the settlement by German-Russian and Norwegian-Swedish immigrants.

Haynes Livery Barn and Dray Line, J.C. Warbis, owner - 1910

Hazelton

The history of Hazelton actually begins several years before her founding, in another town entirely. Williamsport had served as the seat of Emmons County since 1883. A shift in population to the south and political maneuvering, however, sent the county records and government to Linton in 1898. About that same time the Soo Line Railroad reached Braddock, establishing it as a railhead. Previously, the Northern Pacific Railroad announced plans to build a branch line from McKenzie to Linton. Both bypassed Williamsport. Stripped of the county seat and forgotten by the railroad, Williamsport's days were numbered.

John I. Roop, a farmer living several miles west of the former county seat, responded to these developments with plans for a new town to replace old Williamsport. He recorded a townsite plat on his homestead in 1902 shortly after the Northern Pacific started grading for the McKenzie-Linton branch. Located on the border of the branch line's right-of-way this community would have the

one ingredient for success all turn-of-the-century settlements needed, the railroad. Roop named the site Hazelton, after his five year old daughter Hazel. Hazel Roop Moyers died in March 1987.

The construction of Hazelton began in the spring of 1903. Before winter set in, the town boasted a population of nearly 200, several blocks of completed buildings, an elevator and telephone lines. Her inhabitants consisted primarily of Germans and Scandinavians whose families had first settled in Ohio, Michigan, Wisconsin, and Minnesota.

Samuel F. Wright established the first business, a livery stable, in 1902. The next year William F. Yeater tore down his Williamsport general store and rebuilt it in Hazelton. On his heels came two more general stores and a host of other businesses, including an implement dealership opened by Roop, the Bank of Hazelton which remains in operation to this day, and a newspaper, the *Emmons County Republican* which has since relocated in Linton and been renamed the *Emmons County Record*. By 1906 Hazelton became a major marketplace for the surrounding area, replacing Williamsport. The old town was abandoned entirely when the post office was discontinued in 1903.

Religious life in the young commu-

nity also flourished. In 1904 the Catholics of Hazelton moved Woodman Hall from Williamsport to Hazelton's Main Street. This building served St. Paul's Catholic Church until 1917 when the present structure was built on the town's south side. The Williamsport Presbyterian Church reorganized in Hazelton as the First Presbyterian Church on February 19, 1905. After holding services in the schoolhouse for several years, the congregation constructed a church in 1909. Today it remains their place of worship. St. Paul's Evangelical Lutheran Church was organized in May 1923. The first church was built and dedicated in 1924, the second and present one in 1947. Hazelton also was served by a Baptist Church from 1924 to 1964.

Another major concern of Hazelton's early citizens was their children's education. Beginning with a one-room grade school, which had served area homesteaders before the town was established, they outgrew one schoolhouse after another. Soon they began to offer two years of high school, then four. A new two-story brick building was erected in 1923 to handle the growing student body. When the school district reorganized in 1960 this building became the high school and plans were set to erect an elementary school. It was built in 1963. At present these buildings serve the Hazelton-Moffit School District in the same capacities.

Agriculture remains at the heart of the town's economy and the key to

Northern Pacific RR camp, 1902 - earliest photo of townsite

her success, or failure. Already in 1915 the area surrounding the township was recognized for its land's potential. Hazelton at one time supported four grain elevators, but hard times, three elevator fires, one caused by arson, and bad management put all but one of them out of business. Today only the Farmers Union Elevator remains.

Over the years Hazelton has received a number of bynames. At various times during her history the town has been labeled "Little Chicago," a misnomer brought on the community by the criminal activities of a few individuals. More positively, during the thirties and forties residents built several dozen windmills. The picturesque view this made from the highway gave her the name "Windmill Town." During the late fifties, more flax, the grain from which linseed oil is made, passed through Hazelton than any other shipping point in the country, making her the "Flax Capital of the Nation." In the seventies the town's Airport Authority promoted the city as the "Flying Town" because of her over 25 private airplane owners. Sadly, today there is little more than a handful of windmills, airplanes, or even flax.

Hazelton became North Dakota's 132nd city in January 1950. The disastrous set-backs of her early years, outbreaks of typhus and flu, the Great Depression and drought, the so-called Dirty Thirties all had been overcome. Business thrived and the population swelled. In recent years, however, a slow decline has set in. Due primarily to farm difficulties the population has fallen below three hundred. Many stores and other small businesses have either closed or moved. Still, Hazelton struggles forward. The town and area continue to support two service stations, several mechanics and a repair shop, a blacksmith, an oil and implement company, the Farmers Union Oil Company, and the Farmers Union Elevator, a bank, grocery store, hairdresser, tavern, alcohol distributor, and cafe. The town also retains her community spirit.

That spirit has often expressed itself in the civic improvements the resi-

Hazelton, North Dakota - 1910

Hazelton, North Dakota - 1990s

dents have sponsored. In 1956 the town installed a modern water and sewage system. In 1975, as a part of the nation's Bicentennial celebration, Hazelton Park was built. Financed by the community, this facility includes modern brick restrooms, a picnic area, campsites, and tennis courts. The streets were paved at great expense in 1977 and a combination city hall, fire station, and repair shop was built shortly thereafter.

Hazelton's citizens also have shown their community mindedness with their support for various clubs and annual events including the

children's Santa Claus Day each December and Community Day, an event that includes contests and a street dance, in June.

Hazelton has aged and changed in her eighty-some odd years. But she is, as she always was, a community of people who, as one old timer remarked, "stand on their own two feet and make do."

Hazelton's N.D. Centennial Committee, Arlene Davis, chairwoman. Article contributors: Russell Buck, Herman Gimbel, Dewey Geil, Ruth Klein, Catherine Rosendahl, E. I. Roop, Steven Nowicki.

azen probably would not have appeared on North Dakota maps if it hadn't been for the railroad which crossed central North Dakota in the early 1900s. In 1912 it was widely known that the Western Dakota Railway Company, part of the Northern Pacific would extend its Mandan-Stanton branch line westward along the Knife River. The Tuttle Land Company was chosen by the Northern Pacific to acquire lands for townsites, and they purchased the plat for Hazen from Benjamin Oster in 1912 for $5,000. By 1913 the townsite had been surveyed, and the plat filed with the Mercer County registrar of deeds on November 7, 1913. Lots immediately began selling fast, ranging in price from $300 to $500. When the town was only one month old there

2,818 North Dakotans live in H*azen

by Ferd Froeschle & Kathy Huber

were already 40 buildings and 200 residents.

The area was not entirely unoccupied prior to the establishment of the town, however. Alexander F. "Sandy" Roberts came and squatted in the Hazen area in 1882. He filed an application for and received a post office on February 12, 1885, naming the post office Hazen after the Third Assistant Postmaster General, Abraham D. Hazen. Thus, Hazen appeared on a United States map, but the town was not to appear for another twenty-eight years.

The first European settlers arrived in the area about 1883 and settled along the Knife River. These settlers were known as the "Knife River Irish." These folks were responsible for establishing St. Martin's Catholic Church which still exists today. The German-Russians began arriving

after 1886. They were a hard working people who held on to their language, especially in their churches, until after World War II. Also settling in the area were Scandinavians who had established Lutheran churches six years before the arrival of the railroad.

Many of the first residents came from nearby towns of Krem, Mannhaven, and Expansion all of which had been bypassed by the railroad. Many buildings were moved from Krem, located about six miles north of Hazen. Some families even lived in their houses as they were being moved!

One of the first to purchase a lot in Hazen was Dr. L. G. Eastman. Moving his clinic from Krem and setting up practice in Hazen, he also was a major investor and business leader, helping to get many businesses and buildings started. Frank Wernli was another early town father, setting up a lumber company seven months before lots went on sale. Other early promoters were J. E. Stephens, a sheep rancher on the Knife River between Stanton and Hazen; J. F. Smith, owner and operator of a blacksmith shop and auto garage in Krem; C. N. Janzen, cashier of Krem's Citizen's State Bank and a United States commissioner charged with verifying homestead proofs.

Businesses were quickly established: Wernli's Drug Store, Knife River Lumber & Grain Company, Farrington's Hotel, Mandan Mercantile Company, a blacksmith shop, Keeley Hotel, a livery barn, and Doherty's pool hall. And of course as more and more people moved in, the demand for more businesses arose. Hazen's first newspaper began publishing on December 5, 1913 as the *Mercer County Star* which was the forerunner of the present weekly newspaper, the *Hazen Star*.

The early residents did take time to enjoy themselves. It was reported that on November 22, 1913 the first

75th Jubilee Celebration - 1988

"ball" in the new town was held at Ed Doherty's new pool hall building and was attended by thirty-five couples. A few nights later a Thanksgiving dance was held in the loft of the Strong Livery Stable, with a midnight turkey dinner served at the Hazen Hotel. A New Year's Eve dance was held at Keeley's Opera House. A dramatic society was organized in 1914, and had fifty-five members attending its second meeting.

The early business leaders formed the Hazen Boosters as part of the Commercial Club, and did a fine job of promoting their new town. From its fast and furious beginnings in 1913, Hazen grew to a population of 520 by 1920 and to 1,230 by 1950.

The Dakota Star Mine mined coal north of Hazen from 1944 to 1966, with as many as sixty employees which added to the population. During this same period in the late 1940s and early 1950s the Garrison Dam was constructed, bringing in another population spurt and nearly doubling the population that decade. The population stabilized until the coal energy boom in the 1970s brought Basin Electric, United Power, and Great Plains Coal Gasification plants to the county. Hazen experienced growth as never before increasing its population from 1,240 in 1970 to

2,365 in 1980 and to 3,351 in 1983. Construction and industrial payrolls from these plants lent a stability to the otherwise farm-based community and to the local economy, and Hazen acquired facilities its taxpayers might not have otherwise afforded.

In 1885 the Hazen School District was organized to educate the children already in the area. The school in the town of Hazen was started in 1914, and a three-story new school was built and used from 1917 to 1986. The first high school graduating class, five students, received their diplomas in 1920. Over the years the school complex has now expanded to cover a forty-five acre area, and the enrollment in K-12 rose to 951 students in 1990.

Hazen acquired its first hospital in 1941 when temporary quarters were established to handle a Spanish Influenza epidemic that took the lives of twenty-six people in one month. Starting in 1947 Hazen has had a permanent hospital that has served Mercer County and the surrounding area continuously. Housed in three different buildings over the years, it moved to its present location on the east side of Hazen in 1970. In 1986 it became affiliated with St. Alexius Hospital of Bismarck, and changed its name to Sakakawea Medical Center.

One of Hazen's "elite" is John Moses, a local lawyer who left Hazen in 1938 to serve three terms as governor of North Dakota. He was elected to the office of United States Senator in

Main Street Hazen, North Dakota - 1940s

1945. He died after only a few months in that office.

As with many North Dakota towns, weather caused difficulties over the years. Many blizzard stories exist, of course, but the blizzards of 1949 immobilized the entire Hazen area, and the 5th Army came to clear roads and help get feed to farms. Ski equipped planes were used for some missions. Spring floods were also a problem, disastrous ones occurred in 1938, 1966, and 1969. After the latter, a new highway bypass system was built to control flooding into the town itself, and to take highway traffic off main street.

One of the most costly fires occurred on a cold December day in 1973 when three local businesses burned: Bentley's V Store, Jack and Jill, and Eddies Lanes.

The airport was built in 1947 by John and Lyle Benz who were World War II aviation veterans. They established a flying school and even acquired a war surplus B-17 bomber

that was an educational attraction here for three years before it was sold. Hazen continues to have an active airport with a paved runway, located one mile east of the city.

Sports have always been popular in Hazen, beginning with the boxing exploits of Jacob "Bat" Krause in the early days. He was state welterweight champion for a number of years. Baseball and tennis were other early favorites. Besides school sport activities, the city boasts a well developed hockey program, and a winter sports facility which includes an indoor hockey rink that was completed in the 1980s. The nearby Garrison Dam and Lake Sakakawea is a popular fishing and water-recreation spot and has provided good geese and duck hunting.

A well-known annual event is the Christmas Chorale Concert. The Knife River Chorale was organized in 1956 and has performed annually ever since. It has also performed on such occasions as our nation's Bicentennial and Hazen's Jubilee celebrations. Dave Schoenrock, director since 1957, also designs the chorale's backstage settings and transforms the gymnasium into a tree-filled wonder for this annual concert. Singers from Hazen and the surrounding area faithfully participate.

Hazen proudly celebrated its 75th Jubilee in July 1988 with a ten-day celebration. The Hazen Jubilee History Book was printed for this occasion and is available as a resource for anyone looking for more information on Hazen and its people.

Aerial view of Hazen, North Dakota - 1948

As the site of the last great buffalo hunts in North America, the Hettinger community celebrates this heritage with an annual Buffalorama mountain man encampment on Mirror Lake, western entertainment and storytelling. Tours of the hunt and butchering sites, tepee rings, buffalo wallows and a live buffalo herd recall the great Sioux hunts of 1882 and 1883. Then 50,000 bison, the last of the vast herds once numbering 60 to 75 million, made their final stand here on the Dakota border.

Hettinger is located near the corners of four states and just four miles from the border, so the community includes a part of South Dakota.

1,574 North Dakotans live in
Hettinger
*
by Francie M. Berg

Friendly western hospitality is a tradition.

Today this is cattle and sheep ranching country. The NDSU Research Extension Center on sheep research, and more recently, crops, is located here. Coal mining has been important.

Hettinger is nationally known as a rural medical center serving six satellite clinics in a wide area of North and South Dakota. The town is served by a staff of specialists which includes 16 physicians, a well-equipped medical clinic and hospital, and an 88-bed nursing home.

Mirror Lake Park, near the center of town, offers varied recreation with swimming beach, picnicking, exercise equipment, walking trail around the lake, Mother Goose playground, boat dock with paddle boats, canoe and sailboat rentals, fishing, a Centennial bandshell, and quiet, inexpensive RV campground. The town also has an indoor swimming pool.

Long-standing traditions that take on a modern flair are summer ice

Parade on Main Street marks annual Fourth of July Festival

cream socials in the park, Friday night music by the Hettinger Cowboy Band, and an old-fashioned free 4th of July celebration that ends with fireworks over the Mirror Lake. Bird watching tours are conducted by local ornithologists.

Dakota Buttes Museum, with extensive pioneer home and machinery displays, and Pioneer Centennial Square are places to visit. Dinosaur and mammal fossil beds, petrified wood, Indian artifacts, petroglyphs and tepee rings are prevalent here.

Hiddenwood Creek, which flows through Hettinger and Mirror Lake, and surrounding buttes and plains were the scene of the Last Great Buffalo Hunt. In June 1882, 2,000 Sioux, arrayed in their finest regalia and including the head men of the Sioux Nation, came here from Fort Yates and in three days killed 5,000 buffalo.

Just down Hiddenwood Creek near Haynes is the spot where the Custer Expedition camped in 1874 — with 2,000 men, 150 wagons and 300 head of beef cattle — on their way to investigate reports of gold in the Black Hills.

Not far off is the trail on the Grand River where mountain man Hugh Glass was mauled by a grizzly bear in 1823 and left for dead by Major Henry's fur trading party. Severely injured and without weapons, he traveled 200 miles at night through hostile Indian country, recovered and soon headed west again.

Here the old west meets with a homestead and ethnic heritage. This is a country cut by old trails: the Gold Rush trail, the Custer Trail, Indian trails heading east and west to hunting grounds, and south to ancient Black Hills ceremonial sites. Texas trail herds cut through on their way north to the Missouri River and into Canada. Near here Dilts emigrant train ran into hostile Indians and threw up a sod fort. Much later, in 1912, the Yellowstone Trail to Yellowstone Park was laid out and marked with yellow sandstone obelisks.

Cattle kingdoms were established here in the early 1880s, running tens of thousands of Texas longhorns. Famous old brands of the region are the Mill Iron, Turkey Track, the Hash Knife, L7, Triple V, and the E6.

Survey opened up the land for homesteading in 1900, and the days of open range were over. A rush of homesteaders quickly settled the area. Impetus was a period of good rainfall, the westward progress of track laying for the Milwaukee Railroad, and strong promotional efforts.

Homesteaders were required to live on the land for five years (at least seven months a year), build a livable home, cultivate 20 acres and show improvements such as a well or

fences. After 14 months residence, the claim could be purchased at $1.25 per acre.

Adams County was created in 1907, named for a Milwaukee Railroad townsite agent, and on the same day the town of Hettinger was named county seat, although it did not yet exist. A tent town soon flourished on the designated site.

Pioneer folk architecture attests to the ethnic diversity of people who settled here. Examples of these can still be seen and include sod houses, rock houses built with and without mortar, dugouts, tarpaper shacks, rammed earth homes, and low log ranch houses with grass growing on scoria or dirt-covered roofs.

Old west and last buffalo hunts are celebrated in Hettinger

Mirror Lake Park offers varied recreation
Camping, swimming and boating are favorite activities.

Hunter *

by Mrs. Billy Battagler

Hunter is located along North Dakota 18, in north central Cass County. The first known settlers were Even Johnson, Peter Erickson, and Jorgon Anderson who dug into a coulee bank for shelter. Johnson bought 160 acres of government land at $2.50 an acre. He then sold four acres to William Kindred who had the land surveyed, platted, and registered as the original townsite of Hunter on May 28, 1881. Hunter was named after John C. Hunter, a major landowner in the area.

The railroad was important in Hunter's early history. Tracks were laid into the area in 1880 by the Casselton Branch Railroad Company, originally a subsidiary of the Northern Pacific Railroad Company, but sold a short time later to the St. Paul, Minneapolis and Manitoba

Railroad Company (Great Northern). The station was probably established the next year. It provided mail service, freight, and passenger service. A rail terminus now, grain is shipped out in unit trains.

In June 1880 a rural post office named Delno was established a short distance north of the present townsite. The next year it was moved and renamed Hunter. The first general store, Gale and Duffany, was built and was soon followed by the Citizen's Bank, a school, and the Barrett Store. There was an abundance of good, pure water at depths of 10 to 20 feet, and in 1890 a 345-foot artesian well was dug. Today's water needs are met by a rural water system.

Hunter grew very rapidly from the start, by 1899 there were six grain elevators with a capacity of 225,000 bushels and an average shipment of 500,000 bushels. The community supported three churches, one of the best grade schools with four teachers, a bank with capital assets of $10,000, two hotels, two weekly newspapers, and long distance and local telephone

service. The Great Northern Railroad provided passenger and freight service.

The town boasted of two general stores which claimed they carried the most complete stock in the county. Other businesses were: a hardware store, a store which sold shoes and "gents" furnishings, two farm machine dealers, a foundry, three blacksmith shops, two livery barns, a drug store, a millinery shop, a jewelry store, two meat markets, and a fruit and confectionery store. The town also boasted of a harness maker, a veterinarian, and a physician-surgeon. Lawbreakers were housed in a city jail.

Tragedy struck the community early in the morning of December 28, 1899, when a fire wiped out all but the Gale and Duffany store in one block of Main Street, the business was saved by a fire wall. Within a few years this area was substantially rebuilt.

Hunter's population peaked in 1906 with a count close to 600 persons.

Volunteers have been fighting Hunter's fires since 1888 when a hand pump was purchased. Today a five-unit fire fighting force protects the community. A new fire hall was built in 1985. A volunteer ambulance service was organized in 1971.

Telephone service started in 1898; Polar Communications of Park River serves the area today. Limited electric service started in 1911. Today's needs are met by the Cass County Electric Cooperative of Kindred.

The first church services were held in the school in 1882. The Presbyterian church was built in 1886; the building was used until it burned in 1980. A new structure was built. The Methodists started their church in 1887 and built their first structure in 1889. The congregation outgrew those facilities, dedicating the present building in 1917. The first Roman Catholic Mass was conducted in 1887. They built their first church in 1898, but they also outgrew their facilities and constructed their present building in 1954. Early records of the Lutheran Church tell of their or-

Hunter's Volunteer Ambulance Service - established in 1971

Public School in Hunter, North Dakota - built in 1895

ganization in 1892. They dedicated their building in 1902, with services being conducted in Norwegian. They, too, outgrew their meeting place and dedicated the present structure in 1948. An addition was completed in 1985.

Hunter School District No. 68 was organized in 1881 and a school was built. This structure was replaced in 1895; the new building itself was replaced in 1923 by a brick building. A gymnasium was added in 1953 and four grade-school rooms were added in 1960. The school graduated its last high school class in 1967, after providing eighty-five years of continuous high school education. Hunter, Arthur, and part of Erie and Blanchard reorganized on a trial basis and the 1969-1970 school year operated as the new Dakota School District No. 3, with the high school in Arthur and the elementary school in Hunter.

Like most small towns in North Dakota Hunter's population is declining. During World War II several people moved to California to work and never returned. Most of the local young people go to colleges and look for work elsewhere.

The businesses operating in Hunter today are: Nelson's Food Mart, Hunter Liquor, Security State Bank, with branches in Galesburg and Hope, the Bronze Hut, Hunter Grain Company with branches in Blanchard, Gardner, and Amenia, Moen's Gasoline Alley, Nola's on Main, a beauty shop, Sharon Shear Shop, another beauty shop, Fietzek Repair, Bil-Bilt Products, Bilenes Gift and Hobby, Blazek Construction, Peterson and Son Excavating, Hunter Equipment, a John Deere dealership, Scott's Body Shop, Hunter Taxidermy, David Madsen's furnace and air-conditioning, Eastern Dakota Construction, Ramstad Construction, Hunter Lumber Supply, Standard Bulk Service, Pearson Investment Company, the post office, and several home-based sales operations.

There are many active clubs in the community: Community Club, homemakers groups, 4-H, Odd Fellows, Hunter Friendship Seniors, American Legion and Auxiliary, Garden Club, TOPS organization, Rebekah Lodge, Royal Neighbors, and various church groups.

Hunter has two buildings which were moved to Bonanzaville in West Fargo, the *Hunter Times* building and a part of the David Houston home. The latter, considered a mechanical genius, invented the roll principle of the Kodak camera and was responsible for other photographic breakthroughs. Bertin Gamble spent the first seven years of his life in Hunter and William Muir, a nationally known sculptor, was also from Hunter.

Main Street Hunter, North Dakota - 1899

Kenmare was described in 1907: "Back long before the advent of the iron horse and quite a number of years before the Soo Line came into being in this community, this section of the country constituted the northern part of the cattle range which extended clear across the central United States from Texas to the Canadian border. . . .These prairies surrounding our city were predominated by the cowboy and the wild steer, most of which were under the management of N-N Cattle Company. . . . All over this country roved the cowboys, hardy, buxom, living the natural life; living in the saddle by day, sleeping on the ground and in the open, communing with the stars—an army like that of the Indian."

(Kenmare Journal, **June 1907)**

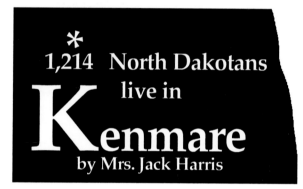

1,214 North Dakotans live in Kenmare
by Mrs. Jack Harris

It was from this hardy mold that E. C. Tolley seemed to be cut. He came to this region in April 1896 to explore the coal regions, study nature, and determine for himself whether the land was fit for developing. Convinced of its worth, Tolley set about interesting prospective settlers in the waiting abundance of the area.

On July 27, 1896 James Crane filed a plat under the act granting soldiers of the War of the Rebellion an additional homestead and it was deeded to the Minnesota Loan and Trust Company in trust for the Townsite Company, consisting of W. D. Cassedy, W. T. Smith, and E. C. Tolley. Others filing on land that later became Kenmare were Miss S. I. Stanley, an early-day milliner, Judge Niederriter, Math Guinn, and E. J. Brown. While there were several others filing in 1896, there was no real settlement until 1897.

Some of the first businesses were owned by George A. Robertson, J. H. Banning, P. M. Cole, Tasker and Company, and Tracy Brothers.

The business district itself was built around a city park which occupied the center block of the district. Two attempts were made through the years to divide the city park up into lots and sell it, but the people of Kenmare defeated both attempts.

The Soo Line Railroad played a part in the development of Kenmare when it came through the area. In 1897 the railroad built immigrant shacks to house people until they could build homes of their own. One season it was noted that some 1,200 cars of immigrants arrived in Kenmare.

Lignite was the name of the first post office and Augustine Rouse was the postmaster. However, it was short-lived, as he was killed in 1896 and the post office was abolished. When it was re-established in 1897, George Robertson was appointed postmaster. Mail was received daily via the Soo Line. Rural service was established in 1903.

Fire destroyed the entire west side of the city square in 1899. But the businesses were quick to rebuild and the town prospered.

In 1901, an election was held and the settlement was incorporated and named Kenmare.

Religion has always played a big role in Kenmare, with the first churches in the city being established in 1900. Among those first churches were the Seventh-day Adventists, Lutheran (Nazareth Danish Evangelical), Baptists (Union Sunday School), and the German Baptist (Dunkard) Brethren, established in 1897. Their congregations were Danish, for the most part, with Swedes and Norwegians. Methodist, Church of the

Kenmare's Danish Mill
(SHSND)

Nazarene, and the Presbyterian Churches were quick to follow.

The first Kenmare School Township was organized in June of 1897. The school building was completed in 1903, but burned to the ground in February 1904. A new building was ready for occupancy later in 1904. In 1908 another school building was built to accommodate the 400-plus students attending school.

It was in 1917 that Kenmare first took part in what was to be a lengthy line of state basketball tournaments. They participated in 1920, 1922, 1924, and 1925. In 1940 they went to the Class B state tournament and they were the state Class B Champions in 1963, 1965 and 1966.

In the fall of 1970, a new school was built and opened to house the middle and secondary schools. It was one of the first of its kind in the nation. The oldest standing school building was torn down.

St. Agnes parochial school served Kenmare from 1912 until 1970. It was staffed by the Ursuline Sisters.

Today, the Kenmare community lists 100 members in the Association of Commerce. There are hospital, clinic, dental, and optometry facilities as well.

The city park still stands in the center of the business district as the Founding Fathers had intended. An old Danish Mill was renovated and moved into the park in 1965. It stands as a monument to the pioneer spirit and dedication of our ancestors.

"Market Days" in Kenmare, North Dakota - 1909
(SHSND)

There isn't much to be seen in a little town, but what you hear makes up for it.

Frank McKinney (Kim) Hubbard

Main Street Kenmare, North Dakota - 1990s
(DPDP - Todd Strand)

The land on which Kief is located today was homesteaded in 1898 by Anton Bokovoy, a Russian immigrant. He patented the land in 1905 and sold half of it to the Tri-State Land Company of Minneapolis, Minnesota in 1908. The other half was deeded to Sam Bokovoy in 1937. The land company resold the land to other immigrant families from Norway, Sweden, Russia, and Germany.

The custom in those days was for the first homesteader to name the town. Anton Bokovoy named it after his birthplace, Kiev, located in the Ukraine in the Soviet Union. Through an error in spelling it became Kief.

Kief officially became a village in 1918. At that time it had a population of approximately 300. Through the years many commercial ventures were established: four general stores, one lumberyard, four elevators, one bank, a drug store, a photographer, two blacksmith shops, one livery barn, a post office, an outdoor theater, one Chevrolet dealership and implement company, three service stations and garages, a cream station, a shoe repair shop, one saloon, one grinding mill, a hotel, one cafe,

24 North Dakotans live in K* Kief
by Jackie Farrin

one barbershop, one pool hall, a bowling alley, one general repair shop, an autobody shop, and one green house. Five churches were also established.

The schoolhouse in Kief was built in 1910. At that time there were about 128 high school and grade school students and four teachers. The school was closed in 1959 because of declining enrollments.

Through the years Kief has been plagued with fires and tornadoes. Fire destroyed the John Deere building in 1946; an elevator was burned in 1968. Other buildings destroyed by fires were a pool hall, a bowling alley, the M and K Grocery Store, and in 1981, the Kief General Store, owned by Sam and Irene Karpenko for 51 years, burned.

In June, 1958 a tornado roared through town demolishing the Seventh-day Adventist Church and

twisting steel grain bins. The Soo Line's outhouse flew through Earl and Ruth's Bar window, and the outdoor theater building and other small buildings were never found.

Though Kief is loosing population several businesses remain: Kief Farmer's Elevator opened in 1967, Krueger Standard began pumping gasoline in 1956, Karl and Ruth's Bar has been operating since 1957, and the A & R Body Shop opened its doors in 1980. A post office has served the town since 1909.

The Soo Line Railroad terminated passenger service in the 1940s; however, freight trains still run through town twice a day.

One of the town's natives rose to prominence in state government. LaClaire Melhouse served for many years as Adjutant General of the North Dakota National Guard.

The largest celebration in Kief's recent history was the town's 75th Jubilee and an All School Reunion in July 1983. On one day of the celebration some 2,000 people gathered in Kief.

Residential district of Kief, North Dakota - early 1900s
(SHSND)

Main Street Kief, North Dakota - 1976
(DPDP - Todd Strand)

While residing in a small town I had often heard people say what a friendly place it was, how kind and neighborly the people were, and what a fine place it was in which to live. From my own experience I had to agree. And yet, evidently not everyone in the town shared the same favorable image. On the highway sign at the town entrance one night somebody crossed out the town name and painted over it the word HELL.

Father Bernard Quinn, 1970

Home Town of 722 North Dakotans

K*illdeer

by Mae Booke

The name Killdeer, from the Sioux Indian phrase *Ta-ha-Kouty* w h i c h means "the place where we kill the deer," was given to a short-lived rural post office established in February 1911 and located on Isaac Tift's homestead; his wife Ida was named postmaster. Discontinued in October area mail was forwarded to Oakdale. Two other rural post offices used the name Killdeer; the Brooks post office established in March 1908 eventually was named Killdeer and it was moved into the railroad town in 1915. When the Northern Pacific Railroad completed its branch line from Mandan into the northwest counties in October 1914 it named its terminal station, Killdeer, after the Killdeer

Mountains some nine miles northwest of the town. There apparently was little agreement in the area about doubling the "l" in the name.

Early Killdeer consisted of tarpaper shacks and frame buildings on a prairie surrounded by homesteaders and ranchers. Residents were provided electric lights, the system being powered by a generator at the Odenthal mill. It was turned on at dark and ran until midnight. Ethnic groups settled together to form communities of German-Russians, Norwegians, Swedes, Germans, and some Irish and English.

As a result of the coming of the railroad many businesses were established and the town grew to a population of 700 by 1915. It became a major shipping point for cattle and grain, at one time being the primary shipping point in the world for cattle. The branch line is now abandoned, the rails and ties have been removed.

Fires have taken their toll of business places; five were destroyed at

one time. When the Nord Hotel burned, the adjacent newspaper office which was on skids, having just been moved to town, was pulled into the middle of Main Street where it stood for some time before being returned to its original location.

The oil boom which began in western North Dakota in the 1950s had a substantial effect on the town. In addition to many new homes being constructed numerous businesses were established including a shopping mall, bowling alley, cafe and bar, lumberyard, auto repair shop, sports marina, greenhouse and landscaping services, implement dealership, and construction companies. Government services also expanded with the addition of a fire hall, a county shop, and a water treatment plant. A Masonic Lodge facility was constructed and a nursing home is being built. The recent loss of oil-drilling activity has had an adverse effect on the community.

In April 1908 Killdeer's children attended school in a one-room country school, a half mile west of town. In 1915 a site in town was chosen for a schoolhouse and in two years a three-story brick building was completed which continued to serve the community for over two decades. It remains part of the school plant, although part of it now is unsafe for use. In 1939 under a Works Progress Administration (WPA) program which provided work for the unemployed a much-needed gymnasium was built.

The Killdeer Special School District was created in May 1921 and following embattled reorganization in 1958 the Killdeer district was consolidated with neighboring districts and became the largest in Dunn County. Eight bus routes serve the district. Today, the school plant includes a new high school, a shop, new grade school rooms, and a much larger gymnasium. One hundred seventeen students were enrolled in high school in 1990; the grade schools enrolled 297 students.

Trees in memory of those Killdeer men who gave their lives in World War II were planted on the school

Killdeer Fire Department - 1927

grounds. Today, they stand tall to remind everyone of their sacrifice.

Since the 1930s Killdeer has become the center for all government offices serving Dunn County. Some offices during that period were housed in the Killdeer Hotel. Later, a frame building was constructed to house them and, eventually, a brick and block structure was added to provide needed space.

Several new churches have replaced those which served the religious needs of early Killdeer and the surrounding area. St. Joseph's Catholic Church built a new facility in 1950; St. John's Lutheran Church built one in 1966, and the Baptists also constructed a new facility in the 1950s. The Seventh-day Adventist Church purchased the Congregational affiliates building; it is the oldest church building in town.

Killdeer's unique public library of stripped logs and native rocks was built during the Great Depression with WPA labor and National Youth Administration funds providing part of the cost. Arrangements were made with Fort Berthold Indian Reservation to cut trees along the Little Missouri River at Elbowoods for the logs. The library's basement and large fireplace were constructed of native rock and cement. Originally built for use by 4-H clubs and Scout organizations it became the town's library; in 1983 it was remodeled and enlarged to make use of the previously unused basement. It is picturesquely situated back from Main Street with a picnic ground and city park in the foreground. To approach it one must cross a footbridge.

A young pioneer doctor moved to Killdeer in 1915. He delivered babies, set broken bones, and treated ailments until his retirement. Killdeer now is served by a medical doctor and a clinic, a dentist, and an optometrist. The community also supports two ambulances manned by trained personnel.

To cater to travelers Killdeer boasts

Killdeer Mountains Round Up - early 1900s

of four motels, two night-clubs, and restaurants. Good camping and picnic sites are convenient, trail rides through the nearby, scenic Badlands are available, and good fishing exists in the area.

The Killdeer Mountain Round-Up, now part of the annual 4th of July celebration, is one of a kind. Old-time cowboy, Sam Rhoades, who came to Killdeer with a long-horn cattle drive from Texas, is credited with starting the rodeo with facilities constructed on his land at the foot of Killdeer Mountain. Since 1956 it has been held on grounds on the outskirts of Killdeer and is now managed by the

Killdeer Saddle Club. Top riders, some arriving by plane, come to try their luck on the stock. One year 10,000 tickets were sold for the rodeo. Rhoades moved his livery stable from Killdeer to his farm and converted it into a house. An attractive dwelling, it was moved back into Killdeer and is now occupied by a rodeo-minded couple who treasure its history.

Killdeer's history is filled with nicknames of old-timers such as Big Pete, Little Pete, Dude, Gube, and Six-Cylinder Pete.

Killdeer, the City with the Pep, lives on!!!!

Winter in Killdeer, North Dakota - 1914-1915

Kramer is located in Stone Creek Township. During the summer of 1905 the Soo Line Railroad established a station by that name on Secs. 11 and 14, T160N, R78W along the railroad's "Wheat Line Branch" which runs from Thief River Falls, Minnesota to Kramer. The railroad bought a wider right-of-way at the site so they could build the grade and bridge across the Mouse (Souris) River, four miles west. In June the site was platted and the rural Ely post office was moved to the new town. The office was renamed Kramer a short time later with Alfred G. Chadbourn postmaster. The town was named after a New York importer and wholesaler who came to inspect the townsite with other eastern businessmen.

Main Street Kramer, North Dakota - 1916

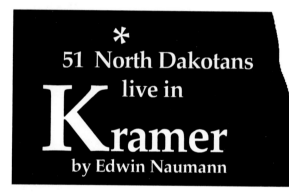

★ 51 North Dakotans live in Kramer
by Edwin Naumann

The first building located in the new community was an old boxcar moved in from Souris, some distance to the north. It was used as a meat market, supplying meat for the rail workers. Lumber was hauled from Omemee, several miles to the east, in 1904 for the first buildings that were constructed. By the spring of 1905 tracks were laid and trains carrying supplies came to Kramer. By the fall of that year Kramer was a busy village of 151 people. Never a boom town, its population remained around 225 people for several years.

Some of Kramer's first businesses were the Eagle and Forthun Hotel, C. T. Kretschmar Hardware, the First Chance-Last Chance Saloon and Pool Hall, Butz Meat Market, the Wright Livery Barn, First State Bank, Ronning-Grogen and Loven Hardware, Horning Dray, Kirkeby

Brothers General Merchandise, and J.J. Wittmayer General Merchandise. Wittmayer moved his store to Kramer from its original location south of town near the Mouse River. By 1906 Kramer had six elevators and boasted of a two-story wood building.

The new schoolhouse was completed by 1907 and by 1912 a brick school building was in use. The Stony Creek School District served the community until 1954 when it was reorganized as Kramer School District No. 46. In 1956 the last, new, modern school was built. The school merged with Newburg and students in grades one through six were taught in Kramer. The Kramer school was closed permanently in May 1991. Most of the grade school children will be bussed to Bottineau.

The village was chartered and incorporated April 9, 1908. The first elected officers who were also pioneer settlers were Hans V. Kirkeby, Fred Horning, George A. Butz, Simon M. Ronning, Henry Boehnke, J. N. Wright, J. J. Wittmayer, and John Walsh who served as marshall.

At one time Kramer had three banks, four hotels, a drug store, two meat markets, three general stores, two hardware stores, two barbers, an implement dealer, two bars and pool halls, a millinery shop, a bakery and a cafe, a feed mill, two livery barns, two drays, a photo shop, a newspaper, a harness and shoe repair shop,

a blacksmith shop, a veterinarian, and two doctors and a hospital.

In 1900 Zion Lutheran Church was started. A small church was built southeast of Kramer where the cemetery is located now. In 1905 a large church was built. The Reverend Albert Rubbert served the church for fifty years.

In 1910 the village hired Ted Redlaczyk to build a fire hall and jail. That same year the volunteer firemen organized. A community orchestra was also organized and used the new fire hall for practice. It was in demand for dances and celebrations throughout the area.

Kramer was always a sports town. Its baseball teams were invited to play at the Minot and Brandon fairs for several years. Two mens' basketball teams were also supported. North Dakota state wrestling champion Len Shong had his headquarters in Kramer. Several matches were held in Kramer with opponents coming from throughout the state and from Minneapolis, St. Paul, Milwaukee, and cities in Montana and South Dakota.

The hub of the city was probably the Soo Depot with agent Bill Voight in charge. Kramer had mail, express, and passenger service twice daily except for Sunday. The train had three cars, the ladies' car, a smoker's car, and the United States Mail and Express car. The coaches had red velvet seats, brass kerosene lamps, and a newsboy who sold sandwiches, candy, fruit, and magazines. The conductor and brakeman wore beautiful blue serge suits with gold buttons. Their caps were trimmed with gold

Aerial view of Kramer, North Dakota - 1979

braid and read "Conductor" or "Brakeman."

Kramer was settled by Germans, German-Russians, Swedes, Norwegians, Irish, Scots, English, and Icelanders. They were Protestants, Catholics, and Jews.

One of the community's best known enterprises was Arthur White's Meadow Lawn Farm, located just northeast of Kramer. He raised blooded Percheron horses and shipped carloads by rail to distant markets. He advertised his business with a large banner which nearly covered half of a freight car. It declared: "Meadow Lawn Farm, Kramer, North Dakota."

At one time Kramer had a brick and block works, a broom factory, a farmers' cream station which sponsored a cattle and horse show each summer, a farmers' shipping association which shipped cattle direct to market, a movie theater, a cabinet and woodwork shop, and a radio broadcasting station owned by Marvin Kirkeby.

The church building erected in 1905 is still in use; a parish hall was added in recent years. The business community has been reduced to a service station, two elevators, one bar, and the post office. A new fire hall which also houses the Senior Citizen's Center was built in 1978. The fire department which was organized in 1910 with a two-wheel cart pulled by men has grown to a three-truck modern department that includes a Rural Fire District.

Kramer has a small city park with playground equipment, well-used by local and visiting children.

More common sense can be induced by observation of the diversity of human beings in a small town than can be learned in academia.
Louis B. Wright
Barefoot In Arcadia
University of South Carolina, 1974

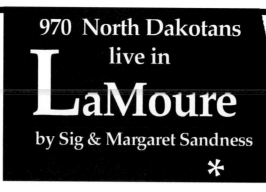

970 North Dakotans live in LaMoure

by Sig & Margaret Sandness

*

Nestled in the scenic and fertile James River Valley in southeastern North Dakota is the city of LaMoure, founded in 1882. It received wide notoriety in that year when the Northern Pacific Railroad designated the spot as the terminus of its Fargo and Southwestern Branch, then being built. It was one of the era's major boom towns. The townsite was platted August 1882 on land owned by E. P. Wells, a land agent from Jamestown who had close ties to the railroad company. Town lots went on sale in Jamestown two months later and by May of the next year buyers had invested some $120,000 in town property. Wells, himself, built the Leland Hotel. By the time the railroad reached the town in late 1883 a fair-sized community had sprung up, including sixty-nine buildings. It was incorporated as a city in 1905. The city added the Wakefield Addition in 1961; it was named for Harold Wakefield, the local superintendent of schools for thirty-three years.

The town was named in honor of Judson LaMoure, a long-time, prominent political figure in North Dakota.

In 1881 Mary Foss homesteaded land which became the south side addition when LaMoure was platted. The first permanent business building, a blacksmith shop, was built in 1883 and the first depot was built that same year. It burned in 1911, was rebuilt that same year and burned

again in 1914. The following year the present depot was erected.

In 1881 Dakota Territory governor Nehemiah G. Ordway appointed the first LaMoure County government. The following year in December the post office was established with Norris B. Wilkinson as postmaster. In 1883 the town's first medical doctors, Moxley and H. M. Boyd, arrived and that same year the first newspaper began publication. It was purchased in 1888 by the *LaMoure Chronicle* which has been published weekly since that time. Today, it's the official county newspaper.

The first school opened its doors on October 30, 1884. In 1905 a new brick schoolhouse was built. A new gymnasium and several elementary classrooms were built in 1955.

In 1886 the county board designated LaMoure as county seat and ordered records transferred from the Grand Rapids courthouse. In 1910 the present courthouse was completed. In 1981 LaMoure County bought the former Grand Rapids courthouse and

had it moved to Memorial Park. The contents of the Henry Arndt Museum which was located north of the LaMoure Courthouse were placed in the building.

In 1889 Roman Catholics and Baptists built churches.

The community suffered a disastrous fire in 1894; the entire business district including thirty-six buildings and many homes burned.

Civic improvements and various government projects have benefited the community since the 1920s. A community building was erected in 1923 and replaced fifty years later by the Milton Young Civic Center. In 1935 during the Great Depression a dam was built west of LaMoure on the James River by the Civilian Conservation Corps. The next year the city paved its streets. The Omega Station, a United States Coast Guard Tracking Station and the only one in North America, was built in 1972. It is one of a network of eight stations located throughout the world. That same year man-made Lake LaMoure was constructed. LaMoure has been the home of many state and county leaders including: Joseph M. Devine, two-term state lieutenant governor who acted as governor for five months in 1898 after the death of Governor Frank Briggs; Milton R. Young, United States Senator for

Main Street LaMoure, North Dakota - 1990s

thirty-five years; two state Superintendents of Schools; and a supreme court justice, Joseph M. Bartholomew.

The town has won honors several times in the Community Betterment Contest and in 1977-79 was designated as one of eleven "All America City" award recipients.

Today, LaMoure has: a nine-hole golf course with a club house; a lighted athletic field; a tennis court, outdoor ice rink, bowling lane, movie theater, swimming pool, motel, and parks; apartment buildings, a condominium, a low-cost housing unit for senior citizens, and a sixty-bed nursing home.

The town also supports and maintains the following services and business enterprises: a volunteer fire department, police protection, garbage pickup, a sanitary landfill, lagoon-type sewage treatment, an abundant water supply, a dental clinic, pharmacy, twenty-four hour ambulance service, a public library, six churches, trailer court, public airport, medical clinic, laundromat, a chiropractor and optometrist who serve the area weekly, mortuary, three grain elevators, two law firms, a trucking firm, a certified public accountant, electricians, an abstract company, two television and radio repair shops, a hardware store, three bars, three service and gas stations, drug store, depart-

LaMoure County Court House built in 1910

ment store, floral shop, bank, investment center, three beauty salons, two grocery stores, three lumber companies, a locker plant, two restaurants, a supper club, a drive-in, seven insurance companies, a sports shop, two implement companies, an auto parts center, a bulk milk service, a concrete ready-mix plant, a Soil Conservation office, an A.S.C.S. office, a Farm Credit Service, credit union, feed plant, veterinary clinic, excavation company, greenhouse, aerial service, Toy Farmer, auto body shop, two bulk oil stations, four carpenter crews, septic tank service, taxidermist, landscaping service, auctioneer, furniture and upholstery service, a

monument company, a county bookmobile, and a gunsmith.

The town also has supported organizations such as Fortnightly which was organized in 1916, the Order of the Eastern Star organized in 1896, 4-H clubs, American Legion and Auxiliary, summer baseball, horse riding club, Boy and Girl Scouts, Sportsman's club, square dancing, boosters, retailers, and a Lions Club.

The town's annual events include: Pancake Day, 4-H Achievement Days, a chicken barbecue, a Horse Show, Crazy Days, and a Craft Show.

Parade down Main Street LaMoure, North Dakota - July 4, 1923

L*ansford

by Margaret Undlin & Colleen Carlson
Home Town of 249 North Dakotans

Locals believe the date of the founding of their community was 1902 and that its original name was Gordon, but the state already had a town by that name. In 1903 the Great Northern Railroad built their Granville-Mohall branch line through the area. That year Arne Roen and Martin Olson sold part of their homesteads for a townsite which was platted under the ownership of Fred H. Stoltze, of St. Paul, Minnesota, a townsite developer for the railroad. Martin is said to have reserved the right to name the site when he sold his land. Apparently he proposed several names, but Lansford was chosen, after his home town of Lansfjord, Norway.

A post office named Bjelland was established in October 1901 some three miles southeast of Lansford. Mail was brought from Minot by people who went there for supplies. After the new town of Lansford was established the office was closed and mail went to the Lansford post office, established in July 1903 with Clarence C. Banks as postmaster.

Two years after the Great Northern completed its project the Soo Line, called the Wheat Line, constructed its tracks on the northern edge of town and established its station of Lansford.

In 1903 the *Golden Sheaf,* a weekly newspaper began publishing; later its name was changed to the *Lansford Journal* and then to the *Lansford Leader.*

Throughout its history Lansford has provided for the education of its children. A two-room schoolhouse was constructed in 1903, followed by a four-room brick building in 1908. In 1912 the high school was added; the old structure was razed in 1959 and replaced by a modern new school.

The first telephone service came to Lansford in 1905. The next year the Farmer Telephone Association was organized. The town's volunteer fire department was organized in 1907 and in 1909 the city used newly discovered natural gas to light the town. Unfortunately, the supply ran out in a couple of years. In 1914 the Lansford Light Plant was built, giving the city electric lights.

Lansford was a booming city in its first few years, having seven elevators and a flour mill which was destroyed by fire in 1931. It was a $45,000 loss to the community. The city also boasted of two banks, three hotels, seven stores, three meat markets, two confectioneries, and three lumberyards. Medical services were sporadic in the early years, but the city had a dentist and by 1910 it had a hospital. The hospital, Dr. J. L. Devine was the physician and surgeon, closed after four years. The community was also served by a veterinarian.

There were four restaurants in the city and three implement dealerships selling McCormick and Rock Island machinery. One of the city's three blacksmiths, George Baggenstoss came in 1912 and retired in 1954.

Edward Haroldson, an attorney, came in 1903 and retired in 1950.

The city dray lines were very important as were the livery barns. During the day it was common to see twenty to thirty teams lined up to unload lumber and supplies. Travel in the early days was done by stage, livery, bicycle, or walking.

The city also boasted of: tailor shops, dressmakers, photograph galleries, jewelers, barbers, bakeries, a steam laundry, painters and decorators, harness makers, shoe repairmen, dancing classes, and vocal and instrumental instruction.

Lansford had its own city band and orchestra which entertained in the Dammann Opera House. Dances were held there and silent movies were also shown there. Later a city auditorium was built and movies were shown there every weekend; dances were held on Friday nights. A bowling alley operated from 1906 to 1918.

Garages were opened in 1910, selling a variety of automobiles: Northern, Overland, Ford, Buick, Maxwell, Reo, Studebaker, Oakland Six, Pullman, Saxon, Allan 37 and the Chambers.

The following churches were constructed in Lansford: Presbyterian, 1903; Methodist Episcopal, 1905; St. John's Roman Catholic, 1906; Norwegian Free Lutheran and Trinity Lutheran, 1906. The Methodist, Catholic, and Lutheran congregations are still active, having built new

The Post Office in Lansford, North Dakota

structures in the later years.

Lansford has been plagued by fires throughout its history. In 1906 a $75,000 fire destroyed five businesses including two general stores and a bank; two years later the south side of main street burned down. During the next decade several more businesses burned down, the Atlantic Elevator in 1911, the Hotel Ruford in 1917, and the Blevins Restaurant and the Occident Elevator in 1920. The business community suffered losses again in 1926 as a result of fire. Destroyed were the *Lansford Leader*, the First State Bank which housed the post office, various other businesses and the Masonic Lodge. In 1952 the Dan LaFortune Hotel fell victim to flames, ten years later Sagsveen Implement was destroyed, and in 1973, within a two-week period the Peavey Elevator and the B. J. Wolf Elevator went up in flames. Lansford Hotel, Bar, Cafe and Western Wear burned in 1981; three years later the Lansford Country Club and the Senior Citizen Center were destroyed.

Businesses operating today are: Archie Lyon's & Son's Honey, the First American Bank and Trust, Lee Brother's, Inc., Souris River Grain Co-op, O'Keefe Oil, Homestead Bar, Johnston's Chevrolet, Inc., Midwest Heating, Lansford Lanes, Lansford Mini-Mall (cafe, game room, motel), Lansford Post Office, Lansford Food Mart, Gates Manufacturing, Inc., Undlin Sales & Service, Tri-S-Sales, Souvenirs by Audrey, Adams Simmental Ranch, Helmings Repair, Triplett Insurance Agency, Vendsel Trucking, Dave's Repair, Talley Quarter Horse Ranch, Gunning's Repair, and Hair Palace.

Current annual events which draw people to the community include the Country Club Golf Tournament, a Threshing Show, and American Legion Post No. 279's Memorial Day service.

Community activity is centered around the Country Club, with a nine-hole golf course. The clubhouse was destroyed by fire on March 9, 1984 and was rebuilt the same year. Activities there include Sunday

Center building is the Lansford School - 1919

Main Street Lansford, North Dakota - early 1900s

morning breakfasts, steak fry suppers, and bingo. The building is also used as a Senior Citizen center and as a meeting place for the Hi-Neighbor Club which has 135 members. The club was organized in 1968.

Other centers of community activity include the Threshermen Historical Society which is located on the south edge of town, the Ambulance Squad, the Fire Department, the Masonic Lodge, the Order of the Eastern Star, Girls and Boy Scouts, Women of Today, Jaycees, and the Community Club.

The community is proud of its Mall, constructed entirely with local funds in 1982. To finance the project almost 1,200 shares were sold and several fund raisers were held. All labor was donated with the exception of the electrical and plumbing work.

Enrollment in the school is small, but it continues to be accredited. A large number of graduates have gone on to many professional careers, although the main livelihood in the Lansford area remains agricultural.

Lansford was incorporated in 1904.

Three hundred years after the first permanent settlement was established by the English on the North American continent, the Great Northern Railroad completed its line to Larson in 1907 and established a station. Like other towns in North Dakota Larson owes its existence to the many settlers who came to farm the new land. Although the first settlers came from many places most were from Minnesota of Scandinavian and German ancestry. Some came directly from Europe.

Columbus Larson, an important early pioneer homesteader and businessman in the area, had the distinction of having his name chosen for two towns, Larson and Columbus, a community four miles east. In its de-

Main Street Larson, North Dakota

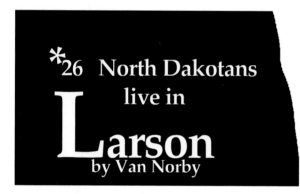

*26 North Dakotans live in

Larson
by Van Norby

sire to compete for business with Columbus, a Soo Line town, the Great Northern named their town for the same man.

Although there was some postal service out of Portal it wasn't until the railroad came that Larson had good postal service and a post office. It was established in September 1907 with Herman deVilliers as postmaster. About 1910 rural mail service was established with August Klienschmidt as the first carrier.

Larson developed quickly and in a few years had all the necessary businesses to serve the surrounding area. A grain elevator and a stockyards were built and soon the land began to produce and the first freight began to move east out of Larson.

The Farmers Co-op Telephone Company organized in 1910 to serve Lar-

son and the surrounding area. Its first operator was Sarah Lorence.

St. John's Lutheran Church was built in 1908 and in the early years services were held in the German language. The first pastor to serve was Reverend A. C. Stolt. Among the original organizers and builders of the church was Herman Pasche whose son Otto and some members of his family were still active in the congregation until 1989. Now they attend church in Columbus.

Nordre St. Olaf Lutheran Parish was organized in 1912 and held worship services in Norwegian in the schoolhouse. Its first pastor was Reverend Buckneberg. Later they rented St. John's Lutheran building. The congregation disbanded in the 1930s and members transferred to First Lutheran in Columbus.

By the early 1920s Larson had reached its peak. Steady decline then set in and continued through the drought and depression of the 1930s. Fires helped speed the town's decline. Only a grain elevator, a grocery store, a liquor store, and the post office along with the school survived the 1930s. The school closed in 1962 when the students were bussed to Columbus. Loretta Marston was the last teacher.

The post office and grocery store closed in 1976 and now Larson is

served by rural carrier out of Columbus. Mrs. Clarence (Minnie) Witty was postmistress for many of the last years; she also managed the local grocery store. The grain elevator burned down in 1980. The train depot has been moved to the historical village at Crosby.

The only business remaining in Larson is the Border Triangle Club, a bar, dance hall, and steakhouse, owned and operated by Myron and Gerdius Watterud.

Although there were coal mines operating in the area they had little effect on Larson. Some people in Larson were employed in the mines; now the mines no longer operate and the workers have moved away.

For many years the railroad moved much freight, grain, cattle, and coal through town on a well-kept track. Now only occasionally, Burlington Northern and Dakota Missouri Valley Western trains move slowly through town with their loads of grain.

Once a busy little town, now a quiet little place where fewer than thirty people live, Larson still survives.

Larson's Main Street no longer has a dirt or gravel surface as in the earlier days. It is ironic that today with better streets and roads, there are few to use them.

Present residents appreciate the effort made by early inhabitants to make a town of Larson. Trees are planted like they had done. Residents keep the town clean and neat and wonder how long it will continue.

South Main Street Larson, North Dakota - early 1900s

North Main Street Larson, North Dakota - early 1900s

The first people to settle in and around Leeds were "squatters" who came to make their homes by filing on land under the Pre-emption Law and later under the Homestead Act. On June 5, 1886 the St. Paul, Minneapolis and Manitoba Railroad Company (Great Northern) laid track through what is now known as the city of Leeds. The siding was named Leeds after the city of Leeds, England. On October 11, 1889 the Northern Pacific Railroad reached the town. Local passenger service on the Great Northern was discontinued in 1971, but grain is still transported from two local elevators which serve the area. Amtrak trains pass through town on a regular basis. Passenger service on the Northern Pacific ended in 1965 and train service was discontinued in 1971; its tracks have now been removed. The Great Northern and the Northern Pacific have merged to form the Burlington Northern Railroad Company.

The original townsite was part of a strip of land one mile long on the south side of the Great Northern tracks. Part of Ole Gronbeck's homestead, he was the first to file in the area in 1884, became an addition to the original townsite. Other early settlers whose land became part of the original townsite included: O. P. Larson, Francis Howrey, Thomas Howrey, and Peter Anderson.

In 1886 a grain warehouse, a store, and a post office were located near

*542 North Dakotans live in Leeds

by Alice A. Smeltzer

the Leeds siding. That same year a school was established and a Lutheran congregation began holding services.

The town grew rapidly. Before 1900 it boasted of having a saloon, pool and billiard room, cheese factory, bank, bottling works, dray and livery services, hotel, confectionery store, elevators, bakery, tailors, jewelers, newspaper, blacksmiths, general stores, doctors, dentists, opera house, flour mill, cream station, lumberyard, and a millinery shop. Electric and telephone exchange service began in 1902.

Leeds Village was incorporated in 1899 with five trustees elected. Ordinances were passed, a village marshal was appointed, a calaboose was erected, and a volunteer fire department was organized. By 1903 the town had expanded with the annexation of four more areas of land, a park had been built, and more ordinances were passed. In 1903 Leeds officially became a city; its population was 589. E. B. Page was elected the first mayor of the incorporated city.

Soon after 1903 sidewalks were built, street lights were erected, and streets were improved. A landfill was opened and a city water and sewer system were installed by 1910. US 2 passed through the city in the 1930s; in 1986 a four-lane by-pass was constructed south of the city.

Today the town has over 50 businesses and 350 homes and apartments. It has many paved streets, an excellent water system, sewer system, garbage service, and sanitary landfill. An airport, ball diamonds, swimming pool, park, library, tennis courts, golf course, and a new community center also serve the community. Businesses include service stations, grocery stores, implement dealership, hardware store, cafe, barber and beauty services, TV repair shop, plumbing services, a funeral home, laundromat, several bars, and a lumberyard. The city also supports a grade and high school, an ambulance service, a fire department, a dentist, and a clinic. The community is also served by two Lutheran and one Catholic church; many clubs and organizations are also active.

In 1986 the city celebrated its hundredth birthday with a huge centennial celebration. As part of the observance a comprehensive history of the Leeds/York communities was published.

Main Street Leeds, North Dakota - early 1900s

Leeds's public pool - 1986

Businesses along US 2, Leeds, North Dakota - 1990s

The Chicago, Milwaukee & St. Paul Railroad established its Leith station about six miles southwest of Carson on Secs. 4 and 5, T133N, R87W along its branch line in 1910. It was named after a townsite promoter's home in Leith, Scotland.

The earliest settlers were of Scandinavian and German descent. The village was incorporated in 1915.

The first trains through the area carried passengers and freight. The depot closed in 1964, freight trains continued to run until 1982, and the train era ended for the community when the tracks were taken up the next year.

One of the first buildings constructed was a bank, today the building houses the post office. It was established August 24, 1910 with Elmer E. Carter as postmaster.

By 1913 various businesses were in operation: two implement dealerships, two restaurants, two pool

Leith Jail - early 1900s

halls, two real estate offices, a blacksmith and machine shop, a newspaper, a bakery, cream station, two lumberyards, two grain elevators, one harness shop, a shoe repair shop, veterinarian office, livery barn, and a dray line. There was also a tin shop, an ice house, an insurance office, and a drug store. In addition there were two contractors and builders, three painters, and two paper hangers to serve the community. There was one church building in town.

As the town grew other businesses were opened: a hotel, two grocery stores, a hardware store, barbershop, two banks, a meat locker plant, and a Standard Oil bulk station. A jail was also available.

A schoolhouse was built in 1914, but it was destroyed by fire in 1921. In 1923 a new school was built; it was closed in 1970. The building was sold and torn down.

Two churches were organized in 1916, the Presbyterian and Lutheran. The churches closed in 1973 and 1975, the members transferring to their respective churches in Carson.

The first fire department was organized in 1914. Through the years Leith was beset by fires, even threatened by prairie fires. Telephone service reached Leith in 1916. And electric street lights were installed in 1918; the village had its own light plant.

The Knights of Pithias built a town hall in 1916. Because it was the largest hall in Grant County at that time it became the focal point for political gatherings. The village was visited quite often by state officials including Governor William Langer and William Lemke.

The hall also served as a movie theater for many years, drawing people from a considerable distance to enjoy the shows. It was remodeled in 1984 and is still used for local dances, parties, township elections, 4-H meetings, and other occasions.

Joe Lawfer organized a cornet band in 1911 which was very popular throughout the community. It led many parades and performed at many celebrations. Joe and his wife, Mabel, also were proprietors of the Lawfer Studio, a flourishing photo business for many years.

The first Grant County Fair was held in Leith in October 1917. A race track was constructed on the fairgrounds so that horse racing could be one of the main attractions. An exhibit building was erected to shelter the many displays of farm products, fancy work, and other exhibits. A carnival with two tent shows and a merry-go-round provided entertainment. Many teepees were set up near the fairgrounds by the Indians who came from the Standing Rock Reservation to participate in the events each year.

The 1918 flu epidemic struck the community during the County Fair; it took a heavy toll. A temporary hospital was set up in the hotel and nurses were brought from Mandan to care for the patients.

Leith which was once a busy, thriving place, now has few business establishments, but it remains a friendly, peaceful place to live. Businesses presently operating include: a post office with Evelyn Bentz as postmaster since 1974; a bar owned and operated by Dan Hoff; a cabinet shop with Keith Olin as carpenter; the Dakota Grain Company managed by Fred Eslinger; the Leith Cream Association owned and operated by Gottlieb "Goppy" Zeller since 1955; and a greenhouse operated by Mrs. Myron Theurer.

Leith supports and maintains a park where picnics and softball games are enjoyed during the summer months. The Main Street was black-topped in 1963.

The many trees planted over the years have helped to beautify the town.

"Market Day" parade in Leith, North Dakota - 1913

Leith, North Dakota - 1912

Lidgerwood was founded in 1886 when the site became the railhead for work on the Minneapolis and Pacific Railroad (later the Soo Line); a boxcar served as the first depot. The townsite which was platted the next year in May was owned by George I. Lidgerwood and Rolla N. Ink of Wahpeton, and William D. Washburn of Minneapolis. It was sandwiched between the Minneapolis and Pacific tracks on the north and those of the St. Paul, Minneapolis & Manitoba Railroad (later the Great Northern) on the south; both roads had established stations called Lidgerwood there.

Named after George I. Lidgerwood, who became the Minneapolis and Pacific's right-of-way agent during the road's extension into Dakota Territory in 1886-1887, the town acquired its unique reputation as being "one of the toughest towns on the road from Minneapolis to Aberdeen" after Ralph Maxwell, the town's first real promoter, acquired Lidgerwood's interests.

The town's first actual residents were members of the Jacob Eckes family

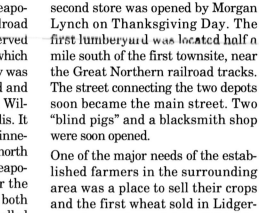

799 North Dakotans
live in

Lidgerwood
by Charles & Louise Frost

who opened a hotel in August 1886. The first store was opened soon afterwards by the Hilliard Brothers and a second store was opened by Morgan Lynch on Thanksgiving Day. The first lumberyard was located half a mile south of the first townsite, near the Great Northern railroad tracks. The street connecting the two depots soon became the main street. Two "blind pigs" and a blacksmith shop were soon opened.

One of the major needs of the established farmers in the surrounding area was a place to sell their crops and the first wheat sold in Lidgerwood was bought by Phillip Wirtenberger from Anton Duerr. No accounting books or checks were available. Two large grain elevators now serve the city. Lidgerwood Farmers Elevator is the oldest business in town to operate under its original name. Produce houses also opened to buy poultry and dairy products. Lidgerwood also met the needs of the surrounding farm families for supplies and for entertainment.

Early settlers had established rural schools for their children and Lidgerwood residents soon felt the same need. By 1889 the first small brick school replaced a two-room wooden building which still stands. Lidgerwood had the first accredited high school in Richland County and was sometimes called the "Athens of the West." Pearl

Movius became its first graduate in 1904.

Churches were quickly established. Today St. Boniface Catholic, Holy Cross Lutheran (Missouri Synod), Bergen Lutheran (ELCA), and the United Methodist continue to serve the community.

The Movius family was significant in the town's early development. Several brothers and a sister established various enterprises including a bank, a land agency, a flour mill, a general store, and later an automobile agency. Buildings they erected still remain in spite of several disastrous fires. Not one member of the family resides in Lidgerwood today.

Other outstanding sons and daughters include: Arnie Oss, the Lidgerwood Flash, who led local school teams to many victories and earned nine letters at the University of Minnesota; Zdena Trinka, author of Medora and other books; Albert Mikesh, a popular musician who has several original compositions and recordings to his credit; Gerald "Spike" Movius, who "ghosted" speeches for President Dwight D. Eisenhower and had several articles published; Anna Murry Movius, Gerald's mother, who published several volumes of poetry; Chester Fritz, who has donated millions of dollars to the University of North Dakota and other educational institutions, including $40,000 for scholarships at Lidgerwood High School; Ida Bisek Lee, whose Prairie Pictures originated in Lidgerwood; and Pat Smykowski, who led Lidgerwood girls' basketball and softball teams to state victories and was

Bird's-eye view of Lidgerwood, North Dakota - 1902
(SHSND)

named the first Miss Basketball in North Dakota.

The city has adapted to the changing needs of the surrounding agricultural community. Although the business district has suffered because people choose to shop in larger cities the community has provided more recreational facilities to meet increasing demands for more leisure- time activities. An active Park Board manages several recreational areas: two parks with playgrounds and picnic facilities, a swimming pool that offers Red Cross lessons every summer, an enclosed stage, several softball diamonds , and a summer recreation program for both boys and girls.

Many clubs hold meetings and promote varied activities. An aggressive golf association supports a nine-hole course with grass greens; a bowling alley keeps many people occupied during the winter months; and modern legal "blind pigs," bars with lounges attract women as well as men.

The city library, established in 1913 and now open six days a week, offers a more quiet sort of diversion.

Lidgerwood maintains a small rest home and a Senior Citizens Center for its increasing number of older residents.

A sign of the times was the community's decision to feature Ralph Maxwell, Lidgerwood's "bad man," during its 1986 centennial celebration. King Max and His Gang, a group of local merchants, accompanied by a bevy of flirting fancy ladies, disrupted pre-centennial events by discharging pistols and letting the ladies practice their talents.

One of the main attractions of the celebration itself was *Gossip*, a play that re-enacted the wild, old days of Maxwell and his men. What was a matter of embarrassment to many old-timers has become the most interesting part of the Lidgerwood's history.

Czech Fraternal Order established in 1908
(DPDP - Fred Schumacher)

Any well-established village in New England or the northern Middle West could afford a town drunkard, a town atheist, and a few democrats.

Denis William Brogan,
***The American Character*, 1944**

Main Street Lidgerwood, North Dakota - 1900
(SHSND)

The city of Lignite was named for the low-grade coal which was dug from underground mines in the area at the time of its establishment. It began in 1906-1907 when the Great Northern Railroad Company extended its branch line from Berthold to Crosby. The townsite was platted in September 1906 and building on the townsite began in 1907.

The town grew quickly and soon had three general stores, two hardware stores, two drug stores, and a one-room school. Lignite's first doctor was one Dr. Johnston. Thorwold Kopsland was the town's first postmaster, the post office was established in April 1907. And Charles Hamblin was the first depot agent.

More businesses sprang up in the next three years. They included two pool halls, a lumberyard, a barbershop, three grain elevators, a feed mill, a bank, a butcher shop, a livery barn, and yet another grocery and dry goods store.

A fire in 1911 destroyed a general merchandise store and the post office. Lignite also had a bank robbery in its early days.

Four churches were built in Lignite in 1914: Congregational, First Lutheran, Bethany, and St. Mary's Catholic. Three lodges were built the same year.

Growing numbers of school children necessitated the building of a two-story school. In 1918 the building was improved with a brick facing, and in 1930 a third floor was added. In 1950 five school districts reorganized to form Lignite School District No. 36. A new school was built on the southern edge of town in 1958. In the fall of 1968 the Lignite and Portal districts merged, forming Burke Central School District No. 36. Further consolidation of the school system occurred when Flaxton joined the district. This seems to be the way of life now. Families are getting smaller, the economy is weakening, and the cost of living and operating expenses are rising. Bethany Church was sold

242 North Dakotans live in Lignite

by Marlis Glaspey

and donated to the Williston Historical Society. It is preserved in its original state and open to visitors. Many weddings are held there today. The First Lutheran, St. Mary's Catholic, and Church of God still serve the city of Lignite.

Main Street still thrives, hosting these businesses: a grocery and dry goods store, barbershop, beauty salon, the Exchange of the First National Bank of Crosby, two liquor stores, a cafe, the post office, bowling lanes and cafe, Wheatland Oil Company (a gas and repair shop), two bulk gas dealers, two propane dealers, a grain elevator, two oil field offices, two welding and repair shops, and an independent repair shop. Four oil field service companies, a senior citizen's center, and a gas plant are located a half-mile east of Lignite.

The town is well-lit at night by automatic mercury lights. Residents have the luxury of using the city propane system to heat their homes. An abundant supply of good water is also available.

The city has a Lions Club, American Legion and Auxiliary Clubs, several Homemakers' clubs, Girl and Boy Scout troops, and 4-H clubs. Bowling and curling teams are active during the fall and winter. Every winter a skating rink is available for everyone to enjoy.

A beautiful city park is now located where the old school once stood. It is well-kept and used for picnics, meetings, gatherings, and family get-togethers. Shelters, tables, grills, and playground equipment are available for public use. The original bell from the old school is mounted in the park.

Low-income and senior citizens can choose from two four-plex housing units. A volunteer fire department, complete with new equipment and trucks serves the city.

The Lignite City Council has five members, a secretary, and a mayor. The city hires a man for the dual purpose of policing and maintenance. The city council dedicates a lot of manual help to city projects. When you add the volunteer help of residents, any special occasion or celebration is a certain success.

A public bus serves the community four days a week, transporting citizens from Crosby to Minot and back. Although Burlington Northern Railroad picks up grain cars in Lignite, there is no longer a depot.

Lignite boasts one novelty, an oil well within the city limits. After the oil boom of 1957 the community's population stabilized at 365.

Today Lignite is a pleasant place in which to live or to visit. It offers paved streets, shady trees, a beautiful school, city park, new church buildings, and attractive homes bordered by well-kept lawns.

We are proud of our community and the people of the area.

A small country town is not the place in which one would choose to quarrel with a wife, every human being in such places is a spy.
Samuel Johnson
Letters, Vol. I, p. 107, 1760

Main Street Lignite, North Dakota - 1987

The City Park of Lignite, North Dakota

Because the county seat, Williamsport, was inconveniently located in the northern part of the county, a central location SE1/4 sec. 7, T132N, R76W was chosen by county voters in November 1896. Several days after the election Wallace E. Petrie, the landowner, surveyed and platted the town. It was named for George W. Lynn, a native of Monroe, Wisconsin, who settled in Emmons County in 1886. Lynn practiced law, farmed, and became the county's first State's attorney. He also published the *Emmons County Free Press* for many years.

One of the town's first buildings, a hotel, was erected by Charles Patterson who became the first postmaster. He rented the building's lean-to to the county for office space. The *Emmons County Record*, still being published, was moved from Williamsport by Darwin Streeter that same year.

A business section rapidly developed and by 1901 the population numbered 118. A one-room schoolhouse and Petrie's store building were moved from Winchester; other buildings were moved from Winona. A two-story frame courthouse and a large schoolhouse were built in 1905,

but it was not until 1911 that a four-year high school was realized.

Incorporated as a village in 1906, Linton citizens voted to change to a city form of government in March 1914. The town's expansion, however, began when, in 1902-03, two competing railroads, the Northern Pacific and the Chicago, Milwaukee & St. Paul agreed to extend branch lines to a junction point just east of the platted townsite. Harry F. Hunter, representing the Milwaukee Road, quickly platted a new townsite known as Hunter's First Addition in August 1902. With its focus on the railroads it immediately drew many commercial firms to the new location, leaving the original townsite as a residential section. It was dubbed "Old Town," a name still used for the west side.

A sandstone quarry northeast of town provided durable material for the permanent structures that soon

replaced false-fronted buildings. Street lighting came to Broadway in 1909 in the form of gas lights which were replaced by the electric "White Way" in 1917. Seeman Park was donated to the city and became a recreational center for the entire county.

One redeeming feature of the Dirty Thirties was the building of the Memorial Courthouse with funding from one of the New Deal programs, using local labor.

North Dakota 83 links Linton to the outside world; it passed through the center of town from 1930 to 1941 when it was re-routed, bypassing Broadway for St. Paul Avenue.

The town's greatest expansion occurred directly after World War II. Municipal projects included the building of a swimming pool, a 250,000 gallon reservoir, a new mercury vapor street lighting system, and an expanded water and sewer system. Streets were also oiled. The following projects also kept the economy humming: community hospital, drive-in theater, livestock sales pavilion, modern motel, green house, and a parochial school.

Because "Old Town" is situated near the confluence of Beaver and Spring Creeks, it has had a serious flood problem. The worst floods occurred in 1943, 1952, and 1987.

Seven churches now serve the community: St. Anthony's Roman Catholic, First Baptist, United Methodist, Peace Lutheran, Bible Baptist, Seventh-day Adventist, and the Assembly of God. A fine ecumenical spirit has developed between these groups in recent years.

Of eight banks that served the community at one time or another, only one remains, the First National Bank of Linton.

Today, many business places are being operated by third or fourth generations of the pioneers who cast their lot in Linton, and found it good.

The business section of Linton, North Dakota - 1930s

Patrons stand in front of the Hotel Linton

County officials count gopher tails
Chas Carley, E.D. Fogel, W.W. Irwin and Wally Kyes

We believe that the Makoti community is a "Good Place— in which to live," and we really believe that there is truth to our slogan: "Makoti Community—The Best In The West."

In the spring of 1901 the territory was opened for settlement. The entire territory was a vast expanse of prairie. The only roads were Indian trails from the Fort Berthold Indian Reservation. A trip to Minot for supplies was a three-day trip for the early settlers.

One homesteader's wife found that her provisions were getting dangerously low when her husband was away at work in Minot. She took her small baby in the baby carriage, and with their small dog started walking

145 North Dakotans
* live in
Makoti
by Mrs. Ethel Aamot
& Mrs. Margie Beyer

cross country to Minot. When nearing the hills, she came upon a large herd of grazing cattle. Fearful of what might happen should the cattle see the dog, she put the dog in the carriage with the baby, covered them tightly and proceeded on her way, frightened but undaunted. That's what we call spirit and determination.

Orlien Township was organized in 1905, before Makoti was organized. It was given the name of the first white child born in the township, Orlin Gudmunson; however, when the township clerk sent in his report he misspelled the child's first name.

There was unusual activity in the region in 1906. The Soo Line Railroad Company began building a line from Max to Plaza. The grading was done by mule and horse power. With the

Main Street Makoti, North Dakota - 1986

coming of the railroad, towns began to spring up.

The story of how Makoti got its name is unusual. Edward Kamrud was the leader of a group of men that wanted to establish a town near the Fort Berthold Reservation. He was also a farmer who wanted to establish a farm machinery business. To reach these goals he asked the railroad to establish a rail siding at a chosen site. Granting his request the railroad then asked him to propose an Indian word for the name of the town. Having recently learned that James Holding Eagle had been employed to build an earthlodge on the state capitol grounds in Bismarck he thought that the Mandan word for earthlodge would be a desirable name. Advised by Holding Eagle that the largest type of Mandan earthlodge was called a *Maakoti* Kamrud submitted the name to the Soo Line officials, but suggested that the extra "a" be dropped and the place be called Makoti.

On July 12, 1911 the village was platted and townsite lots were sold. Nearly two hundred people attended the sale; many businessmen purchased property. Makoti was incorporated June 10, 1916.

By 1914 Makoti could boast of two banks, two hardware stores, three merchandise stores, two lumberyards, one meat market, one barbershop, two elevators, one bakery, two implement dealers, two blacksmith shops, two livery and feed stables, three coal dealers, one city dray line,

one feed mill, one tailor shop, two hotels, two churches, one consolidated school, a telephone company, post office, Soo Line Railroad with two trains daily, one newspaper and "more children to the square inch than any town in the county."

The Makoti Threshing Show, North Dakota's largest, was organized in 1961 around Clarence Schenfisch's collection of thirteen tractors. Each year the show expanded and today visitors can view over 300 operating units, including steam and gas engines, and antique cars and trucks. The show also includes antique exhibits of various kinds and the world's largest collection of stationary engines under one roof. Demonstrations at the exhibition include plowing with a 10-bottom plow, hand-fed and hand-tie hay baling, and hand-fed threshing. The community provides free shuttle bus service as well as facilities for campers.

At one time the community was served by four churches: three in town and one in the rural area. The Methodist church closed its doors in 1970; the building was moved to Pioneer Village on the threshing show grounds. Today, Hope Lutheran and St. Elizabeth's Catholic, and one rural Lutheran church serve the area.

Throughout the years Makoti has improved its appearance and its quality of life. Currently, the town boasts of paved streets, an adequate water supply, a swimming pool, a paved tennis court, beautiful park facilities, a baseball field, improved school facilities, a new senior citizen building, a modern fire department, an ambulance service, an electric shop, a locker plant, and a new bank.

The town of Makoti, North Dakota in 1917

Rumely Oil Pull, Makoti - 1912

The town of Marmarth was established and named in the fall of 1907. The townsite originally laid out on the east side of the Little Missouri River was known as Neva, named for the first postmistress, Neva M. Woods, daughter of a pioneer homesteader.

The first few structures in the village were built on the east side of the river, but the land was owned by a rancher who refused to sell for a fair price. Consequently, the site was abandoned and another was laid out on the west side of the river. This site became the town of Marmarth, named after Margaret Martha Fitch who was the granddaughter of Albert J. Earling, president of the Chicago, Milwaukee & St. Paul Railroad.

The town grew rapidly because of the railroad, and in 1909 a village form of government was established. Its first officers were Ben F. Meinecke, president; E. S. Warren, clerk; and David M. Milne and Richard Harrison, trustees. By 1915 the population had increased to about 1,000 and a city commission form of government was adopted in that year.

The first electric light plant built for the city was in operation in the fall of 1915. One of the most important projects which contributed to increased business activity in the city was the building of the first-class steel bridge across the Little Missouri River east of town (completed June 20, 1916). The bridge provided needed access to the Marmarth business community for many farmers and ranchers from east of the river.

In December 1917 natural gas was piped into Marmarth from a Montana gas field southwest of Marmarth by Montana-Dakota Utilities Company. The city became the first town or city in the state to have natural gas available for use in both domestic and commercial quantities. City water works with a tall water tower and complete sewer system were built in 1918. Drainage was into the Little Missouri River which afforded excellent disposal.

Frank Gibbs came to Marmarth in 1908 and bought a small hardware store. He built a small two-story house at the back of his store before his wife joined him with their children, Buster and Florence. Next door was a laundry run by a couple named Sherp. Many early residents lived in tents. Vandervort, the jeweler, for example, lived with his wife in a tent near his store. Dr. Bordwell operated a small hospital at the old townsite, but moved it to the new site and opened an office staffed with a nurse.

In the beginning Marmarth supported two banks, the State Bank managed by Fred DeLange and the First National Bank managed by Allison. It also supported two hotels,

Looking south down Main Street Marmarth
On the left, the Mystic Theatre, on the Register of Historic Places, site of community and regional productions, including *Marmarth's Hamlet*

the Woods Hotel which burned and the St. Charles Hotel. Gus Jorns operated the drug store. There was also a store run by Divine, a post office and a telephone office, and a meat market run by Tabor.

The local newspaper, the *Marmarth Mail*, was edited by Cramer. A movie theater, the Mystic Theatre, was operated by Guy Johnson and a gas station was owned by Bude. A Ford agency and garage and a mortuary were operated by R. Gibbs. The railroad maintained a roundhouse and scheduled three east and three west passenger trains each day, besides providing freight service. Many traveling theatre groups and Chautauquas stopped for appearances, especially after the Barber Block was built. There were also many saloons which thrived and a few undesirable businesses — which citizens forced to close.

The Marmarth Congregational Church was founded in 1908 with the Reverend John G. Dicky as its first pastor. The first Roman Catholic Church, St. Mary's, was built in 1910. Father Karl Hierlmeier served this mission as well as those in Beach and Hettinger.

One of the most important projects constructed in Marmarth was the Barber Block, built in 1909. It was 75 by 90 feet with the ground floor occupied by businesses. The upper floor was an opera house, the stage equipped with four dressing rooms with lavatories and hot and cold running water. Without a doubt no play house between the Twin Cities and the Rockies could match its expansive theater, with no posts or obstructions to spoil the view. The Barber Block burnt in January 1918 and was re-

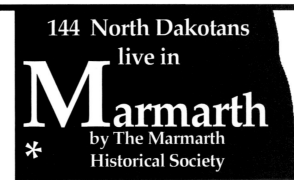

144 North Dakotans live in

Marmarth

by The Marmarth Historical Society

built in the same year by financiers F. O. Barber and C. P. Allison.

Marmarth School District No. 12 was organized in the spring of 1908, taking in eight congressional townships. The District was reduced in size, but it is still in operation and now includes some territory from Bowman County. The old school was built by the B. F. Meinecke Building Company in 1909 for $19,500. It was ready for occupation in February 1910. The first high school class, two students, graduated in 1912.

The town still nestles under the towering buttes that surround it. It enjoys the conveniences that its planners built for them. The railroad now only goes through Marmarth. The city has two cafes, a mini-mart, one bar, and a post office. Dr. Hegge, a dentist, also maintains a practice in the community.

The Marmarth Historical Society is very active in the community, trying to keep the little city alive. It has restored the Mystic Theatre and sponsors numerous activities including local talent performances and professional acting companies. Both undertakings provide entertainment for the surrounding communities and draw business to the city.

The city has a volunteer fire department which managed to build a fire hall with the help of the city and county. A new fire truck was recently purchased. The Firebelle's, a ladies auxiliary, raised enough money to finish the kitchen in the fire hall and with the help of the city commission they sponsor the 4th of July parade and award prizes. Another active local organization is the Little Missouri Saddle Club which, with much community help, sponsors the annual 4th of July rodeo.

Looking north on Main Street, Marmarth
On the left, the Barber Block, which the Marmarth Historical Society seeks to restore.
Mayor Patty Perry walks past the old St. Charles Hotel.

Home Town of 2 North Dakotans

*Marshall

by Sharon C. Gjermundson

The first settlers who came to the area in 1885 were mostly from Norway. In July 1901 through the efforts of Senator Thomas Marshall a post office was established on John Kyseth's ranch, located along the Knife River. Two years later the office was moved a short distance southwest when his nephew, Charles O. Kyseth, became postmaster. The facility was named after the senator.

In 1908 Edward Carson and his wife, Clara, built a general store and post office on their homestead two miles southeast of the present site. The facility was a godsend for the area's settlers; they came from miles around to trade and get their mail which was brought by carrier H. P. Dinius from Richardton.

The Northern Pacific Railroad had originally staked out a branch line along the Knife River. In 1913, however, tracks were laid through Halliday and the plans for the Knife River route were abandoned.

The Marshall Store changed hands in 1917 when the Carson family moved to California. Ed Hemple and his wife took over the duties at the store and post office and later moved the building to the present site.

These were the only businesses that Marshall ever had, other than a blacksmith shop and garage operated by Oscar Vangness. He left in 1951 to open a business in Leonard. Clarence Hansen ran the garage for a short time after he left.

Early church services were held in a school east of Marshall by a Reverend Armstrong who came from Dickinson. The Marshall Lutheran Church was organized in 1929 when a church was moved from north of Dodge to Marshall. The church and school were the centers of activity for the Marshall community.

Flood waters from the Knife River forced several families to leave their homes in 1943. In 1971 flood waters reached the steps of the store before receding.

The store has changed hands several times throughout the years. Owners or operators have included: Ed Carson, Ed Hemple, Abel Hoovestall, Hartwig Anderson, Lester and Adam Jacobs, and Stanley and Sharon Gjermundson who purchased the business in 1970.

Marshall has remained the same throughout most of its history, mainly serving the farmers and ranchers along the Knife River and those in the community north and south of it. The village has, however, experienced several "boom" periods. When North Dakota 8 was paved road workers rented vacant homes and brought trailers in for temporary housing. During the "oil" boom seismograph crews and exploration projects brought business to the area and more recently the construction of the southwest water pipeline brought more activity to this rural community.

Marshall was recognized world-wide when Brad Gjermundson became the World Champion Saddle Bronc Rider in 1981 and again in 1983, 1984, and 1985.

Families who have lived in Marshall over the years include: Mr. and Mrs. Tom Perhus, Mr. and Mrs. Frank Allen and Beulah, Mr. and Mrs. Oscar Vangness and children Kenneth and Marion, Olga and George Rynning, Mr. and Mrs. Hartwig Anderson and children Duane and Beverly, Mr. and Mrs. Adam Jacobs and Annabel, Mr. and Mrs. Lester Jacobs, Fred Hueske, Mr. and Mrs. Keith Perhus and children Scott and Vickie, and Mr. and Mrs. Stanley Gjermundson and children Tammy, Brad, Casey, Lyle, and Connie.

Why is it that in all ages small towns and remote villages have fostered little malignities of all kinds? The true answer is, that people will backbite one another to any extent rather than not be amused. Nay, so strong is this desire for something to go on that may break the monotony of life, that people, not otherwise ill-natured, are pleased with the misfortune of their neighbors, solely because it gives something to think of, something to talk about.

Sir Arthur Helps
Companions of My Solitude

The town of Marshall, North Dakota - 1988

Billboard honoring town's Brad Gjermundson

Norseman Statue

Dedicated in September 1973 to all pioneers who settled the state, the work designed and created by Professor Dean Bowman of Concordia College was part of a promotional effort to make Tioga a Scandinavian village. Constructed of welded tubular steel surrounded by brazed copper sheeting, the statue became weather-beaten and vandalized. Eventually, it was torn down.

Ryder News Office, Ryder, North Dakota - 1935

The Hagerty House Hotel in Monango, North Dakota - 1909

One of Stanley's Bicentennial projects was to decorate the city's fire hydrants as famous Americans.

Fire Department in LaMoure, North Dakota - late 1930s

Page 138

Rode Motor Company in Ryder, North Dakota - 1932

Main Street in Max, North Dakota - 1911

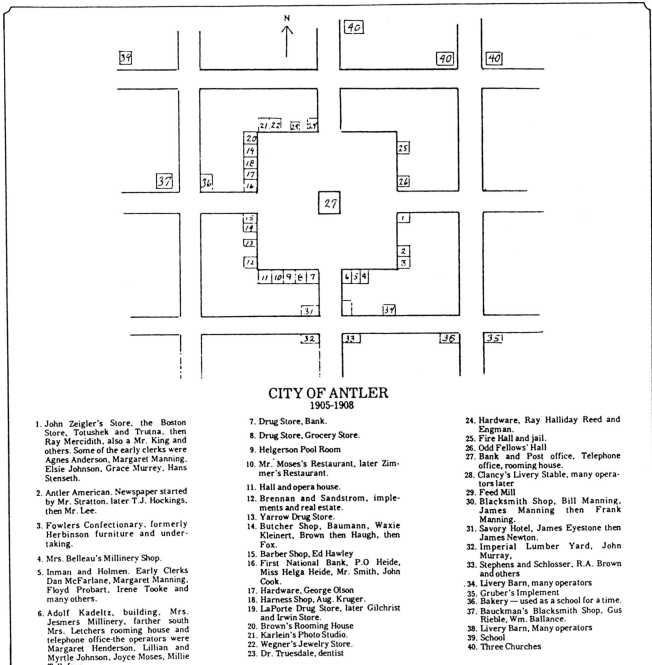

CITY OF ANTLER
1905-1908

1. John Zeigler's Store, the Boston Store, Totushek and Trutna, then Ray Mercidith, also a Mr. King and others. Some of the early clerks were Agnes Anderson, Margaret Manning, Elsie Johnson, Grace Murrey, Hans Stenseth.

2. Antler American. Newspaper started by Mr. Stratton, later T.J. Hockings, then Mr. Lee.

3. Fowlers Confectionary, formerly Herbinson furniture and undertaking.

4. Mrs. Belleau's Millinery Shop.

5. Inman and Holmen. Early Clerks Dan McFarlane, Margaret Manning, Floyd Probart, Irene Tooke and many others.

6. Adolf Kadeltz, building, Mrs. Jesmers Millinery, farther south Mrs. Letchers rooming house and telephone office-the operators were Margaret Henderson, Lillian and Myrtle Johnson, Joyce Moses, Millie Tollefson.

7. Drug Store, Bank.

8. Drug Store, Grocery Store.

9. Helgerson Pool Room

10. Mr. Moses's Restaurant, later Zimmer's Restaurant.

11. Hall and opera house.

12. Brennan and Sandstrom, implements and real estate.

13. Yarrow Drug Store.

14. Butcher Shop, Baumann, Waxie Kleinert, Brown then Haugh, then Fox.

15. Barber Shop, Ed Hawley

16. First National Bank, P.O Heide, Miss Helga Heide, Mr. Smith, John Cook.

17. Hardware, George Olson

18. Harness Shop, Aug. Kruger.

19. LaPorte Drug Store, later Gilchrist and Irwin Store.

20. Brown's Rooming House

21. Karlein's Photo Studio.

22. Wegner's Jewelry Store.

23. Dr. Truesdale, dentist

24. Hardware, Ray Halliday Reed and Engman.

25. Fire Hall and jail.

26. Odd Fellows' Hall

27. Bank and Post office, Telephone office, rooming house.

28. Clancy's Livery Stable, many operators later

29. Feed Mill

30. Blacksmith Shop, Bill Manning, James Manning then Frank Manning.

31. Savory Hotel, James Eyestone then James Newton.

32. Imperial Lumber Yard, John Murray,

33. Stephens and Schlosser, R.A. Brown and others

34. Livery Barn, many operators

35. Gruber's Implement

36. Bakery — used as a school for a time.

37. Bauckman's Blacksmith Shop, Gus Rieble, Wm. Ballance.

38. Livery Barn, Many operators

39. School

40. Three Churches

A classical center-square town in Bottineau County

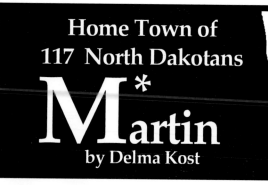

M*artin

by Delma Kost

Martin can trace its history to 1893 when the Soo Line finished laying its tracks on its new main line to Canada, through McLean County where good land was available in the area.

The first townsite, located about one and a half miles to the east of the present site, was named Casselman, after the railroad had established a station by that name. Because few settlers had reached the area a post office was not established until January 1898. Then an office was located in the railroad's section house and its section foreman Patrick Walsh was named postmaster. Three years later it was moved to a general store operated by Christ Heer.

The name Casselman caused confusion for both railroad and postal authorities. Equipment, merchandise, supplies, and articles were mistakenly sent to Casselton in Cass County; consequently, in 1902, both the railroad and the postal department changed the name to Martin, after William Leslie Martin, a railroad vice-president. The townsite itself was platted in 1909 and the following year Martin was incorporated as a village.

The first pioneers to settle in the area in 1896 were Gottlieb Kalk and Frank and Phillip Putz who were of German descent, and who, having emigrated from Rumania to Edenwald, Saskatchewan and having suffered several years of poor crops there decided to migrate to North Dakota. Later the Rust, Gaul, Friesel, Michelson, Bauman, and Helm families followed.

In 1897 the Christ Heer family arrived, acquired land, and opened the first general store which expanded through the years. It was destroyed by fire in 1948. Community needs in the early days were served by Moellendorfs Store, by a hardware store operated by Fiesel & Nickalaus, and by a large complex operated by the Samuel Brothers. Gottlieb Kalk also established a general business enterprise during the same period.

From late 1909 to 1914 the town experienced a boom, the population reached 500 in the latter year. Many new businesses opened including a drug store, two livery barns, three lumberyards, two blacksmith shops, a barbershop, a photography studio, three banks, a hotel, three bars, and German and English newspapers.

The first settlers were mainly Baptists who built the town's first church which was also the first church in the county. In 1907 a Lutheran church was built next to it; in 1926 churches were built by the Roman Catholics and the Evangelical United Brethren. Today, only the United Methodist Church which originally had been moved into the city and the Baptist Church remain. The Baptists replaced their original structure with a new facility in 1965.

A small school, also the first in Sheridan County, was built near the railroad tracks in 1897. It soon became overcrowded and a new two-story facility was constructed, but it was destroyed by fire in 1923. The next year a larger brick building, at the present site, was constructed. A gymnasium was added in the early sixties and in 1967 the school district was merged with Harvey. BoCats of North Dakota, a small manufacturing firm purchased the school property.

War, depression, fire, and other factors took their toll and by 1927 the population was reduced by half. At present, the city has about one hundred residents made up of businessmen, retired farmers, railroad workers, and teachers, with some of these still active in their field.

A few businesses remain; namely a Farmers Elevator, a garage-store-post office combination, a bar and fishing tackle shop, upholstery shop, sport shop, and the BoCat firm.

Though the city is not experiencing a population growth, the pride of its citizens is seen in the many well-kept homes and yards, upkeep of the City Hall and Park, the number of paved streets, and a sewer system. The city joined the Harvey Rural Fire Department and the Rural Water System; its people enjoy living in a small town.

Present day Main Street Martin, North Dakota

Interior of the Martin Bank - 1915

Main Street Martin, North Dakota - 1914

Max traces its origins back to 1904 when a post office was located on the homestead of Paul W. E. Freitag. It was a corner in the kitchen of the Freitag farm house. Freitag, the postmaster, named the office after his son Max and later moved it to the new town.

During 1906 the Soo Line, the Minneapolis, St. Paul & Sault Ste. Marie Railroad, extended its branch line north from Garrison and built another branch line west from Drake. When the site of a new town was platted on August 8, 1906 just northeast of the junction of those two branch lines railroad officials wanted to name it either Junction or Junction City. Local residents, however, persuaded them to name it Max.

301 North Dakotans live in *Max

by Ruth Whiting Bernsdorff

Since then the city has grown with the annexation of the West Side Addition, the Carvell Addition, and the Whiting Addition. Once a busy railroad town, there is no longer passenger or freight service. Max is located on US 83 between Bismarck and Minot.

Various ethnic groups settled in the area, Scandinavians, Germans, German-Russians, and English. Many came from eastern states, especially Minnesota. These groups were reflected in the early churches.

The first meeting to organize a Congregational Church was held in 1906; the church was legally incorporated March 22, 1907. Its first minister was W. E. Shaw and its building was first used as a community church, services were held by several denominations. Some church services were also held in homes in the area.

Active churches today include: Immaculate Conception Catholic Church, Our Savior Lutheran Church, St. Matthew Lutheran Church, First Baptist Church, and Seventh-day Adventist Church.

Among the first places of business were a cafe which was first opened in a tent and later located in the Vendome Hotel, the Boston Department Store, The Citizens State Bank and First State Bank, a harness shop, butcher shop, eventually five general merchandise stores, two hardware stores, grain elevators, lumberyards, and a millinery shop. The community was also served by a barber and a medical doctor, a Dr. Ivy who also owned a drug store. Telephone service was provided by the Max Telephone Exchange.

The *Max Enterprise*, a weekly newspaper, began publishing in September 1906 with Mr. Whitney as the editor.

The first school in Max was located in the old Steinhaus Store building. Lena Linn was the first teacher. In 1908 a two-room frame schoolhouse was ready for use and four years later a brick building was erected. Later it was enlarged. In 1955 the voters favored reorganizing the Connors School District, which initially served the town and was created in October 1904, as the Max Special School District No. 50. The district was reorganized again in 1958. A

Max's WWI Home Guard - 1918

new school was dedicated September 17, 1961.

Fire destroyed many of the original buildings on Main Street. A fire in October 1931 destroyed a large part of the business district. A municipal water system was completed in 1952.

The community has always had active clubs and organizations. Among the present ones are the Max Civic Club, the Business and Professional Association, the Over 55 Club, a senior citizen's group, the Fire Department, the Max Development Corporation, and Max Community Enterprises, Incorporated.

Max has entered a community incentive program, the Community Betterment Program, since 1975-1976. Max ranked in the top ten communities each year it participated. In 1979 it was first in its category.

The annual Max Rodeo is one of the city's special events. Every five years an All School Reunion is held; it has proven to be very successful.

Max is a progressive small town with all the conveniences of a modern city including paved streets and a pleasant city park.

Grandma's Kitchen & Grandpa's Laundromat - 1988

Huettl Brothers Garage - burned in 1987

When the Great Northern Railroad built its branch line northwest from Towner in 1905 it created several villages, one of which was Maxbass. The railroad hired the Tallman Townsite Company to plat the site. It was named after Max Bass who was an immigration agent for the Great Northern Railroad.

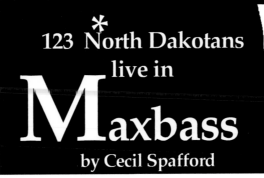

123 North Dakotans live in Maxbass
by Cecil Spafford

Maxbass grew rapidly, a core group coming from the trading post of Renville. At the end of four months it was a full-fledged village with the following business places: two banks, the Security Bank and the State Bank; four general stores; four lumberyards; six elevators; one track buyer; three restaurants; three pool and billiard halls, one weekly newspaper, the *Maxbass Monitor*; one drug store; one real estate office; two hardware stores; one confectionery store; two meat markets; one livery barn; one barbershop; three contractors and builders; three dray lines; two blacksmith shops; and two doctors. As the village grew older there were other places of business, including a hotel, implement dealers, and an attorney-at-law.

Some of the first events in Maxbass were the following: the first lot was sold on July 11, 1905; the first edition of the weekly newspaper, the *Maxbass Monitor* which published until 1919, was issued on August 17, 1905. The post office opened for business on August 17, 1905. Its first postmaster was John Staub. The first telephone system began operations on August 24, 1905, its first sidewalk was laid on August 20, 1905, and the railroad provided its first passenger service on November 13, 1905 and its first mail train service on November 20, 1905. Its first band, a twenty-two piece brass band, traces its history to November 21, 1905.

The Village of Maxbass was incorporated on March 17, 1906; its first election was held on April 16, 1906.

The first child born in Maxbass was Cecil Loucks, born on February 26, 1906 to Mr. and Mrs. Ed Loucks. The first person buried in Graceland Cemetery at Maxbass was Sarah Bodal, the eighteen-year-old daughter of Anton Bodal. She died of tuberculosis in April 1915.

The first church services in Maxbass were held in the Renville Store building. The first Congregational minister was E. E. Cram; the first Methodist minister was C. D. Locklin. The Grace Methodist Church was erected in 1909 and dedicated on November 21, 1909. Its first trustees were Vern Kemp, W. M. Martin, Abe McCaslin, D. L. Lewis, and George Arnold. The Congregational Church was also erected in 1909; it was dedicated on December 12, 1909. Years later a decreased membership made it necessary for the Congregational Church to close and its church building eventually became the church home of the English Lutheran Congregation.

That church was organized on April 24, 1930. Its first trustees were H. B. Gunderson, John Haakenson, and Ole Brendsel. In 1964 a new English Lutheran Church was built in Maxbass. St. Patrick's Catholic Church in Maxbass was built and dedicated in 1916. Its first trustees were Fred Weber, Sr., and Tom Galvin. Father Andrieux of Bottineau served as priest until 1948. The Catholic Church closed in 1980.

Before Maxbass was three months old a meeting was held in the Security Bank building to plan a school for the thirty or more children living in or near the village. Jennie Stokes was hired as the first teacher and held school for a short time in the Renville Store. School opened January 4, 1906. In 1907 a two-story brick schoolhouse was erected; Max Bass gave a bell to the new school. A new one-story school was built in 1961 and the old brick structure, in use since 1907, was razed the next year. In 1913 Minnick Fossum, then president of the school board, presented diplomas to the first graduates of Maxbass High School. The first graduates were Anna Anderson, Clifford Cram, Estella Kirn, and Lottie Kirn. The high school closed in 1981. Maxbass now operates an elementary school for kindergarten through grade six. Grades seven through twelve attend school in Newburg.

Fires have destroyed many businesses in Maxbass. The last fire destroyed the grocery store on December 11, 1978. The grain elevators were destroyed by fire on April 2, 1969. After the elevators were de-

Downtown business district of Maxbass - early 1900s
(SHSND)

stroyed the railroad was removed from Maxbass. The only businesses which remain today are a bar with cafe and groceries, a service station, a beauty shop, and the post office.

The Maxbass City Park was established around 1955. R. C. Streich planted and cultivated the trees for many years. In 1972 the Maxbass Park Board was organized. It has purchased playground and picnic equipment, planted trees, and bought baseball equipment. A golf course has been established and annual golf tournaments are held.

In 1955 the city celebrated its 50th Anniversary by holding a Golden Jubilee on July 22-23. Also in 1955 Mrs. Minnick (Gussty) Fossum was North Dakota's Mother of the Year. Maxbass celebrated its 75th Anniversary on June 27-29, 1980.

For many years the population of Maxbass was fairly stable. It had a population of 240 in 1910; forty years later 259 people lived in the village. By 1990 the population had decreased to 123.

Maxbass also had the distinction of a suburb, "West Maxbass," being platted.

One of six elevators in early Maxbass, North Dakota
(SHSND)

State Bank in Maxbass, North Dakota - ca. 1936
(SHSND)

Mercer was built on the homestead of a Civil War veteran, William Henry Harrison Mercer, sometimes spelled Musser, who settled along the Missouri River in 1869. Establishing one of the first farms north of Bismarck he cultivated about 120 acres of land and harvested about 2,000 bushels of wheat.

In 1905 the Northern Pacific Railroad extended a branch line west to Turtle Lake and established the Mercer station. That same year the McLean County Townsite Company platted the townsite and the federal government established the Mercer post office and appointed Nels Olesen postmaster.

When the world officially recognized Mercer, with the establishment of the office, there were many people in the area who had already staked their claims as homesteaders and no doubt were happy to have an address. Scandinavian farmers came to the area as early as 1900 and German-Russian immigrants arrived soon after.

Early in its history the community adopted a slogan: "Mercer is growing, all roads lead to Mercer, come to the land of plenty." Within five years it became a hub of activity and in September 1909 the *Mercer Telegram*, its weekly newspaper from 1907 to 1917, interpreted the pride of the villagers by featuring the following poem on the front page:

We have two general stores right now,
Who's (sic) prices are in reach;
To the Hardware store we proudly bow
Because it is a peach.
A Meat Market. A Hotel fare,
With everything to eat,
A rest in our new barber chair
Just simply is a treat.
Three lumber yards, with prices right,
Two Livery barns as well,
A Printing office right in sight
Where all the truth we tell.
The Implements that are handled here
Are certainly all right;
The Feed Mill run by Johnie dear
Is simply out of sight.
The First State Bank so nobely (sic) stands
Beside our great Pool Hall,
But Hedahl's Furniture so grand
Just simply beats them all.
Of Real Estate men we have but two
And that is quite enough,
The rest we had did not much do
But left with people's stuff.
Of Elevators three we score,
Blacksmith shops just two;
If we should tell of any more,
It hardly would be true,
But in another year from now
It would be no surprise
To see our little bumper town
Just twice its present size.

The hardware-furniture store of Edwin Hedahl, the general store of George McFadden, the feed mill of John Ketterling, the meat market of Christ Sackmann, and the livery stables of Adolph Singer and J.R. Washburn were owned by the original operators twenty years later. The grain elevators were in operation until 1973 and the lumberyards went out of business during the 1950s.

The blacksmith shops became a part of history with the advent of modern technology, but one smithy will be long remembered. Karl Rennick was the artist who designed many of the iron crosses called Iron Spirits, found in area cemeteries where German-Russian immigrants are buried.

The First State Bank folded during the depression; however, a second bank, the Mercer State Bank which opened for business in 1910 with F. O. Freeberg as cashier remained in the Freeberg family until 1967 when it became part of the First National Bank of McClusky.

In later years there were general stores owned by the Dakovna, Freeberg, Hjelle, and Gardiner families.

The Belmont Hotel survived until the 1940s but had continuous turnover of proprietors. The Belmont, the city Pool Hall and Cafe and the school were the centers of early community activity.

Mercer had organizations like the Mercer Dramatic Troupe, the Literary Society, the Commercial Club and one organization that was destined to be short-lived, the Bachelor's Protective Association of Mercer, a secret meeting of bachelors. This became a casualty of decreased membership as visits to the Washburn and McClusky courthouses and to Pastor Keller to exchange marriage vows became frequent occurrences.

Religion was an important part of the lives of Mercer residents, but a church building in the village was not built until 1916.

A German Lutheran missionary pastor, Reverend W. W. L. Keller, was an early homesteader and was instrumental in building Zion Lutheran Church south of Mercer in 1906 and Saint Paul's Lutheran Church, locally known as the Braun Church, four miles northwest of Mercer in 1909. Pastor Keller continued to serve the Evangelical Lutheran congregation and was succeeded by his son, Walter, who served from 1914 to 1921. Hope Lutheran Church was built in Mercer in 1916 and served the German Lutherans until 1957.

Church services for the Scandinavian

Our Savior's Lutheran Church

Lutherans, Methodists, and Baptists were held in the Mercer school building by visiting preachers.

In September 1916 Pastor Ragnvold Ulvilden became the resident Scandinavian Lutheran minister and in 1928 the present Lutheran church was established. All the Lutheran parishes in the area merged in 1976 and are now known as Our Saviors Lutheran Church.

The Mercer Baptist congregation from north of Mercer moved into the city in 1947 and the Mercer Church of God has been in the community since the 1940s. The EUB, Methodist, had a church which was established in 1916 south of town and was in Mercer from 1952 until 1981.

School sessions were first held in a frame building which is still standing. Olga Natwick was the first teacher in 1907 when thirty-three students answered roll call. The frame building was replaced by a brick structure in 1916 and the first high school graduation occurred in 1922 when two young ladies received their diplomas. The last class graduated in 1972 when re-organization resulted in the establishment of the Turtle Lake-Mercer school district and the Mercer school closed its doors in 1976. There are four hundred loyal Mercer High School graduates and many of them return for school reunions. The brick schoolhouse is now the Mercer Recreational and Senior Citizen Center.

The health care needs of early Mercer residents were attended to by Dr. G. E. Heinzroth of Turtle Lake who made house calls on horseback, by horse and buggy, later by train and then by automobile. Early residents recognized the need for a hospital and on July 1, 1915 the Mercer Hospital opened for business with Dr. Ralph Deming and nurse Anna Krogmoe in charge. The hospital operated for two years; the

building became a family residence.

Musical groups provided recreation and entertainment for early Mercer residents. Church and community choirs and dance bands were in existence soon after the community was organized. The Mercer Booster Band of thirty-one members started practice in March 1910 and even though the membership changed frequently, continued to be part of the activities until the 1930s with many of the concerts on the Mercer band stand.

Athletic activities were well attended and both men and women participated on town teams. The present relationship between Mercer and Brush Lake, two miles north, began early in Mercer history. A gasoline launch was operating on the lake during the summer of 1909 and combined activities have continued. The present Memorial Day rodeos sponsored by the Brush Poppers Horse Club have a statewide reputation.

Like many early prairie communities Mercer had its share of fires, the most destructive was in August 1910 when three major businesses burned to the ground. In its effort to fight the blaze the water brigade literally ran out of water. The first town well was dug in 1915 and the present water and sewer project was completed in the 1950s. A fire in the 1950s de-

stroyed the early City Hall which served as a church in its final years.

At the present time Mercer has one general store, a bar, a post office, a bank, a machine shop, three contractors, three churches, a service station, a fire department, an airport and flying school, and an active senior citizen group.

Mercer's population is about one hundred. A woman mayor, Martha Diede Thompson, was elected in 1980 and still serves on the Mercer City Council.

The village has produced some prominent North Dakota citizens: John Hjelle, son of pioneers Ole and Ella Hjelle, was the editor of the *Bismarck Tribune* from 1948 until 1980; his cousin, Walter Hjelle, son of Ben and Cora Hjelle, served as North Dakota highway commissioner; Walter Christensen, son of Jonas and Julianna Christensen, was the North Dakota state treasurer for ten and a half years until his death in 1979; and the grandson of pioneers Christ and Christine Sackmann, the Reverend Robert Lynne, is the first bishop of the Western North Dakota Synod of the Evangelical Lutheran Church in America.

For the past eighty-six years Mercer residents have been involved in keeping their village alive and the Mercer Booster Club is still actively promoting Mercer and declaring that "all roads lead to Mercer."

Main Street Mercer, North Dakota - 1910-1912

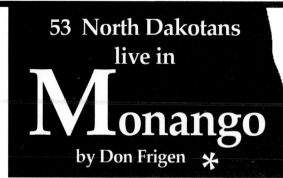
Monango was settled in 1886 by a group of emigrants from Pennsylvania who in 1882 first founded the town of Keystone three miles northeast of its present site. Keystone was short-lived because the route of the Chicago, Milwaukee & St. Paul Railroad extension from Ellendale to Edgeley was surveyed some three miles to the west. When the railroad established a station named Monango along the extension in 1886 anyone who owned a business or a home in Keystone was given a free lot of their choice in Monango. Keystone residents moved to Monango in the winter of 1886-1887 after the snow covered the ground. Sled runners were built under many buildings which were pulled to their new destination.

The origin of the town's name is obscure; some of the stories which offer an explanation follow. One early tale tells about a tiny Indian baby, strapped to a travois harnessed to a dog, who was rescued by soldiers at the Battle of Whitestone Hill in 1863. The troops decided to name the baby and chose a name they thought sounded like an Indian name, *Monango*. Another story suggests that the town was named after a famous Indian chief, still another has it named after a Milwaukee Road offi-

cial. One more traces the story of the name back to the original Keystone settlers, some of whom had come from the Keystone State of Pennsylvania. The town was named for a landmark in Pennsylvania, the Monongahela River Valley, after changing the word Monongahela.

W. A. Caldwell, J. F. Hagerty, and Beriah Magoffin and his son, Ebenezer, were the community leaders at the time of Monango's settlement. At the turn of the century this rapidly growing town had two fine hotels, the Monango House and the Hagerty House. The community was served by the Milwaukee Road which provided daily north-south service; east-west service was provided by the Soo Line which was built one mile south of Monango in 1891.

The Presbyterian Church was moved from Keystone; it was the first church built in Dickey county and operated until 1962. A Methodist Church was built in 1890; the congre-

gation disbanded in 1902. In 1907 and 1908 St. John's Catholic Church was built with substantial amounts of money donated by William A. Caldwell, Jay F. Hagerty, and George B. Hall, all non-Catholics, to make Monango a "complete" community. This congregation disbanded in 1941. St. Paul Lutheran Church was moved into Monango in 1947. It was established three miles west of town in 1894 and continues to hold weekly services. It is the oldest operating Lutheran Church in Dickey County.

The area was first settled by the Scotch and Irish. In the early 1890s German-Russians settled the area west of Monango, mainly in the townships of Hamburg and Potsdam. Many descendants of these early German-Russian settlers, to the fourth and fifth generation, are still living in the area.

Monango's first school was held in homes in the town. The first permanent school, a wooden structure, was built in 1901. A large brick school was erected in 1920 and the wooden structure was then used as a gymnasium. This building was destroyed by fire on January 30, 1937. In 1938 a modern gymnasium was built with Works Progress Administration help. The cost of the project was $29,776. Both the school and gymnasium are in use today. A cooperative school arrangement with neighboring Fullerton in 1977 moved the K-6 grades to Fullerton and 7-12 stayed at Monango. The 1945 girls' basketball team won the state tournament and the 1972-1973, 1973-1974 girls' team were undefeated.

Like many prairie towns, Monango suffered from fire damage. Magoffin's Store burned to the ground in 1916 along with many other businesses and homes. In 1946 and 1947 fires again ravaged main street. The latter fire destroyed the Modern Woodman of America building, a town landmark.

Monango's Juvenile Band organized in 1908

The first house built in Monango, North Dakota - 1887

Monango had a newspaper, the *Monango Star*, from its very beginning. In 1908 the name was changed to the *Monango Journal*, it printed its last edition on February 13, 1920. A second paper, the *Monango Mirror*, published from 1892 to 1896.

Medical help was available to the town and the surrounding area from 1886 to 1933. A total of six doctors served here, with the last being Dr. Gundermann who is buried in the city cemetery.

Monango boasted of a cheese plant from 1895 to 1905. Monango Full Cream Cheese won first prize at the North Dakota State Fair in 1895; cheese sold for $.09 per pound.

Two banks served the financial needs of the area. The first to open was the Bank of Monango owned by William A. Caldwell. It operated from January 1, 1887 to November 18, 1930. The Farmers and Merchants State Bank opened April 7, 1907 and closed its doors on March 31, 1923. Both bank buildings are still being occupied. The Caldwell Land Agency was the oldest land agency in North Dakota.

A Monangoan, Theodore Northrop, was largely responsible for creating a historical site at the Whitestone Battlefield. The battle was the most serious confrontation between the Indians and the military in the state. The site and monument were dedicated on October 13, 1909.

Monango began to decline in the early 1930s. The Milwaukee Road discontinued operation in 1979. Present businesses are the Triple R Bar and Grill, Harry's Gun Shop, Wolff's Apiaries, and Smith Brothers Livestock.

Monango has an active Community Betterment Association which sponsors the annual Turkey Barbecue held in September. The community also has a very fine men's softball team. In the past many excellent amateur baseball and basketball teams provided many hours of entertainment.

Monango celebrated its Centennial June 27-29, 1986. More than 5,000 people attended the Saturday events.

Main Street Monango, North Dakota - 1909

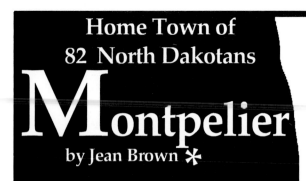

Montpelier
by Jean Brown ✱

Montpelier was named by Jerome J. Flint and his partner, Bailey Fuller, after Montpelier, Vermont, the capital of their native state. They purchased the land in 1881, and in October 1885 a part of this land was deeded by Flint and Fuller to the James River Valley Railroad, and in December it was deeded by the railroad to Edward G. Bailey, who in 1886, deeded it to Frank A. Seymour, trustee, who platted it.

Charles E. DeWar, of Billings, was the surveyor. There were 14 blocks, a main street and 8 avenues called Livingston, Flint, Fuller, Bailey, Holbrook, Billings, DeWar, and Merriam. The Hilsinger Addition of four additional blocks was platted April 17, 1914. The first settlers to Montpelier Township came in 1880. They were the F. A. Carley, Elliot A. Tarbell, and John and Joe Cumber families. Tarbell built the first dwelling in the spring of 1880. Lumber was hauled from Jamestown by team and carried across the James River on a raft. The bridge was not built until 1882.

The first post office was in the Tarbell home and was called Tarbell Post Office, but later it was moved to town and called Montpelier. The stage running from Jamestown to LaMoure brought the mail. The F. A. Carley home was the local stage stop, for dinner and a change of horses.

In 1883 grading was done for the James River Valley Railroad, but the road was not completed until 1886.

On August 12, 1883 Flint and Fuller deeded a piece of land to School District No. 7. The first school was built in the spring of 1882, on the same site where the present school stands. In 1889 it became School District No. 14.

Roman Catholics erected the first church in Montpelier in 1896, however, services had been held in homes for some time previous to this. Lutheran and Presbyterian churches were built in 1915 and a new Catholic church was constructed in 1916.

Montpelier also grew to boast of two farm elevators, three general stores, a livery stable, blacksmith shop, barbershop, newspaper, bank, lumberyard, billiard parlor, two cream stations, a meat market, a drug store and doctor, an express and telegraph office, funeral parlor, a telephone company, and a population of 200.

On November 26, 1985 one of the town's last landmarks, Stott's Store, was lost to fire. At one time it housed the Opera House on the top floor. It was the site for many and varied community affairs: school carnivals, school plays, graduation exercises, elections, farmers' meetings, basketball games, roller skating, dances, vaudeville shows, and movies.

In 1986, one hundred years after being platted, Montpelier celebrated with a wonderful three-day birthday party, which was unanimously agreed to have been the best Centennial celebration ever.

Today, in 1991, Montpelier supports an elevator, post office, saloon, antique and salvage operation, and a trucking and excavating business. Only one church survived the passing of the years.

Only 82 residents live in the small community, but the many farm families in the surrounding area are as much a part of the town as if they, too, lived in Montpelier.

Aerial view of Montpelier, North Dakota - 1985

Downtown Montpelier, North Dakota, looking east - 1914

Main Street Montpelier, North Dakota, looking west - 1914

Mooreton can trace its origins to the development of Bonanza wheat farms which focused the nation's attention on northern Dakota during the latter 1870s. After the Northern Pacific went bankrupt in the early 1870s the company developed a scheme to dispose of its land grant to producers rather than speculators. It began selling land for a cash outlay of 37 cents to $1.65 an acre and to offer discounts to buyers who would begin cultivation immediately. James B. Power, the railroad's land commissioner, sold some 1,700,000 acres to 2,988 buyers during the period 1873 to 1878.

By 1878 Hugh and Henrietta Moore, from Newburgh, New York, had acquired some 17,300 acres of land

Main Street Mooreton, North Dakota - 1976
(DPDP - Fred Schumacher)

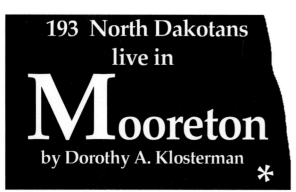

193 North Dakotans
live in
Mooreton
by Dorothy A. Klosterman

known as the Antelope Farm. Five thousand of its acres bordered the Hafener land on the northern part of what is now Mooreton.

The St. Paul, Minneapolis and Manitoba Railway Company (commonly known as the Manitoba, later the Great Northern), under the management of James J. Hill, was in the process of constructing a line through the area in 1881. However, before the rails were laid, and to avoid competition, the Manitoba and the Northern Pacific divided North Dakota between them. The Northern Pacific sold its branch line from Casselton to Mayville to the Manitoba and bought from the Manitoba its line from Sauk Rapids to St. Paul and another of its lines running west from Wahpeton.

In 1881 Mathias Butala, a native of Austria-Hungary, and his wife, Susanna, settled on land in the area,

Sec. 6, T132N, R49W, and built a store. The next year in October Butala was named postmaster when a rural post office named Triest was established in his store; Triest was his former home and his native country's major port on the Adriatic Sea.

In 1883 the Northern Pacific established a station called Griffin on that same section of land, naming it for F. F. Griffin, then the Assistant Superintendent of the railroad's operating division between Milnor and Wadena, Minnesota. In April the next year the station's name was changed to Mooreton for Hugh Moore who managed the Antelope Farm and who had given right-of way to the railroad. The Triest station also changed its name to Mooreton that same year. In May 1884 Batala and two of his neighbors, John and Anton Hafener, platted the Mooreton townsite, adjacent to the railroad station.

By 1895 the town had developed a sizable business section but it suffered considerable loss when a fire broke out in October of that year. On Friday, October 11, 1895 the *Richland County Gazette* reported that "Mooreton was nearly exterminated by fire a little past one o'clock last Sunday. The fire started in a stable, and owing to the compact manner in which the buildings were erected and a stiff breeze from the northwest,

spread with considerable rapidity. As the town had no adequate means for fighting the fires, about the only thing the people could do was stand by and see it burn. Among the buildings burned were the hotel, three stores, a meat market, a station house and a number of small buildings; the depot, elevator, two stores and a few other buildings remain. A citizen, when asked how the fire originated, said he did not exactly know, but it is thought that someone threw a cigar or something of the kind, as the fire was under good headway when first discovered. So here is probably a loss to charge to the smoking habit, which will equal all the profit on smoking materials ever sold in town."

Mooreton was quick to recover. With large bonanza farms rapidly developing in the surrounding area old businesses were rebuilt and new enterprises sprang up.

In the early 1900s the town consisted of the following businesses: a blacksmith shop, Chernich's general store, Radovich's livery stable, a boarding house and meat market, August Bumpke's "Blind Pig," John Schmitt's harness shop, John Tomz's "Blind Pig," three elevators, a telephone office, a mill, a depot, a coal shed, a lumber store, and Hafener's general store.

Mooreton's main street has changed through time. Today, its main street businesses include: Cenex service station, formerly a Standard station owned by Leslie Bossman; Hermes

Hardware, owned by Dana Hermes; and the Central of the Valley Farm Management, Greg La Plante, general manager. Other enterprises include: Menne's Grocery Store and Meat Market, owned and operated by George and Tommy Menne; the Farmer's Bar, owned and operated by Don Merchant; Ward's Recreation, owned by Lester Ward, the City Centre Cafe and senior citizens' room, Joel Willyard, manager, and the Welding Rod owned by John Cox. Also located on main street is the Mooreton post office with Sharon Merchant, postmistress. The former George Feneis Garage now houses Jan Weber's gift shop, and the Southeast Grain Company, formerly the Farmers' Elevator with its fertilizer plant and 54-car load-out facility is located on the Burlington Northern Railroad, previously the Northern Pacific.

Mooreton has two churches and one school. St. Anthony's Catholic Church was built in 1884; its present and third structure was erected in 1956. A parochial school, built in 1920, closed in 1932. The present pastor is the Reverend Father Albert Binder.

Ferd Evenson Drug Store in Mooreton, North Dakota - 1912
(SHSND)

The American Lutheran Church was built in 1919 and has undergone several renovations during the years. The present pastor is the Reverend John Holt.

The school district was reorganized in 1966 and Mooreton became a part of the Wahpeton School District. The present school building houses the entire 5th grade section of the district.

In 1949 Mooreton received national press coverage when it completed the installation of a lighted ball park. Achieved through the cooperation of the Mooreton Commercial Club and surrounding communities the park symbolized the importance of baseball to the area.

The present Mooreton Community Club, originally organized as the Mooreton Commercial Club, began in 1941. The town is noted for its annual Labor Day celebration which began in 1947.

Mooreton, in the center of a fertile agricultural area, is a community-supported city that is alive and growing in a time when small towns are threatened by modern highway systems which make it easier to travel to larger cities, by adverse economic conditions, and by the isolation of living in a rural area.

Radovich Butcher Shop in Mooreton, North Dakota - 1912
(SHSND)

Home Town of 663 N. Dakotans

New England

*by Joe Bohlman

New England was one of the earliest settlements west of the Missouri River in Dakota Territory. It was settled by an advance party of eighteen from the New England states who were sponsored by the New England Colony Association for Dakota, organized in Boston, Massachusetts in the winter of 1886-1887 and presided over by Thomas H. Bicknell. The group arrived in Dakota Territory in May 1887, traveling south from Dickinson to the Cannonball River. They arrived there on May 2, 1887 and established New England City, their headquarters.

The colony was successful in petitioning the government for a post office; it was established on August 26, 1887, but it was named Mayflower. The settlers were able to have the name changed to New England City the next month, but several years later the name was shortened to New England.

On June 17, 1887 the first issue of the newspaper, the *Rainy Buttes Sentinel* was printed by M. L. Ayers. In 1907 the *Hettinger County Herald* was established and is still publishing.

School began in the fall of 1887 with five pupils. By spring of 1888, twenty-seven houses had been built and the Congregational Church was dedicated in July of that year.

The community struggled for survival because of bad weather, poor crops, the failure to attract a railroad, and the migration of many of the early settlers who moved farther west or returned east. The expected coming of the railroad, however, improved the community's prospects.

Looking ahead, William C. McKenzie, a prominent merchant and postmaster, platted New England's townsite on the old village site in April 1909. Several months later the Chicago, Milwaukee & St. Paul Railroad's subsidiary, the Milwaukee Land Company, platted an addition to the town. And in November 1910 the railroad reached New England.

The Northern Pacific Railroad was but twenty-five miles north and both companies encouraged immigrants from Scandinavia, southern Russia, and Hungary to settle the area. The town grew rapidly; by 1912 at least fifty business places and professional offices were flourishing. New England had the largest livery stable in the state; McKenzie opened a department store which was the largest store west of Minneapolis at the time; and New England claimed title as the largest primary wheat market in the world for a number of years.

New England School District No. 9 was organized in June 1907. A three-story brick public school building was erected and dedicated in 1914. A diploma was presented the high school's first, and only graduate that year, on June 5, 1917. The original building was replaced in 1955 with a modern one-level building. Recent additions have enlarged the facility.

A Catholic boarding school, New England St. Mary's, opened in the fall of 1924 in the former McKenzie Department Store building. It was staffed by the School Sisters of Notre Dame. Between 1950 and 1980 a modern grade and high school, dormitories, convent, and gymnasium were built. The school boards students from out of state and from various foreign countries. Education has always been important to New Englanders. Both public and parochial schools have graduated a host of students who have proven themselves throughout the world. Their achievements have kept New England "on the map."

There are four active churches in the

212 teams wait for unloading on Elevator Row - 1912

The first building built in New England - late 1880s

community today: St. Mary's Catholic, Our Redeemer's Lutheran, United Church of Christ, and the Assembly of God.

There are two notable buildings in the city. One is the World War I Memorial Hall, built in 1935. It serves as the primary center for community events and it also houses the public library. Extensive renovation was accomplished in 1988. The other is the Riverside Apartment building, formerly the McKenzie Hotel, which is listed in the National Register of Historic Places.

New England commemorated its 75th Anniversary in 1961 with an elaborate celebration. The Centennial celebration held in June 1986 was an extravaganza! Thousands viewed the parades and the locally produced historical pageant. A history of the area and of local families can be found in *1886-1986: Century of Change.*

4th of July parade passing the McKenzie Hotel - 1914

New * Hradec

by Betty Pavlish

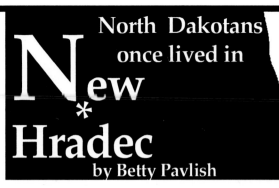

Early settlers in the area first worshiped in their homes, their spiritual needs being served periodically by one Father Studnicka who traveled across the state from Wahpeton. In 1898 the Northern Improvement Company, a division of the Northern Pacific Railroad Company which looked after its land holdings, deeded forty acres to the Right Reverend John Shanley, Bishop of the Fargo Diocese, for the purpose of establishing a parish in southern Dunn County for the immigrants who had come from the old Austrian province of Bohemia, now part of Czechoslovakia. In that year the Bohemian settlers held a meeting, decided to form a parish, and by October had erected the first church in Dunn County, a frame structure, called Saints Peter and Paul Roman Catholic Church. For the next few years the parish was served by priests from Dickinson, one of the most regular being Father Rabstinek.

At first the community was known as *Novy Hradec*, a Czech term meaning "New Castle;" however, a post office called New Hradec was established there in February 1908. Edward Kasal was appointed postmaster. The town wasn't incorporated until 1903; in 1911 the land went through probate and was officially turned over to the parish.

Held together by religious and social ties the community dreamed of having a priest of their own nationality. While on a trip to Chicago Vincent Kovash visited the Benedictine seminary in Lisle, Illinois and made the request. Father Grunt was sent to the parish in late 1904 or early 1905; he remained only a few months, but was instrumental in getting a parish house built.

Father Edward Kasal, energetic, ambitious, and known as the "Cowboy Priest," helped bring the community into the modern world. Although his territory included parts of North Dakota and Montana he was instrumental in getting a post office for New Hradec. He encouraged the settlers to build a community hall, he introduced the first cream separator into the area and brought the telephone to the community, and he was asked by Governor John Burke to help organize Dunn County and suggest names for county offices. He left the parish in late summer of 1910.

Father John Smoley, a Slovak priest who had served in his country's army but who could not speak the Czech language very well, followed the "Cowboy Priest." His successor was a Polish nobleman, Father John Przytarski, who served until the fall of 1916.

Father Tomanek served the parish from 1916 to 1920. In the summer of 1917 the small frame church was destroyed by fire; but the parish decided to rebuild immediately. They also decided the community needed a new school of its own. The project cost $26,000. Christmas Eve Mass was celebrated in the new church in 1917; in early 1918 a teaching order of nuns from Mankato, Minnesota arrived to staff the school which opened with twenty-six students, many of whom boarded with the sisters. Its enrollment peaked in 1942 when 143 students were in attendance, 92 were boarding students. In October 1945 ground was broken for a new school complex and five years later classes were held in the new building. It remained a boarding school until 1969 when nuns became unavailable to staff the institution. The school was leased to the New Castle school district for a few years after which it closed permanently.

The parish was served briefly by Father Emil Bubik. His successor was Father Joseph Vytisk who served the parish from 1922 until 1934. An eloquent speaker whose sermons were well received, he labored to meet the social needs of the community, encouraged the young people to preserve their heritage by presenting Czech plays, inspired the parish to retire its debt, and succeeded in increasing the size of the congregation.

In 1934 one of the parish's own sons became its spiritual leader. Father Ladislaus Brydl served the parish for fifty years. It flourished under his leadership: organizations like the Catholic Workman, the Rosary Society, the Knights of Columbus, the Catholic War Veterans, and the Sodality of Our Lady were organized and youth groups were promoted.

A view of New Hradec, North Dakota - early 1920s

After serving the parish for fifty years Father Brydl retired in January of 1984.

The parish was without a permanent pastor until the summer of 1984 when Father Raphael Stovik OSB of the Assumption Abbey in Richardton was appointed pastor. He is still serving the parish.

Peak family membership in the parish at one time numbered two hundred fifty; only ninety families are members today.

Business flourished in the community in its early days. Zimbrick operated a general mercantile store and a cream station and faced competition by the Kostelecky store. Later Lucas Adamski and Vincent Kovash operated a general store, purchased cream and eggs and when John Karsky entered the partnership machinery and twine were sold. The Adamski family operated the store until 1952 when it was sold to Bill and Dagmar Urbanec who operated it until 1954. Shortly after that the building was torn down. The post office was also housed in the store until it closed.

For a time the building was given to the Katolicka Delnik society and used for plays, meetings, and dances. It was later traded for a section house which was torn down and its lumber used by the association to

SS. Peter & Paul Church and its parish - early 1900s

build a new hall. During a wedding dance in July 1963 the hall was destroyed by fire; a new structure was built immediately after.

Automobile services were also provided for the community. Anton Market operated a garage for many years. Joe Franchuk and Tony Kovash also serviced the community's automobiles and Jim Gulka operated a similar business for about twenty years before he closed his shop in the 1960s and moved to Dickinson. The post office was housed in Gulka's garage when the store was closed and remained there until recently.

The New Hradec community also supported a bar which like many

other businesses was located outside the city limits. For many years it was owned and operated by the Joe Jablonsky family. Steve Heiser, Ray Bullinger, and Ray Bren also owned and operated the facility. Some years ago Bren closed the bar, dismantled the building, and used the lumber to build a house.

The last of New Hradec's businesses is now just a memory. But it remains a viable religious community; Assumption Abbey at Richardton has now taken the community "under its wing."

The parish has been named to the National Register of Historical Places.

Funeral procession in New Hradec, North Dakota - ca. 1918

In 1895 the village of Leipzig was established in west central Grant County. Most of the settlers who moved to the site were German-Russians; they named their community after Leipzig, Germany.

In 1910 when the Northern Pacific Railroad built a branch line from Mandan into the area and the Chicago, Milwaukee and St. Paul Railroad built its branch line from McLaughlin, South Dakota, into the same area, the two lines converged at a point where each road located a station. In May 1910 a townsite there was platted by the Milwaukee Land Company of Chicago, a Milwaukee Road subsidiary. A post office was also established there in May and named New Leipzig after the village of Leipzig which was located about

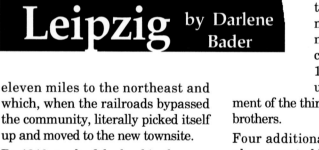

326 North Dakotans live in New Leipzig
by Darlene Bader

eleven miles to the northeast and which, when the railroads bypassed the community, literally picked itself up and moved to the new townsite.

By 1910 much of the land in the area which had been part of the Northern

Pacific land grant had been acquired by two men from Dubuque, Iowa, William Lawther and James Shields. There was an effort to name one of the new towns in the area after Lawther and in 1910 the Northern Pacific did so by using his name for a station between Elgin and Carson, but the next year when a town and post office named Heil was established the railroad agreed to adopt that name for their station. When the New Leipzig post office was renamed Lawther in January 1912 the community protested and in August the postal authorities changed the name back to New Leipzig. The name Lawther was too similar to Lawton, North Dakota and created postal delivery problems.

Hertz Brothers Hardware is believed to be the oldest firm still doing business in Grant County. Organized in Leipzig as the Farmers Commerce Company by principal stockholders Christ, Henry, and Emanuel Hertz, and several minor stockholders, it was one of the enterprises to make the move to the new railroad town. It changed its name in 1912 and is now under the management of the third generation of Hertz brothers.

Four additional firms in town are also operated by third generation managers: First State Bank, Birdsall

Elevator, Roehl Trucking, and Stelter Repair. The business district today provides almost entirely farm-related services.

The spiritual needs of the community are met by the following churches: Seventh-day Adventist, New Leipzig Baptist, St. John's Catholic, Christus Congregational, and Immanuel Lutheran.

School classes were held in rooms furnished by various business firms in 1910. Two years later the first school house was built; it was leveled by fire in February 1915. That same year a brick, fire-proof structure was erected. Additions were made to that structure in 1926, 1957, and 1961 to care for increased enrollments resulting from annexation of rural school districts.

In recent years the community has been responsive to the needs of its elderly citizens. The New Leipzig Development Association, organized in 1966, has provided four dwellings which contain 18 one- and two-bedroom apartments for low income senior citizens.

In 1971 New Leipzig introduced North Dakota's first authentic German funfest, Oktoberfest. The three-day festival has grown through the years with the combined efforts of city and rural residents. Oktoberfest is "both a reflection and a means of recovering a sense of identity in our German heritage" and a Thanksgiving to God at the end of our harvest season. A highlight, since its inception in 1978, has been the Oktoberfest Musical presented by area residents.

New Leipzig, like other rural North Dakota communities, faces the sad truth that after it gives its youth a solid religious upbringing and educates them locally to the best of its ability, it then sends them to college for training in fields, that in most cases, takes them out of the community and the beloved state of North Dakota.

Moving the four-story Michelson Star Mill - 1910
(SHSND)

Oktoberfest billboard welcomes visitors to New Leipzig

Present day Main Street New Leipzig, North Dakota
(DPDP - Bruce Severy)

N iobe's original townsite map was dated November 23, 1906; the following month townsite lots began to be sold. The Great Northern Railroad Company laid rails through this Swedish settlement in 1907 and built a depot that year.

The town is located on land originally homesteaded by Michael E. Grady. It lays on the prairie with a small coulee to the northwest. The area children swam there in the summer and used it for skating in the winter. To the southwest is a small hill, known at first as "Knob Hill" and later as "Grady Hill," which was the scene of many winter sled races.

Eric Ericson, a weekly mail carrier, brought mail from Kenaston to Niobe in 1907. On March 27, 1908 the town's post office was established with Andrew Nelson as postmaster.

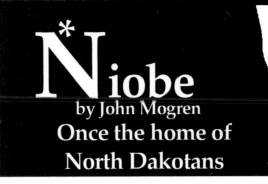

*Niobe
by John Mogren
Once the home of North Dakotans

It was closed on May 1, 1974 with Myrna Nelson the last postmistress.

Business boomed in the first two years of the town's history. Businesses which were established included: A. K. Johnson & Company, Alle Fleckten Confectionery, Andrew Nelson Grocery Store, Anton Mickelsen Feed Mill, Darymple Elevator Company (Ward and Anderson), Erickson & Fleckten Hardware Store, Great Northern Depot, Hotel (Murphy & Woolredge) Mike Grady, Johnson Blacksmith Shop, Joe Nel-

son Pool Hall, Kamps Lumberyard, LaCrosse Pool Hall, meatmarket-butchershop, Mrs. Olsen's Restaurant, Meyer Lumberyard, Peter Larson General Store, Rugby Milling Company, Swedish Baptist Church, Swedish Lutheran Church, Tall & Johnson General Store, Winter & Ames Grain Elevator.

Niobe has always been predominately Swedish. Church services in the Swedish language were not entirely discontinued until the 1940s. The Swedish Lutherans celebrated "Jul Otta" which was an early morning matin service held at Christmas. The entire community would join in the celebration of "Midsummer" with picnics. The Swedish Baptists gathered at the Perry Ledene farm and

Main Street Niobe, North Dakota - 1909

Peter Larson's General Store - 1914

the Swedish Lutherans at Andrew Granlund's.

The Swedish Lutheran Church was organized November 1904. Their church was completed in November 1907. A Sunday school was organized four years later with forty-one children. The church still serves the community. The Swedish Baptist congregation laid the foundation for its church in July 1908; the structure was completed the next year. The congregation disbanded in 1970 and dismantled the church in 1971.

Niobe was a lively little "burg" in her early years. Dances were held in the meeting room above Tall & Johnson's store. The Caroline Hotel was the scene of many gala events and years later the town hall was considered the place to go to dance.

Imagine the excitement when Lawrence Welk played in Niobe! The Niobe Band, organized in 1911, entertained many people when they played in the Niobe Bandstand. It disbanded in 1957. Basket socials at the school house with Aron Erickson, caller, were also well received.

Niobe Public School - 1913

Noonan

by Iola Rosenquist

Noonan was established in 1906 when the Great Northern Railroad extended its branch line from Berthold to Crosby. The townsite was platted that year on land owned by Mrs. Carrie Everson. Many people named Noonan settled in the area as early as 1902-1903; but local stories suggest that the town was named for Patrick Noonan who homesteaded in the area.

The town grew rapidly, aided by railroad promotion. In 1906 J. J. Gits opened the Golden Rule Store. The next year one McKee opened a bank, Rolf Reite started a drug store, and Ole Christianson began publishing the town's newspaper, the *Republican*. Other early businesses were an implement dealership operated by Henry Nelson, a hotel managed by Henry Kostchever, a light plant run by William Nordman, and one Cornwall provided blacksmith services.

The post office wasn't established until March 1907. Henry Kostchevar was named the first postmaster and Alfred Simonson was the first mail carrier.

Noonan incorporated in 1909 as a village and reorganized with a city council form of government in the late 1920s. Its first mayor was Patrick Noonan.

The city became a Port-of-Entry in the mid-twenties. The first immigration officer was Max Andrewjeski; the customs officer was Mr. Roberts. Present officers are Ray Schultz and Mr. Calli.

Coal was discovered in a creek bank one mile southeast of Noonan. Elmer Truax Sr. started the first strip mine in the state. The Baukol-Noonan Company closed in 1987.

Prairie Chapel Methodist Church was built in Coalfield Township on land donated by Ben Wissbrod. Later it was moved to town. Later the congregation voted to close the church and the building was sold to Mr. Eide. In 1914 the Catholic Church was moved from Kermit to Noonan. Father Wagner was the first priest; Father Gavett now serves the parish. Bethlehem Lutheran Church held its first service in 1906 with Reverend Samuel Peterson officiating. In 1919 a building program was begun and the next year Reverend G. W. Tola was called as pastor. Now serving Bethlehem and Zion, a country church, is Pastor Carol Hill. The Assembly of God congregation was organized in 1918; it built southeast of Noonan and moved to town a year later. Both Reverend and Mrs. Reckley served as the first pastors. Pastor Orval Close now serves this church.

On October 13, 1907 the first baby, John Barber, was born in Noonan. Seven years later Dr. J. A. Smith came to Noonan and set up practice in the hotel. Later a hospital was built which is now used as the Good Samaritan Center.

Noonan was first part of the Coalfield School District, but consolidation efforts in the 1920s merged that district with others to form Noonan School District No. 41. It was reorganized into a new Divide County district in the early 1960s. The first schoolhouse was built in 1910. The first high school graduating class received their diplomas in 1925; the last class to graduate from Noonan High School was the class of 1981. The elementary school was closed in 1984 and is now the Noonan Community Center. One of the major celebrations in the city was the all school reunion held in 1972.

The community's early settlers were remembered when Noonan's first Old Settlers Celebration was held on June 26, 1924. And the city now holds an annual Farmers Appreciation Day sponsored by the business places. Other remembered community activities are school carnivals, paper drives, collecting scrap iron, buying war bonds, the rationing of nylons and tires, school operettas, victorious athletic events, shows, dances, and roller skating. Other memories include doings at the Travelers Cafe, Crum's Drug Store, Memorial Hall, and Luther League meetings.

Noonan Train Depot in 1988

Main Street Noonan, North Dakota - mid 1900s

In 1988 the city had a population of about 225. That same year the city boasted of the following businesses: B and B Hardware owned by Jerome Brorby; Chets Super Service and Nygaard Oil owned by Chet Nygaard; the Noonan Farmers Telephone managed by Larry Clemens; Noonan Coop elevator managed by Arden Eide; Noonan Grain Company managed by Dwaine Waller; Ma Fagerlands Cafe owned by Donna Fagerland; Noonan Post Office with Shirley Burner as postmistress; Lund Sanitation owned by Alton Lund; the Good Samaritan Center managed by Bill Brewer; Border Lanes Bowling Alley owned by a local corporation; Noonan Market owned by John Lund; Town and Country and Travel Inn Bars owned and managed by Carla Johnson and Gerald Tanberg; Farmers State Bank Station managed by Gordon Wallin; Zimco Trucking owned by Dale and David Zimmerman; Rosenquist Repair and Salvage owned by Perry Rosenquist; Johnson Backhole owned by Gene Johnson; Verlindes Repair owned by Bruce and David Verlinde; Smithberg Satellite owned by Craig Smithberg; Lumsden Repair owned by John Lumsden; Noonan Greenhouse owned by Dale and Barb Ellison.

Active in the community are the Lions Club, the Fireman, the American Legion, two homemakers clubs, three church aids, five church circles, a Gun Club, a Sportsman Recreation Club, and Senior Citizens Club.

Baukol - Noonan Coal Company - mid 1900s

Early Scandinavian immigrants coming into western Grand Forks County and settling on the rich soil of the Red River Valley along the Goose River spread the word that more friends and relatives should come. So they came, from Norway and from the southeast around Northwood, Iowa.

One of the area's early settlers was Paul C. Johnson who came from Norway, worked for several years as a farm laborer around Northwood, Iowa, and took up land along the north branch of the Goose River in 1875. In December 1879 a post office named Northwood was established on his farm and he was appointed its first postmaster. Three years later when railroad crews constructed a grade north from Mayville and Port-

Early settlers near Northwood, North Dakota - late 1800s

1,166 North Dakotans live in *

Northwood

by Arthur G. Bilden

land through western Grand Forks County the Hougen brothers, George and Thomas, believing that a town would eventually spring up there, purchased land, surveyed it, and platted the Northwood townsite along the grade. The brothers also built a store on the site and the next year in August the Northwood post office was moved to the new town and George O. Hougen became postmaster. In 1884 the railroad was completed as far north as Larimore; that same year the railroad established a station called Northwood on the new townsite.

The town's first newspaper was published on October 19, 1884. It passed through several hands until Dan Campbell became its editor in 1899 and for sixty-eight years it published

news in a way beautifully diversified from all journalists. The *Gleaner* is still published today.

Northwood experienced a holocaust on September 13, 1899 when fire originated in a hotel where a maid was dosing a bedstead with gasoline to exterminate bugs. The entire business area was wiped out; fifty buildings were destroyed. The pioneer spirit prevailed, however, and reconstruction began immediately. The community has had a volunteer fire department since it organized in 1889. Today, five fire trucks manned by well trained local firemen stand ready for immediate action.

Concern for the sick and aged led to the formation in 1901 of a corporation which set out to build and operate a hospital and home for the aged. A pioneer woman, Eli Thingelstad, donated her large farm house for a nursing home, but sensing the urgency of first having a hospital the house was converted into a hospital. Seven years later, a new brick, two-story hospital was dedicated and the old house, hospital, was diverted back to a resthome. The Deaconess Hospital and Home Complex has continued to grow. The new, modern up-to-date buildings now have 90 skilled and 38 basic nursing home beds and 26 hospital beds. It employs 170 full and part-time workers and boasts an annual payroll of $1.6 mil-

lion. Its clinic building, also a part of the Deaconess Complex, houses a four-doctor clinic, a dental clinic, and an eye clinic. In the early years from 1909 to 1921 it also had a school of Nursing.

The first Northwood church was the Norwegian Evangelical Lutheran Church built in 1886. Then, the Ebenezer Free Lutheran congregation first gathered in 1898. The Assemblies of God and Vineyard Christian Fellowship were formed in more recent years.

The Northwood Public School first opened in 1885 and built its first brick structure in 1901. Later remodelings and additions have provided needed classrooms, music rooms, shop, and two gymnasiums.

Many individuals and many things have made Northwood a city of distinction. At one time five young ladies won state and regional queen contests, designating Northwood the "City of Queens." A large residence, built in 1895, is listed in the National Register of Historic Places. One citizen, Peder Nelson, was decorated with a medal by His Majesty King Olav V of Norway for writing and publishing about our Norwegian heritage. Several citizens have worked countless hours to maintain our Pioneer Museum. Television crews from Norway have made films in Northwood to be shown in their homeland.

Yes, Northwood is a beautiful little city. If you don't believe it, come for a visit. You'll love it too, and be glad you came.

Main Street Northwood, North Dakota - 1905

Main Street Northwood, North Dakota - 1990s

North Dakotans once lived in

*Oakdale

by Deloris Chays & William Lubke

Oakdale began as a rural post office, established on July 23, 1889 on Michael S. Cuskelly's ranch. It was located some twelve miles northwest of Killdeer on Sec. 23, T146N, R96W among scrub oak trees on the eastern edge of the Killdeer Mountains. No other post offices were established any distance north except Acorn and Elmgrove in the extreme northwestern corner of the county, suggesting that this section of the county was the last to be settled.

Mail was hauled by stagecoach from Dickinson to the Oakdale post office three times a week. William F. Sperber served as postmaster for several years when the office was located about a mile and a half north of its original site, but it and a country store, in the same building, were operated by Michael Cuskelly from 1902 until 1911 on its original site, Sec. 23. Cuskelly sold the store to Chris Larsen and Hube Dehlinger. The post office remained on its original location until 1941 when Lloyd W. Random became postmaster and it was moved two miles north where it remained until 1958 when it was closed.

The Dehlingers, Larsens, Cuskellys, and Currys all built houses in Oakdale.

In addition to the post office and store Oakdale had at one time a two-story, eight-room hotel operated by Ernest B. Lubke and his family who lived in the hotel, a blacksmith shop also owned by Lubke, a barbershop operated by Miller Powers, and a livery stable operated by Charlie Tress. A dance hall provided weekly entertainment for people in the surrounding region. Masquerade dances were often held and those coming to the frolics on horseback provided excellent business for the stable on dance nights.

The town also boasted of a bank for a short period of time. The Northwestern State Bank owned by A. B. Curry was established in 1913, but it was moved to Killdeer the next year. Its first depositor was William C. Lubke, a young boy who deposited his first hard-earned five dollars. The bank was eventually destroyed by fire.

The Oakdale School District was created in February 1908. Oakdale School No. One was located one-half mile north of the post office. Children came from miles around to attend and there were as many as thirty-six students attending sessions in the one-room school. The district was dissolved in 1958, becoming part of the Killdeer school district.

For several years Allie Palmer served as postmaster and operated the general store. In later years the post office was the only part of Oakdale that was left.

The Dehlinger house was torn down; the lumber was taken down to the Little Missouri River where it was used to build a garage. The Curry house was moved to Killdeer and is now occupied by Walt Bandles. The blacksmith shop was torn down and rebuilt in Halliday.

The only building left standing in Oakdale today is the old Michael S. Cuskelly house in which Allie Palmers and the Leonard Davis's lived in for many years.

Falling Spring in the Killdeer Mts. near Oakdale
(SHSND)

Post Office in Oakdale, North Dakota - ca. 1920
(SHSND)

View of Oakdale, North Dakota - 1902-1911
(SHSND)

The area in which Oakes would eventually be located was officially opened when the Nicollette Fremont exploration party camped at the confluence of Bear Creek and the James River on July 17, 1839. When a stagecoach line running from Columbia, South Dakota to Jamestown, North Dakota passed through the area sod shanties sprang up along the route.

Railroad construction ultimately brought the town into being on land previously homesteaded by William Mills and John Jones.

The James River Valley branch of the Northern Pacific Railroad was extended south along the valley's east side in 1886 to meet a Chicago and Northwestern Railroad line built north from Columbia, South Dakota. The lines met at the townsite of Oakes, platted on September 1, 1886 by the Western Town Lot Company, a townsite subsidiary of the Chicago and Northwestern road.

Although the townsite was jointly owned by the two railroads the town was named after Thomas Fletcher Oakes, the vice president and general manager of the Northern Pacific. Railroads played an important part in the town's early history.

A third railroad reached Oakes when the Minneapolis and Pacific Railroad Company (later the Soo

1,775 North Dakotans live in Oakes

Dahne Kinzler, Marvin Hansen, Karen Tripp & Jon Klein ✳

Line) laid tracks along the townsite's southern edge in 1887.

With their coming Oakes grew rapidly; in the early 1900s daily rail schedules disclosed as many as eight passenger and eight freight trains being routed through town. With settlers arriving by rail from many locations the settlement became a melting pot for many nationalities and religious beliefs.

The Hudson post office which was located across the James River was moved to the townsite and renamed Oakes in December 1886.

The first town lot was sold to the P. S. Peabody General Store which later became the Klein and Sutmar store.

The Bank of Oakes, currently the First National and the *Oakes Republican*, today the *Oakes Times* joined a host of hotels and retail services as Oakes sprang into existence.

The first church was the Presbyterian with the Methodist, Catholic, Lutheran, and others following in rapid succession.

The first formal school was built in 1904. Among the early prominent citizens was Thomas F. Marshall, one of the founders of Oakes's first bank who was later elected United States Congressman in 1900, 1902, 1904, and 1906.

In 1907 a disastrous fire destroyed a large portion of the downtown area. The business community responded by rebuilding with brick and stone. Many of these structures remain in today's business district.

The North American Creamery once had a large plant in Oakes and its owner built the Noonan House. The plant is currently utilized by the Land O Lakes Company and the mansion is known as the House of 29.

When Oakes presented the play *Our Town* by Thornton Wilder, the performance was featured in *Life Magazine*.

Good soil, accessible water, and a strong public spirit have always played an important role in the development of Oakes. Grain production is the area's basis of economy and handling it is achieved with area elevators and three rail lines which still serve the town.

Oakes is noted as the only community in North Dakota still served by three railroads.

The area has actively supported the Garrison Diversion Project. The Oakes component of the project is near completion and is slated to be the first to receive irrigation water. The community celebrates the importance of irrigation with an annual three day event held in June. Irrigation Days features activities for the entire family.

The town's centennial was held in 1986 and detailed information on the first one hundred years is available in a seven-hundred page history.

The House of 29 in Oakes, North Dakota

Main Street Oakes, North Dakota - 1905

Ruins of Oakes after the October 1907 fire

Home Town of 103 North Dakotans

*Oberon

by Eugene Nielsen

In 1883 settlers began arriving in what was known as Antelope Valley, a short distance southwest of Devils Lake. Henry U. Thomas, one of the first settlers, named the area for the many antelope grazing there.

A businessman from Larimore, North Dakota, J. C. Stearns, had collected money from about fifty eager homesteaders to have the valley surveyed. Vernon B. Matthews was a surveyor for the Jamestown and Northern Railroad which was platted through the Oberon townsite. Matthews laid out the townsite and was Oberon's first settler. He and his family lived in a dugout on the east edge of town. From this site he could look out over his town.

The railroad was graded into town by the fall of 1883 and the town was ready for settlers to move into the next spring. Some of the earliest settlers included Edward L. Yager, Walter J. Taylor, William Charles Schaffner, David Wood, the Dan Chance family, and one Dunbar. Abram Baldwin came by stage in June 1884, the same month the townsite was registered. Many of these settlers' descendants still live in Oberon.

For a short time the town was called Antelope Station, then the name was changed to Barkers Station. In January 1886 Matthews was appointed postmaster. He changed the name to Oberon, a name made famous in William Shakespeare's classic *A Midsummer Night's Dream.*

Two of the first businesses established were Harry Rush's blacksmith shop in 1884 and a general store operated by Abram Baldwin and Jacob Fultz in 1884 and 1885. The general store stocked the bare necessities and traded them for buffalo bones which many of the early settlers collected as a source of income; the bones were stacked near the rail site. The first carload of freight shipped from Oberon in the spring of 1885 was a load of buffalo bones.

Both school and church services were held in the railroad depot for the first two years. A school was built in 1886 and was operational during the summer months for a four-month term. A Congregational Church was organized in 1886. This group served and ministered to the community's needs for over twenty-five years, until Calvary Lutheran Church was built.

By 1900 several businesses had started including two general stores, a hardware store, a butcher shop, two livery barns, an implement depot, a lumberyard, a harness and stationery store, two blacksmith shops, two hotels, a millinery, a drug store, a newspaper, two elevators, a barbershop, and a doctor.

The railroad played an important role in Oberon's development. It provided stockyards, an ice house, loading platforms, a huge well to supply the steam locomotives, a section house, and jobs for the railroad crews. Activity boomed in Oberon during the early 1900s. The branch line was extended to Maddock and Esmond in 1904. In 1905 Fort Totten Indian Reservation was opened to settlers. Several settlers came to the area during that time.

Oberon's current school was completed in 1922. Two years later it won the state basketball tournament held in Valley City. From 1910 through 1977, 519 students were graduated from the high school. The school now serves grades one through eight.

Over the years there have been several small fires. In 1925 a major fire destroyed one block on main street including a bank, a drug store, and the Garnaas General Store.

Oberon celebrated its centennial in 1984. The town has paved streets, several sidewalks, a city sewer and water system, two four-unit low-income housing units, and about 100 friendly people.

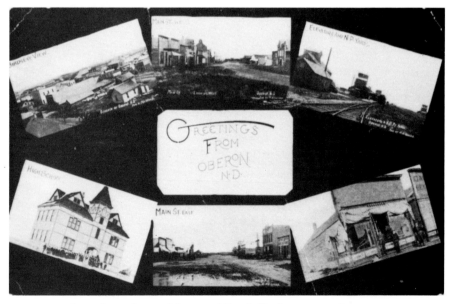

Greetings from Oberon, North Dakota - early 1900s
(SHSND)

Main Street Oberon, North Dakota - 1976
(DPDP - Jerry Anderson)

Main Street Oberon, North Dakota - 1976
(DPDP - Jerry Anderson)

Many people predominantly Scandinavian in origin immigrated to the area because of the Homestead Act. The town owes its beginning to the St. Paul Manitoba Railroad Company (Great Northern) which established a station named Elton at the site in 1887. The name was changed to Palermo during the winter of 1897-1898. It is believed by many that it was named Palermo, for the capital of Sicily, as a tribute to the Italian crews that had worked for the railroad.

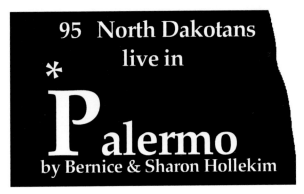

95 North Dakotans live in

* Palermo

by Bernice & Sharon Hollekim

In 1901 John C. Hoff's shanty served as a dwelling and a store. In February of the following year the first post office was opened with Hoff as postmaster and in August of that same year the townsite was platted under his ownership. Two mail routes were established to serve the areas north and south of town. Since then the routes have been consolidated into one contract route.

In 1908 Palermo, then a part of Ward County was officially incorporated as a village. At that time the village had a resident population of 168; by 1930 it reached its peak population of 205.

Hardware stores, drug stores, banks, restaurants, cement factory, lumberyard, harness and shoe shops, elevators, saloons, mercantile stores, and other places of business thrived for many years, but like many other small towns the population and business has dwindled until all that remains is the elevator, post office, and two bars.

The Trinity Lutheran Church was organized in 1903 and the First Lutheran Church was organized in 1904. The first organizational meeting to merge these two churches was held in 1963 and thus the Faith Lutheran Congregation was formed. In 1967 the Trinity Church building was moved and attached to the First Lutheran Church. A new kitchen and an additional dining area was also added to the new Faith Lutheran Church. The 75th Anniversary was celebrated in 1979.

The first school opened in 1902 in a small shanty; in 1903 a wooden building was constructed on the present school site. In 1908 a cement block, two-story building was constructed; it burned in 1934. School was held in the church basements until the present school was completed in 1936. An addition to the brick school in the 1960s added a cafeteria, classrooms, and an office. The yellow schoolhouse which housed the intermediate grades was also built during this time.

The first high school graduation was in 1924 and sadly the final graduation in 1979. Presently junior and senior high school students are transported to the Stanley School with kindergarten through grade six continuing to be taught at Palermo.

The Great Northern Railroad stopped service in 1969 with the depot being moved to the Lostwood area.

In 1977 Palermo held its Diamond Jubilee to celebrate its seventy-five years of existence with many coming from near and far to reminisce and have a good time.

Each summer the community sponsors a school reunion which is looked forward to by many.

A small city park has been established with continued improvements being made, such as tables and benches, picnic shelter, playground equipment and additional trees planted to honor North Dakota's Centennial. The park is a popular picnic area and is used for an annual beef and pork barbecue, which is followed by a street dance.

Main Street Palermo, North Dakota - early 1900s

Sack race at the Annual Beef & Pork Barbecue

Palermo's cement block school constructed in 1908

In 1910, part of the Fort Berthold Reservation became accessible to homesteaders. George Parshall, a Hidatsa Indian, was a member of the survey party. The custom was to apply the name of a survey group member to a probable townsite, in this case the SE1/4 sec. 25, T152N, R90W, and when the Soo Line Railroad came through in 1914 the name Parshall was officially adopted. A monument to Parshall in front of Memorial Hall was dedicated in 1954, the address given by Jefferson B. Smith.

In July 1912 Parshall was described as a "mass of survey stakes on the barren prairie." Main Street was apparently going to be where North Dakota 37 and 1804 now are. Many of these first buildings were clustered about where the Ivol Bartelson farmstead is located.

Platted in October, 1911 the town lot sale was held on November 2, 1914, supervised by a U.S. government official. The first lot was sold to N.O. Sanden for $1,500, or perhaps $1,000.

The village in June 1914 consisted of John Iverson's store, Ed Kjelstrup's bank, Tangedahl's Pool Hall and Restaurant, a barbershop, and a post office.

D.E. Richardson bought the Baker Trading Post southeast of Parshall in

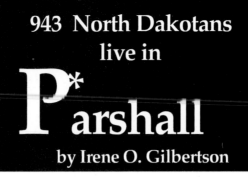

943 North Dakotans live in

P*arshall

by Irene O. Gilbertson

1914 and that fall was the first to move his building onto town lots.

Soo Railroad crews laid rails in the townsite in September 1914. Three depot agents served the community: W.T. Kenady, Hank Lindstrom, and Tom Lynch. The depot is gone and other than hauling grain trains are a thing of the past.

Court Shubert bought the city Dray Line and Feed Barn from William Carmody in 1924, adding an "ice business" the next year. The ice was cut on the Missouri River at Sanish and transported by rail to Parshall where deliveries were made to businesses and homes three times a week until 1936.

David Larin was the "Father of the Parshall Village": first postmaster, first editor, early homesteader. He with E.B. Kjelstrup and Fred Hankins proved to be the "Three Musketeers" of the little town.

Parshall's first primary election was held in June 1914 in John Iverson's store, about a dozen voters turned out. Getting the returns to Stanley proved very difficult because of recent rains. Roads were impassable; it wasn't until Saturday that the official judge hired a horse and buggy to take the votes to the county seat.

Parshall Common School District No.3 was organized on September 7, 1915. In the fall of 1917 it was decided to incorporate as a city, with Scott Hurst elected as the first mayor.

The first 4th of July celebration was held in 1915. The Indians were given beef which they barbecued, and everyone celebrated.

The Reservation Garage built by Ole Njos and George Johnson in 1916 was later sold to Edwin Nelson who had a Chevrolet dealership and repair shop there until in the 1950s. On Nelson's first trip to Elbowoods in the fall of 1916 he met several tractors, each pulling four or five wagons loaded with wheat or flax, coming to the elevators in Parshall, which during the 1940s was designated as "Wheat Center of the World." Millions of bushels of golden grain, excellent for producing wheat flour, have been shipped from the region.

Parshall's first ready-to-wear store, the Parshall Toggery, was opened by M.J. Bohenstingl in 1917. Operating it until 1947, he also served Parshall as assessor, city treasurer, auditor, and school treasurer. Harry Watson opened the first bakery in 1918. In the early 1930s he ran a bread route to Raub, Plaza, and Makoti. During World War I he made a washtub-sized doughnut which was auctioned off in Minot for charity; it brought over $1,000.

The first post office was housed in the Dave Larin house. Since then it has been housed in different buildings: the bank, a part of Ed Nelson's implement shop, and finally in its

Parshall's Governor's Chorus sing to the Legislature - 1962

present location. The first telephone exchange, in a small building east of Yetter's was staffed night and day for forty years. Services are now provided by the Rural Telephone Corporation.

The "Old Swimming Hole" was made during the Great Depression when the Civilian Conservation Corps (CCC) constructed a dam on the creek. Years later a new swimming pool was built south of the elementary school.

The city water system replaced local pumps. Several were favorites, and coffee drinkers took buckets and pails to obtain water at the different backyard wells. A reservoir on North hill replaced the water tower and tank which was dismantled and sold to the city of Ryder. Because problems still existed with the water supply, a new source was acquired by laying a pipeline to Lake Sakakwea in the 1980s.

Charles Wales sold the *Mountrail County Record* to Donald and Chilas Cochrane in June 1964. It's Bicentennial edition was the largest single issue printed in the state. Older generations remember editors "Old Man" Rodgers, Ralph Wales,and his father Charles.

A major attraction in Parshall is the Paul Broste Museum which displays his world-renowned rock collection. It was dedicated July 3, 1966; some 2,500 spectators watched the ceremony.

Hankins Airport, named in honor of Fred Hankins, Jr. a fighter pilot killed in 1944, became a reality in 1946 through the efforts of three local flyers, C.J. Mahowald, Dr. Robert Blatherwick, and Lester Schram. In 1968 the Parshall Municipal Airport Authority was created; many improvements have been made in the past several years.

Today Parshall is a thriving village, many residents are the children of the homesteaders. Various religious groups serve the community: St. Bridget's Catholic, a Lutheran congregation, and two United Churches of Christ. A Senior Citizen organization, the Jet Set, is very energetic and a sixty-bed nursing home, Rockview, benefits the community.

Winter of 1916 in Parshall, North Dakota

An active Legion organization, the Arthur Solie Post No.121, and its Auxiliary sponsor an annual Memorial Day Program. Community youth are served by the Boy and Girl Scouts.

Popular current pastimes in the city include bingo, golf, and organized, competitive ball games which draw enthusiatic crowds. The recent popularity of roping resulted in the construction of several arenas. Even the pre-schoolers have their "go-arounds." Points are accumulated through competitive Barrel-Racing and team-roping events which are held during "slack time" and winter. Prizes, buckles and saddles are awarded to the winners.

The public library is open twice a week. During the summer months it sponsors story hours for the young and book checkouts for the old. The county bookmobile makes scheduled stops in Parshall and serves the school system during the school year.

There are no automobile or implement dealerships in Parshall today. Getting repairs means a trip to Minot, or elsewhere, many are made by farm wives—"Go'fers," who spend hours on the road and who haul anhydrous tanks and are found "manning" or is it "womaning" the grain truck during harvest.

The locker plant closed shop when deep freezers and automatic refrigerators became commonplace. Today it is primarily a custom-meat butchering plant.

Today several businesses thrive in the downtown area: one grocery store, a variety and consignment store, the bank and insurance agency, two drug stores, a bowling alley, three restaurants and a Tastee Freez, a hardware store, a lumberyard, several service stations, carpenters, accountants, a dentist, a satellite medical facility, and the telephone company. That and the Ballistic Cast Company employ the most workers. Two motels care for transient businessmen and occasional travelers who need lodging.

The *Mountrail County Record* continues to publish and the *Minot Daily News*, a daily paper, is distributed in the community.

The elevator complex, a cooperative venture, serves the farmers well. Unit trains and huge semis carry golden grain to terminals. Some years Parshall is the primary wheat center of the Plains, handling over a million bushels of grain.

Parshall has a unique place in the state's history. In 1936, the temperature dropped to -60 degrees F there, the coldest state temperature on record.

Change is inevitable. Early homesteaders didn't foresee the radical changes brought about by farm mechanization, the evolution of the automobile, or the development of modern road systems.

Parshall will celebrate its Centennial in the 21st Century. One wonders what lies ahead for the town?

Home Town of *
642 North Dakotans
Pembina
by Mrs. Hetty Walker

The region surrounding the confluence of the Pembina River and the Red River of the North can be considered North Dakota's oldest area of relatively continuous settlement. Pembina's origins can be traced to competition in the fur trade which developed in the region in the 1780s. As early as 1782 traders of the North West Company operated out of Pembina and in the fall of 1797 Charles Jean Baptiste Chaboillez constructed a post on the riverbanks of the Red River of the North where Pembina now stands; Hudson's Bay Company was also erecting a post in the vicinity. Four years later Alexander Henry, a wintering partner in the North West Company, erected a permanent establishment there.

The town's history is also linked to a Scottish nobleman, Thomas Douglas, the fifth Earl of Selkirk, who thought emigration could solve the difficulties of the Scottish and Irish peasants. In 1812 he founded a colony of Scots and Irish where present day Winnipeg, Canada is located. The colonists, however, lacked provisions and many went to Pembina where they built cabins, a storehouse, and a stockade which they named Fort Daer, after

Selkirk who was also Lord Daer. The fort was built on the south side of the Pembina River, on Chaboillez's former post. Saved by herds of buffalo which were plentiful in the immediate area the colonists wintered there for several years. The original settlers, however, were of French heritage, coming from Quebec, Montreal, and Three Rivers.

It is generally accepted that the town's name derived from the Chippewa Indians who called the area *Anepeminan sipi*, a reference to the highbush cranberries that grow along the rivers. Its proper spelling, however, was a matter of debate for years. Spelled *Pabana or Panbian* the Selkirkers arrived at the current spelling *Pembina* in 1814.

The first marriages in the community were performed by Miles Macdonnell, the man Lord Selkirk had made governor of the settlement.

Pembina's growth was stimulated by the appearance in 1818 of Father Severe Dumoulin who built a chapel, a presbytery, and a store and eventually would baptize 313 persons and perform 53 marriages.

The Metis, a person one of whose parents was French and the other North American Indian, conducted summer and fall buffalo hunts, for provisions and buffalo robes, from Pembina for many years. The size of the hunt increased through the years from 540 Red River carts in 1820 to 820 in 1830 and to 1,210 in 1840, the last great hunt, when some 1,300

buffalo were killed in the vicinity of the Cheyenne River.

Many of the early settlers came through Canada and were of Icelandic, French Swiss, Norwegian, Scottish, or English extraction. After the coming of the railroad in 1887 the town became a melting pot for many different nationalities: Native American Indians, Metis, Norwegians, Swedes, Swiss, Icelanders, English, Russian, German, French, Scots, and others.

All early buildings in Pembina were constructed of logs including the first post office which was established in 1850; one account indicates it was established in 1849. In the late 1800s the town boasted of Fort Pembina, just south of the town, a brick factory, Drewry's brewery, and gas lights.

The town suffered from a major fire in the 1890s when the main business block was nearly totally destroyed. In the 1960s Pembina's fireman held their annual ball in the city hall and the affair received national press coverage when the *Miami Herald* headlined: "Hot Time in the Old Town Tonight! Pembina, N.D. firemen, burn down their fire hall."

Today, the town boasts of an airport, a bus manufacturing plant, several fraternal organizations, and an American Legion Post. A border town, Pembina's economy is based primarily on government services and farming.

The town's "big day" is the annual Fourth of July celebration when everyone turns out.

Downtown Pembina, North Dakota - 1900

July 4th Parade in Pembina, North Dakota - 1890

The Jonesvilles, Smithtowns, Greenfields and all the other -villes, -towns, and -fields of America are essentially alike. No two American habitations are identical, but all of them, big or little, bear the strong family resemblance of the same parentage. The lives of the ten thousand citizens of Jonesville express the basic values of 180,000,000 Americans.

W. Lloyd Warner
Democracy in Jonesville, 1949

This settlement was one of several which came into existence as a result of the construction of the St. John branch line by the St. Paul, Minneapolis & Manitoba Railroad (Great Northern). A station named Perth was established in late 1888 on land owned by Robert J. Laird, a retired Methodist minister. He is connected with the origin of the town's name, but precisely how remains unresolved. The Perth post office was established in his home and he was appointed postmaster in July 1889; mail was hauled by team from Churchs Ferry

22 North Dakotans live in

Perth

by Shirley Jones
& Maxine Hanson

by John Jeanotte, a Frenchman. Laird platted the original four-block townsite in November 1897. Incorporated as a village in August 1905 it became a city in July 1967.

President Johnson and I have a lot in common. We were both born in small towns . . . and we're both fortunate in the fact that we think we married above ourselves.

**Richard M. Nixon
September 5, 1969**

Three buildings had been constructed in the town by the spring of 1897: the Laird home, the railroad section house, and Sam Beggs's blacksmith shop.

Later that year John Nelson built a home. He was manager of the grain elevator which also had been constructed in that year. In the following two years Emory Fitz established a machine business and A. J. Heal opened a lumberyard and general store. By 1898 Perth boasted of eight businesses, the families living in quarters connected to their store.

Before the town had a school, Laird's wife taught classes in their home. Later, a teacher was hired and the classes were moved to the section house. Perth's first school was constructed sometime prior to 1904. In that year a new facility was constructed; it served the community until 1971 when the school was closed and the building torn down. Early teachers were: Miss Springer, Miss Wankle, Miss Cowan, and Neal Williams. Elsie Strandness, Ethel Scobba, and Helen Strand taught in the Perth school in later years.

At one time there were three churches in Perth. The Presbyterians were the first to build. Today, the Lutheran church serves the community; many local events are held in its parish hall.

Perth has undergone many changes in the last ninety years. At one time banks, hotels, cafes, and newspapers flourished. The *Perth Journal* and the *Perth Gazette* have long since ceased publication. Today, the Perth Farmers Cooperative Association is the only business place left. The pride of Perth, it was built in 1976 and stands shiny and new looking.

Few people live in Perth today. One block off main street the home of Bill and Maxine Hanson houses the post office. Maxine is the postmistress; Bill, a retired elevator employee, is the mayor. The Jones family makes up over one-third of the town's population. Bill is general manager of the elevator; Shirley is the elevator's bookkeeper and also serves as the town auditor; and Delane and Sarah are students. The Boe family, Dan, Jocolyn, and little Matthew, farm; and Stan and Barb Bukowiec teach in the Belcourt school system.

When the school had a basketball team, it was called the "Perth Pirates." Today, twenty-two people make up the town's treasure.

July 4th Celebration in Perth, North Dakota - late 1890s

The first automobile in Perth - early 1900s

Sending off the boys to World War I

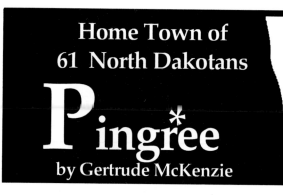
Pingree is located on the Devils Lake Branch of the Northern Pacific Railroad line, now known as the Burlington Northern. It was built through Pingree to Melville in 1881-82 and was completed to Leeds in 1889. The townsite was platted and recorded, September 18, 1882. It was incorporated as a village in 1917 and divided into three wards.

The town was named for Hazen Pingree who came to the area in 1880 to establish a potato plantation and become wealthy. The venture failed and he returned to Detroit, Michigan where he became a successful shoe manufacturer. He entered politics, was elected mayor of the city and eventually served as Governor of Michigan from 1897 to 1900.

It was after these achievements that the people chose to name the town after him. Another version of the naming of the town suggests that it was named by John Alden for David Pingree who was an early landowner in the area.

Some of the people who were influential in building the early town were Jim and Tom Price, G. M. Smith, Mary Buchanan Bartholomew, Augusta Plowe Conant, Fred Wanner, John A. Alden, and Clifford Waters.

At the height of its growth the town had three grocery stores, two banks, a drug store, two lumberyards, three grain elevators, two hotels, a weekly paper, and other shops and services.

Three churches were built. In the 1960s the Catholics and Lutherans built new structures and the Congregational congregation remodeled its facility extensively. Active from the beginning the denominations continue to serve the community.

In 1906 a modern brick school building was erected to replace a small wooden structure. In 1963 that building was replaced by a "new, modern" building.

Cultural life in the community was enriched by the organization of debate, literary, and community clubs, followed in later years by Homemakers, 4-H, and other social clubs. At present there is a Senior Citizens Club which meets in its own center.

Dances, basket socials, card parties, and travelling shows provided entertainment for early settlers. Baseball was also popular. Water sports, picnics, and roller skating drew people to Jim, Arrowood, and Spiritwood lakes.

In 1907 and again in 1911 disastrous fires destroyed most of the buildings on main street. Some of these were not rebuilt, but eventually other businesses were started and the town continued to grow and became a lively and bustling trading center.

Many trees were planted by the early residents to beautify the town.

Pingree business establishments began to suffer with the coming of the automobile, the development of commercial trucking firms, and the improvement of the state's road system, especially US 52. Larger trade centers were now easily accessible. With the coming of school buses the last store closed.

A Memorial Park was established in 1957 through the efforts of the Pingree Womans Literary Club and the support of the community. A plaque listing the names of area service men can be found there. In 1980 a replica of the town's original bandstand was built. Trees, flowers, playground equipment, and a tennis court make it an attractive addition to the community.

Today, Pingree boasts of a community cafe, an upholstery shop, a garage, welding shop, and a paint and body shop. The local Heritage Association purchased the old railroad depot, moved it to main street, and converted it into a museum.

A strong moral fiber brought by the early English, Norwegian, Irish, German, and Swedish settlers remains, making Pingree a good community in which to live.

Bird's-eye view of Pingree, North Dakota - 1912
(SHSND)

County Agent's office & the Pingree Patriot office - 1912
(SHSND)

Early day general store in Pingree - late 1890s
(SHSND)

The community "Portland On the Goose" owes its beginnings to a power struggle between two railroads: James J. Hill's St. Paul, Minneapolis and Manitoba and the Northern Pacific, a transcontinental line forging westward from Lake Superior to Puget Sound. Both roads were interested in the lucrative traffic in this part of the Red River Valley and began to build branch lines into the area to ensure their control. The race was on! Hill, the "Empire Builder," operated two lines in the valley, one on the Minnesota side and one on the North Da-

602 North Dakotans live in

Portland*

by Philip M. Paulson

kota side. In an effort to cut off the Northern Pacific's Casselton Branch, being built north to Mayville, he and fellow stockholders decided to build a third line, the Breckenridge extension, northwest past Casselton and then north toward Mayville. Northern Pacific tracklayers reached Mayville in the summer of 1881; Hill's

tracklayers reached Portland in late 1881. The following spring the line was opened to traffic. The two sites, Mayville and Portland were only two miles apart.

The townsite was plotted in November 1881 by George W. Parke, an employee of the Manitoba line. He laid out main street on the section line, made it eighty feet wide, and named it Parke Avenue, after himself. John Amb, a local man, surveyed other additions.

The two railroad companies soon found it to their advantage to avoid competition. In 1882 they divided North Dakota between them; the Manitoba acquired the Northern Pacific's Casselton-Mayville branch and sold it its line from Sauk Centre to St. Paul. Following this trade the Portland line was extended north. An 1885 time table indicates a schedule for a train running from Breckenridge through Portland and on north to Park River, with another branch from Ripon to Hope, all known as the "Portland Line." Today, several miles of track to the south have been removed. A train from the north serves both Portland and Mayville.

On July 4, 1871 Alvin C. Arnold with his wife and three daughters "arrived" and unloaded their covered wagon on the banks of the Goose River. The family, with two daughters, had left Indiana in 1868, traveling by covered wagon to Yankton, Dakota Territory where they remained three years. They learned of the rich lands to the north and with other members of the wagon train settled along the river. The Arnolds settled "furthest up river."

They were followed by many other parties from Yankton, and many from the east. Mostly of Scandinavian origin, either first or second generation, the early settlers established several Norwegian Lutheran churches. When the townsite was platted two congregations moved their houses of worship into town. Both, the Aurdal and Bruflat, congregations have continued to grow. Other denominations followed.

Legend has it that the first business in the new town was a saloon in a "cook car"; however, another story suggests that the first businessman was E. E. Neste who moved his stock of groceries in from Blanchard. Another early entrepreneur was Colonel W. H. Robinson who opened a lumberyard, the first of a chain of some twelve yards in other towns.

Portland's first newspaper, the *Inter-Ocean*, published its first edition on January 27, 1882. Shortly thereafter

Panoramic view of Portland, North Dakota - early 1900s

two attorneys and two physicians set up practice, a wholesale grocer opened a store, and a harness shop and a livery barn began serving the public. Several hotels were erected over the years. With Mayville just two miles away competition was keen.

The first major fire in town destroyed Neste's store and a saloon. The former was promptly rebuilt in a better location. On September 3, 1883 fire was discovered in the G. C. Koerner Meat Market and "owing to the proximity of the building occupied by the Post Office and the Jas. Power Harness Shop, they were blazing too." A large store was destroyed in 1908 and two years later a grocery store, a furniture business, and a jewelry shop were burned. These buildings were replaced with fire-resistant material. The farmer-owned elevator has been destroyed twice, in 1915 and again in 1950. It has been replaced with a concrete and steel structure.

On January 1, 1916, while preparations were being made for a big wedding, the Bruflat Church went up in flames. It was replaced by a Gothic structure with large stained glass windows. The Aurdal Church has

The Bruflat Academy and Business Institute closed in 1918. The buildings were sold to the Portland Special School District in 1920.

also erected a new, modern building. The only other church operating in the city is the Valley Free Lutheran Church.

Portland has produced several men who have risen to excellence in their chosen professions. The most recent is Gilman Rud, commander of the "Blue Angels," the United States Navy's flying exhibition team.

The community supports several cooperative enterprises. Today, the Farmers Elevator handles more grain each year than six elevators handled in previous years; it also operates a bean facility. Land O Lakes manages a fertilizer blending installation, Cenex runs a bulk and retail gasoline plant, and the town is served by a cooperative credit union. The town also supports a bank which just celebrated its hundredth anniversary in 1986, a large grocery store, a cafe, and an independent service station which also does repair work. One of the town's railroad depots has been moved to a new location and is now a bakery and lunch room.

For many years the local business association has sponsored an annual "Appreciation Picnic" for the surrounding community. It is held in the beautiful park in a bend of the river on the edge of town.

A modern water system and good water have helped the town's development. Two new additions have been platted recently and many new homes have been constructed. Portland and Mayville school districts have merged; educational instruction is offered in both locations.

Former Opera House - now the American Legion Post No. 93

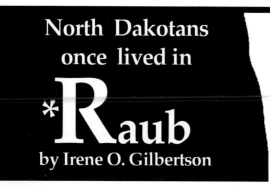
This now-deserted village traces its beginnings back to October 1912 when the post office of Raub, named for homesteader Jacob Raub, was established on his homestead in Sec. 23, T149N, R89W. Nellie Taylor Raub was named postmaster. In 1915 the office was moved to Sec. 8, T149N, R89W when Edythe L. Blonde was appointed postmaster and where A. P. Blonde ran a country store. When T. C. Veum opened a store, confectionery, and telephone exchange and he became postmaster in 1916 the facility was moved to his land. Veum was also a townsite promoter and later Raub developed on his land. The office was operated until the late 1970s when the last postmaster, Ethel Ludwig, resigned and retired to Ryder to live.

Area residents who chose to continue the Raub address, with the Ryder zip code, are served by a star route from Ryder. Other patrons use Parshall as an address.

Raub, although an inland town, prospered for several years. There were two grocery stores, a cafe and pool hall, a bank, a combination dry goods, grocery, and meat market, an implement shop, one or two blacksmith shops, a hardware store with the first gas pumps in front, a garage, a rural school perched on the hill overlooking the town, a community hall, the first of three, and three churches, Methodist, Catholic, and Lutheran.

Several dwellings were scattered hither and yon on either side of the unpaved road which served as Main Street. Forty or fifty residents called Raub home. The earliest settlers were the Nels Larsons, George Ranums, E. C. Dotens, Slatmans, Kothes, Marie Ludwig, J. S. Rapps, and the Schulers. All were business people. They were followed by George and Earl Liebel, Swede Larson, the Fred Propps, the Wilke brothers, "Doc" Wiowodes, John Sholz, DeHavens, Wutzkes, Charles Deardurffs, Kvales, Overlies, Hector Billadeau, and the Frank Dorans. The last businesses in town were the Steak House with Georgie Tomhave as chef, the beer parlor operated by the Engens, and the grocery store owned by Earl Liebel.

Today the town stands deserted. Most of the buildings have been demolished, but one elderly couple still remain in their house. Two other residences are vacant, testifying to a life that once was.

The Great Northern Railroad had contemplated building a track from New Rockford, North Dakota to Great Falls, Montana. Anticipating the coming of the railroad, a townsite, Huberton, had been platted by the federal government a mile west of the present site of Raub. The railroad surveyed a line through the area, but did not build. World War I brought a halt to the project and the Soo Line from Drake to Sanish became the route for the freight that supplied Raub. A schoolhouse was the only structure that was erected there.

Raub School District No. 74 was created in 1914 but that same year the name was changed to Loquemont School District No. 74. When the Raub schoolhouse was built the existing school was moved three miles west where it was used until reorganization with the Parshall District.

Loquemont township was organized in 1919 and was originally named Pershing Civil Township, after General John J. Pershing who commanded the American Expeditionary Force in Europe during World War I. Loquemont is a play on the French *L'eau-qui-Mont* meaning "the water that rises." A creek wound its crooked path just north of the town, through the township, and westward several miles to empty its waters into the Missouri River. Today the creek, known as Deepwater Creek, flows into Lake Sakakawea on the western edge of the township.

The town declined because motored vehicles replaced the horse and buggy and the team and wagon. "Country stores" gave way to sophisticated markets, buses took students to reorganized schools miles away, the advent of rural free delivery changed the system of mail delivery, and the Rural Electrification Cooperatives and Rural Telephone Cooperatives brought conveniences not dreamed of in the days of kerosene lamps and the crank telephone.

These luxuries spelled the end for "community togetherness" and many community activities: "home talent" plays, rural school programs and play-days, 4-H and Homemakers Clubs, Farmers Union organizations, and neighborhood visiting.

Today, the Memorial Hall stands at the end of what was once Main Street. It is used for township meetings, elections, and an occasional community "potluck" supper. Young couples in the area are trying to revive the dying community spirit by scheduling various group activities, basketball for the men, volleyball for the women, and roller-skating for the children.

If you are driving westward from Roseglen, another derelict town, on North Dakota 37 and 1804, take a quick glance before you cross the bridge over Deepwater Creek, and envision the metropolis of Raub as it once was!

The deserted town of Raub, North Dakota

**And in that town a dog was found,
As many dogs there be,
Both mongrel, puppy, whelp, and hound,
And curs of low degree.**

Oliver Goldsmith
Elegy on the Death of a Mad Dog

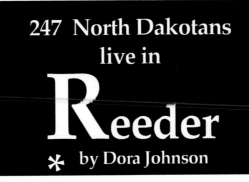

Reeder

In the late 1800s the area which is now the Reeder community was occupied by large cattle barons from the south. After the turn of the century when it was revealed that the Chicago, Milwaukee and St. Paul Railroad would establish a station in the area an enterprising rancher by the name of Albert Leff established a town on his ranch, located several miles east of the present site of Reeder. He built a hotel and restaurant, a livery barn, and established a stage line connecting his town with Dickinson. William Krebsbach erected the First State Bank, and Steel and Muzzy opened a general store. A post office named Leff was also established in November 1907 with Henry W. O'Dell as postmaster.

In 1907 the Milwaukee Railroad bought land from Herman and Mary Hilden for a townsite. Early the next year the station of Reeder was established a short distance from Leff's town and the Leff post office was moved to Railroad Avenue in the new townsite. Its name was changed to Reeder. The new townsite was also platted in 1908. The day the first town lots were sold, May 14, 1908, is considered Reeder's birthday. The event was widely advertised by the railroad. Special train services were scheduled and entertainment, including sports activities, band music, bronco riding, and steer roping, was provided. Even the robbery of an over-land stage coach was re-enacted. That day 149 lots were sold for $30,300. The town was named Reeder for E. O. Reeder an engineer with the railroad.

By the fall of 1908 the population had increased to nearly 300 and three years later it had reached 400.

A surprising number of businesses were in operation in the new prairie town in 1908: three general stores, three banks, three real estate offices, two hardware stores, two implement dealers, four lumberyards, two pool halls, five hotels and restaurants, a drug store, a dentist, a meat market, a blacksmith shop, two livery stables, a barbershop, a photograph gallery, a sign painter, and a stage line that made regular trips to Dickinson.

In July 1908, William Krebsbach who had just completed the new First State Bank building on Main Street had gone to Dickinson and was returning with $10,000 in currency needed to open his new bank. He was sharing the driver's seat, carrying his money in a suitcase under his feet. Unfortunately, the driver had imbibed too freely before leaving Dickinson and so was a bit carefree with his team of four half-broke broncos. Traveling around a curve at a high rate of speed a front wheel dropped into a buffalo wallow, throwing Krebsbach and the driver to the ground. The broncos stampeded across the prairies. Krebsbach had visions of his money scattered over a township, but the suitcase was recovered intact and the bank opened on schedule the next morning.

Medical doctors practiced in Reeder prior to 1910, but Dr. J. L. Dach served as Reeder's resident doctor for the longest period, from July 1910 until the late 1930s.

A grand and glorious Labor Day Celebration was held on September 7, 1908. Shortly after the lot sale in May an energetic group of musically inclined men organized the Reeder Brass Band under the direction of J.L. Hjort. They felt they would be ready for a public performance by Labor Day. Aided by Reeder's businessmen the occasion was turned into a grand holiday. It began at 10:00 A.M. with a market day; horses, cows, household goods, lumber, and farm machinery were auctioned off. The sales netted a little more than $624. In a baseball game in the afternoon Reeder defeated Wolf Butte by a score of 6 to 3. In the evening an audience of over 400 nearly filled the large auditorium to hear the band's concert. It was very successful, netting the band $125.

Caught up in the national sport a meeting was held on April 6, 1908 to organize a local baseball team. The first game along the newly established rail line was played at Gascoyne, some seven miles away. The stage was used to transport the team and fans. Reeder won, 14 to 11.

Reeder was renowned for its large number of highly talented musicians. J. L. Hjort, a man of rare musical ability, directed the community's musical activities. For health reasons he had been advised to go "west," to take life easy among the frontier people. Before leaving Minneapolis he declared that he would bring oratorios to the prairies of North Dakota, and he did.

In January 1911 the Reeder Choral Society was organized. In less than three months of weekly rehearsals, the choir of about seventy voices had mastered Stainer's *Crucifixion* which was presented to the public on April 2, 1911. Major portions of *The Messiah* were presented in 1912; the choir was assisted by soloists from larger cities. For this performance special train fares were offered by the Milwaukee Railroad. After Hjort and his wife went into semi-retirement in Minneapolis the Choral Society disbanded for lack of a director.

The first pioneers faced many hardships: prairie fires once started often spread until they reached the North or South Grand Rivers; winter blizzards often proved disastrous; trying to ford the North and South Grand Rivers when they were swollen from recent rains forced pioneers coming south from Dickinson with wagons filled with supplies to choose between waiting until the waters receded or taking a chance on making it through the high water without their wagons being overturned and the contents washed down the river. Several deaths in the area resulted from cave-ins or breaking into a gas formation while settlers were digging wells for water. Other fatal accidents were associated with horses as most farmers used horses for their work as well as their mode of transportation.

Many homesteaders were deeply concerned about their religious life. Our Saviors Lutheran Congregation organized on May 10, 1908 with sixteen families as charter members. Its first official documents were written in Norwegian. Services in both English and Norwegian were conducted on alternating Sundays. On June 28, 1908 the First Congregational Church of Reeder organized with twenty-one members. They built the first church building in Reeder. In October 1912 the foundation was laid for the Sacred Heart Catholic Church. On January 10, 1911 a group of German Lutherans organized the Zion Evangelical Lutheran Congregation. There were eleven charter members. Services were conducted in German until the 1920s. Pastor Eggers, the first residential pastor, also served congregations in Desart, Bierman, and Marmarth, North Dakota, rural Baker, Montana, and Bratsberg, South Dakota.

Reeder's first regular school term, six months, began on September 8, 1908 with thirty-one pupils being taught by Mabel Howard in facilities on the second floor of the N. W. Steel Mercantile Store. In June 1909 a new building was planned and the low bid for the four-room two-story frame building was $3,520. L. O. McAfee

became Reeder's first high school superintendent in 1912 and under his supervision five young ladies were graduated in 1916.

A more spacious and modern brick building was built in 1923 at a cost of about $50,000. Since then two wings have been added to the main building, one in 1962 costing $142,000 and the other in 1973 at a cost of $77,000. These additions provided a new gym-auditorium, vocational facilities, more classrooms, and a modern kitchen and dining room.

In 1980 Clarence Tweet, a 1917 graduate, presented his personal library to the school. It consisted of about 3,000 volumes as well as many framed pictures of value.

Activities connected with the school throughout the years include: basketball, organized in 1913, baseball in 1917, football in the 1920s, track, debate, speech, orchestra, Glee Clubs, softball, band, and more. Reeder students have made impressive records in these activities. Their awards in basketball and music have been outstanding. Through the years they have placed first eleven times in the district basketball tournaments and have gone to the state tournament five times. Their recent accomplishments in music have been equally impressive.

Postal service began in 1907. Before that time mail was brought by anyone coming from Dickinson or New England. Mail was brought into the community by train for fifty years. Today it is hauled by vans.

The same community spirit that gave Reeder such an excellent start in its formative years continues today. In the early years the Woodmen of America and the Royal Neighbors contributed much to the

First State Bank - 1908

community's social life. They no longer exist. Soon after the town was established the Reeder Fire Brigade was organized. In 1976 a new Fire District was formed.

Music has always been important to the community. For many years the City Band performed faithfully every Saturday night during the summer. During the Depression many families left the community and it was forced to disband. About 1960, under the leadership of Pastor Richard Beckman, a new high school band was organized and continues to be part of the school's curriculum today.

Other organizations which have come into being through the years include: the American Legion and its Auxiliary, The Reeder High School Alumni Association, Homemakers Clubs and 4-H Clubs, Boys and Girls Scouts, Lions Club, Prairie Pioneers, and Sons of Norway.

Reeder is struggling to survive. Businesses still operating today include: one grocery store, two bars, one cafe, two oil companies, a branch of the Hettinger First National Bank, the post office, one beauty shop, one blacksmith shop, and two elevators. The town also supports a Senior Citizens Club and three churches.

Today's leaders are hopeful that ways can be found to preserve the community so that Reeder will continue to be a fine place to raise children and provide a high quality of life for all its citizens.

Main Street Reeder, North Dakota - 1990s

R*egan

by Dawn Storer

The city of Regan was named for J. Austin Regan, a Fessenden businessman who was also an official of the Dakota Land and Townsite Company which platted the town on Sec. 35 of Estherville Township in 1910.

In common with most small towns in this area, Regan owes its beginnings to the coming of the railroad. The last steel on the Northern Pacific Pingree-Wilton line through Regan was laid in November 1911 and coal trains from the Washburn Lignite Coal Company mines at Wilton began runs the next month.

The United States government anticipated the establishment of the town by appointing Miss Lillian Ong as postmaster on October 5, 1911, but it was the next summer before the post office opened.

The first building was Tolchinsky's cream station, quartered in a small shack. An ice house was next to go up, with hopes for a creamery to which farmers could sell their milk. This dream never materialized. Then came the Congregational Church which was dedicated in the summer of 1911.

The town sprang up in the summer of 1912 with a dozen buildings under construction at the same time. By December 1912 the following buildings had been completed and were occupied: two general stores, a hotel, a butcher shop, a land office, a drug store, two banks, a livery and feed stable, a blacksmith shop, a pool room, a lumberyard, two elevators, and a dozen residences.

The next year, 1913, Dr. Phillip Reedy, the town's first and only physician arrived; the maiden issue of the first newspaper, the *Regan Headlight* was published; and the settlement's first big Fourth of July celebration was held.

No population figures are available for the first few years of the town's history, but old-timers said that nearly 300 people lived in Regan before World War I. Census figures show a steady decline: 1920—202 residents; 1930—168; 1940—149; 1950—104; 1970—74; 1980—71.

Hard times came and the closing of business and departure of residents had an effect on Regan. Yet there were bright spots in the gloom. The establishment of the Regan High School in the mid-thirties provided a focal point of activity. The construction of the gymnasium in 1937, with Works Progress Administration funds and labor, gave a place for community gatherings and today remains the focal point for community activities.

Today there is only a grade school. The town has shrunk to a few citizens. The small community, however, still has an important part to play. The grain elevator serves area farmers as does the general store, post office, filling station, and saloon. Regan also has one church. There is still a strong sense of community as was evident when Regan celebrated its 75th year in 1987 with an "old fashioned" Fourth of July Celebration. Several thousand people turned out to celebrate with the citizens of Regan.

Bird's-eye view of Regan, North Dakota - 1973

Bird's-eye view of Regan, North Dakota - 1912

Regan State Bank in 1920

Rhame, in its picturesque setting at the foot of scoria hills, is located in southwestern North Dakota. It is set about 20 miles from the state borders of both South Dakota and Montana.

When the Chicago, Milwaukee & St. Paul Railroad extended this section of its line in early 1908 a station with a depot, simply a derailed box car, was established about a half mile west of the present site of Rhame. It was called Petral. Shortly thereafter Allen G. Elliot was named postmaster of the newly established Petral post office. Some months later railroad officials decided to locate the new town a short distance to the east; the depot, which became Rhame's first building, and several business places along with seven or eight frame shacks were moved. The Petral post office was renamed Rhame and also moved to the new location.

The new town was named for Mitchell Davison Rhame. Born in Long Island, New York he moved to Minnesota in 1872, became a professor of civil engineering at its University, and was employed later by the railroad. Highly respected and well-liked he was the road's chief civil engineer when the town was established.

The first station agent in Rhame was R. W. Cornell. After the railroad built them a house his wife joined him; she was the only woman living in town for two months.

Various businesses were established in quick order: livery barns, blacksmith shops, elevators, hide, fur, and cream buying stations, lumberyards, grocery stores, department and hardware stores.

The *Rhame Review* published its first issue in April 1908; two banks, Farmers State Bank and First State Bank, were founded in June 1908; and by the late 1920s Rhame boasted of 38 business establishments and other services. Pool rooms, barbershops, drug stores, restaurants, hotels, a telephone office, a hospital, a mortuary, a movie theater, a meat market, and an I.O.O.F. Hall, all at one time or another could be found in Rhame. Today, there are only ten business places left in town.

In the early days homesteaders came from the surrounding region to pick up their mail at Post Office Butte, the highest point on the Milwaukee road. The mail was placed under rock ledges after having been brought by stage from Dickinson.

School was first held in a rented shack one mile west of Petral; it closed when the townsite was moved. The first school in Rhame was built in 1908. It burned down four years later and a modern brick building was constructed; it is still in use. An auditorium and a gymnasium were added to the school plant in 1939 and 1940 under a Works Progress Administration (WPA) project. A new elementary school was built in the 1960s. The 1908 brick structure was completely renovated in 1985. In 1961 local school districts were reorganized and consolidated.

The city of Rhame, North Dakota in 1908
(SHSND)

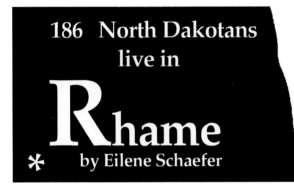

186 North Dakotans live in

Rhame
* by Eilene Schaefer

Early homesteaders were mostly of German, Norwegian, and Swedish stock. Church played a vital part in their lives, but money was scarce; consequently, services were held in homes and later in schools until they could afford to build churches. The Lutheran church was built in 1913; a parsonage was also constructed in 1913. The Roman Catholic church was constructed in 1914 and the Assembly of God erected a facility in 1937. All have been remodeled through the years to accommodate larger congregations.

Rhame is a modern little community. Telephones were installed in 1911; a water system was constructed in 1917; electricity was introduced in 1929; natural gas was made available in 1930; a sewer system was added in the 1960s; and the streets were paved in 1983.

In 1958 Rhame held its first annual Gala Day Celebration, an occasion when many former residents return to renew old friendships. In 1976 the town helped celebrate the nation's Bicentennial; two all-school reunions have been held, in 1976 and in 1983.

Although Rhame has fewer business places and fewer residents today, young people are committed to the area, building homes and operating businesses. It is a good place for the elderly to retire.

Rhame's motto has always been: "Rhame The Friendly City."

A view of Rhame, North Dakota
(SHSND)

Bird's-eye view of Rhame, North Dakota
(DPDP - Bruce Severy)

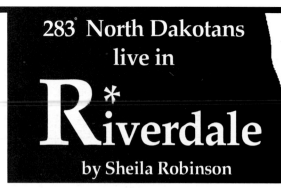

283 North Dakotans live in R*iverdale

by Sheila Robinson

Riverdale became North Dakota's newest incorporated city on July 26, 1986 when the Army Corps of Engineers transferred title to the site to new mayor Bill Lawson. A city council had been elected in September 1985. The city is located on the east end of Garrison Dam overlooking Lake Sakakawea. The name was selected by the Corps from entries submitted in a state-wide contest run by weekly newspapers. Mrs. T. O. Lervik of Granville won the contest.

The federal government established the townsite in 1946 to facilitate the construction of the Garrison Dam; it was laid out in a fan-shaped plan. Contracts were let by the government that year for the construction of a railroad, now removed, and an access highway, now North Dakota 200. The first fifty-two houses were constructed in 1947 to house officers and personnel needed for constructing the dam. Additional housing was built later for construction workers and concessionaires.

By 1948 the town consisted of dusty streets, warehouses, barracks and mess hall, a three-wing hotel, a brick administration building, a school, and many shops. Equipment worked everywhere. A diesel electrical generating plant and a central heating plant for most of the town were soon erected.

Housing facilities mushroomed; five trailer courts were laid out and many company houses were built. The boom town grew rapidly. In 1954-1955 the population peaked at around 5,000. There were nearly 1,100 students in school; four first grade classes were being taught and the community supported eleven Girl Scout troops.

Most of the inhabitants were community minded people. In spite of uncertainty of their stay they supported a great variety of organizations. The American Legion Post organized in January 1948 is still operating. The Women's Club which was organized at Fort Lincoln in Bismarck where many of the engineers lived is still functioning. When housing became available in Riverdale club members moved, bringing their library with them. The collection is now part of the McLean-Mercer County Bookmobile Library.

An active Sportsmen's Club ran a trap shoot, ski tow, and archery range. They built two fish rearing ponds below the dam, now a part of the Federal Fish Hatchery. The old golf course, north of the town, is still used, although two holes on a peninsula recently fell into the lake.

Business places included: a hospital with two doctors; a dentist, a clothing store, a hardware store, a drug store and cafe which later became a sports shop and then the library, a radio repair shop, a barbershop, a Red Owl grocery store, and a souvenir concession. A one thousand-seat theater showed cartoons and newsreels before the main film.

The school was administered for two years by the Corps of Engineers. Then the Riverdale Special School District No. 89 was organized during the 1950-1951 school year and the school was administered by an elected school board, under state supervision. Enrollments fluctuated as various parts of the dam were completed and construction workers left.

The first church services were held in a trailer court utility building; soon a church building was erected. Where else but in a government town would members of the Catholic, Lutheran, Community, and occasionally Episcopalian fellowships utilize the building without conflict? The church was the busiest building in town: church services, meetings and dinners, women's groups activities, Scout meetings, and weddings. There were, however, very few funerals held in the church.

The exodus from Riverdale began about 1956 when construction on the dam was completed and electricity was being generated. As buildings became empty they were torn down or moved out of town. The Air Force recreation area with twenty-eight units was used extensively until it was closed in 1985.

Some years ago Congress approved legislation to sell the three construction towns which had been established to facilitate harnessing the Missouri River, Fort Peck in Mon-

Residential area of Riverdale, North Dakota - 1988

tana, Pickstown in South Dakota, and Riverdale in North Dakota. In Riverdale the Corps of Engineers kept only the Administration building. Their old shops are available for light industry. All homes were either sold to the occupants at the time of the sale or put up for bids.

Over the past few years the town's appearance has changed: buildings have been remodeled, what color to paint your house is now an individual's choice, new homes have been constructed, lots have been sold, overnight rooms are now available in apartments near the school, and a mobile home park is being developed.

Business places today include: the post office, beauty shop, Credit Union and a bank, a restaurant with a bowling alley, Dairy Queen, a gas station which also sells groceries, craft store, a marine supply and repair shop, and medical doctor service twice a week.

The city is now looking forward to new residents and businesses connected to Tourism. The locale is a prime recreational and fishing spot.

Trailer camp in Riverdale, North Dakota - 1953

Chinook salmon abound in Lake Sakakawea along with walleye, northern, sauger, trout, and other game fish. Fishing derbies and tournaments are held each year. The Federal Campgrounds are located below the dam and Lake Sakakawea State Park across the lake provides camping pads, a marina, and concessions.

Riverdale will now appear, for the first time, on the census rolls of the state's towns. The newborn town is well on its way to becoming a tourist Mecca.

Aerial view of Riverdale, North Dakota in 1955

R*ugby

compiled by Dale G. Niewoehner

Home Town of 2,909 North Dakotans

Rugby Junction came into existence in 1886 when the St. Paul, Minneapolis and Manitoba Railroad established the station on its new line west of Devils Lake. The present townsite was platted and opened for sale in July 1889 by the Northwest Land Company of Moorhead, Minnesota whose president Solomon G. Comstock obtained title to property claimed by Thomas Foster and Frank Sikes through the use of Valentine Script. Previous to this platting a village had been started and was doing a flourishing business about 80 rods west of Main Avenue of Rugby on the south side of the Great Northern Railroad track. This village never had a name, but a post office named Rugby was established there in December 1886. As soon as the plat of Rugby Junction, the name given the station established by the railroad, was recorded and the lots offered for sale, the original village disappeared and the business houses which had been erected in it were hauled to new locations.

The first store building to be erected in Rugby Junction, incorporated as a village in May 1897, was owned by C. F. Anderson and Nels Jacobson under the firm name of Jacobson and Anderson, but others followed in rapid succession.

On June 20, 1886 a gang of men, teams, and graders reached Rugby Junction and commenced work on grading for the main and branch lines of the St. Paul, Minneapolis and Manitoba Railroad, (now the Burlington Northern) and on July 19 the track laying machine and work train entered the village, but the first passenger train did not arrive until August 1 and thereafter for some time the trains stopped for dinner. The initial issue of the *Pierce County Tribune*, June 23, 1888 declared that "the west bound trains were thronged with people which unloaded for meals at Rugby and give an impetus to all departments of trade and the hum and bustle of life might be compared with the Union depot of St. Paul."

The first wedding ceremony to be conducted in Rugby took place at the home of C. A. Bigelow on July 2, 1888, the contracting parties being Frances B. Nash and Milo M. Miller, both of Barton. The Reverend Draper of Dunseith performed the ceremony.

In the early days, crop failures were caused by dry weather, gophers, and frost. On September 20, 1888, a disastrous prairie fire did considerable damage for farmers but was stopped before it reached the village.

Good crop prospects of 1891 brought new life into the almost dead village and a Board of Trade and a brass band were both organized in June.

With the exception of the "wildcat" bank established by E. Ashley Mears in the eighties, the Merchants Bank which was incorporated in June 1897 with a capital stock of $10,000 was the first bank organized in Pierce County.

The first church erected in Rugby, First Presbyterian, was also built in 1897. Two years later a raging storm of wind, rain, and hail moved it off its foundation about four feet and tore off its steeple. Sidewalks were torn up and thrown across the street and nearby buildings were also damaged.

In December 1899 A. H. Jones, associated with several capitalists in the eastern part of the state, came to Rugby and organized the Rugby State Bank, later known as the First National Bank. A brick building was erected the following year but the bank failed and the building is now occupied by Don Rupp's insurance agency.

The Cramond Hotel, steam-heated and electric and acetylene gas lighted, was for many years the scene of many gatherings and banquets. It was built in 1901 as was the Methodist Church. The following year fire destroyed several downtown buildings, but a two-story brick block together with the Tofsrud, Jacobson, Merchants Bank and Dr. McBride blocks were a testimony to the area's prosperity.

The population of Rugby in 1900 was less than 500 but by 1905 it was 1,300. At that time there were five large elevators and a flour mill to handle the grain raised in the region.

Other early businesses included the J. B. Buck Hardware which also carried a line of furniture, Jacobson's Big Department Store located on about an acre of land and which did an immense farm machine business,

Downtown Rugby, North Dakota in the 1970s

and Haugen and Nelson who carried a complete line of up-to-date mens' and boys' clothing and were also agents for several made-to-order clothing houses. O. T. Tofsrud's General Store featured an excellent stock of dry goods, groceries, shoes, and gents' furnishings and on its second floor housed the well-equipped local opera house.

Dr. I. M. McBride & Son engaged in the drug business and erected a handsome two-story brick building in 1905. E. A. Frydenlund sold lands and made trades of all kinds. The first restaurant in Rugby Junction, a popular eating place for railroad crews and passengers as diners on the Great Northern did not appear until 1890, was built in 1886.

Among other enterprises doing business in Rugby in 1905 were: Johnson Brothers, a general merchandise store; F. P. Bergman & Company, a land and loan operation; I. N. Harman who had a general store in what was known as the Syndicate Block; Rugby Drug Company, owned by B. Madson and B. H. Stoddard; E. J. Lander & Company, real estate and loans; three lumberyards, St. Anthony & Dakota, Imperial, and Bovey-Shute; Seldon Crockett, real estate and loans; and the *Pierce County Tribune* published at that time by Anderson and Stager.

Rugby, named for Rugby, England is the geographic center of North Amer-

Downtown Rugby, North Dakota - ca. 1926

ica. The continent's center is marked with a stone and concrete monument constructed in the early 1930s by W. B. and E. B. Paterson with the volunteer assistance from the local Boy Scouts, the Rugby Lions Club, and others of the community.

Today, it is a stop for Amtrak's Empire Builder passenger train. US 2, a four-lane roadway, and North Dakota 3 which runs north and south provide a gateway to the International Peace Garden and the Turtle Mountains to the north. The city has served as a regional medical center for many years, but agriculture is the area's largest industry.

It boasts that "Say It With Flowers," the primary slogan used by florists across America for many years, was coined by Nels Lindberg at a national

floral convention in Chicago. He founded the Rugby Greenhouses.

The Geographical Center Museum and Pioneer Village offer visitors an opportunity to see antique farm machinery, automobiles, restored buildings, and a large collection of artifacts associated with north-central North Dakota. The Pierce County Court House, built in 1910, is on the National Register of Historic Places.

I just owe almost everything to my father [and] it's passionately interesting for me that the things that I learned in a small town, in a very modest home, are just the things that I believe have won the election.

Margaret Thatcher
Quoted in *New Yorker*
February 10, 1986

Early photograph of Main Street Rugby, North Dakota

Ruso's townsite was the former homestead of Mrs. Albert Kantrude, the former Emma Helland. The name is claimed to be a Russian word meaning south of us. It was probably named by a land agent who was instrumental in bringing immigrants to the area.

The town traces its beginnings to 1906 when the Soo Line Railroad Company built its Max-Drake branch line and established a station named Ruso on Sec. 5, T150N, R80W. The town grew quickly after the station

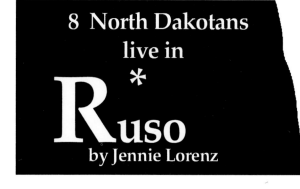

8 North Dakotans live in

*

Ruso

by Jennie Lorenz

was established.

Businesses in Ruso during its early years included the Burgess General Merchandise, the post office which was established in December 1906 with Edwin G. Burgess as postmaster, Hanson Drug Store, the *Ruso Record*, an icehouse, two lumberyards, Bovey-Shute and Rogers, two blacksmiths, Tom Thomsen and Iver Lunder, Charley Halliday's Harness Shop, Emile Roulier Meats and Groceries, Schultz Restaurant, J. A. Johnson General Merchandise, E. W. Wilson Livery Barn, Mrs. Louie Moe's hotel, Art Schultz's barbershop, a pool hall, a dance hall, Ernest Wilson's Hardware and Tin Shop, a jail built in 1907, Sevareid Real Estate, E. W. Pearly Feed Grinding, two doctors, A. O. Aaker and one Robertson, two cream-buying stations, Bronsak's Restaurant, George Okins who ran a dray line, and Whipple's Hardware Store. The First State Bank of Ruso, owned by Paul Wedge, went bankrupt in 1923.

Ruso also had five elevators, the O & M, I. L. Berge, Schmidt-Gulock, Atlantic, and Minkota. One burned in 1914. The others closed or were torn down as the years went by.

A schoolhouse was moved to Ruso from the country in 1907. In 1910 a new school was built and was equipped to teach grades one through eight and high school. In 1931 or 1932 the school burned. A new school was then built, but it has now been converted into a house and still stands.

Two churches were built in the town. First Lutheran, organized in 1907, still serves the community. Reverend E. C. Sargent served the Congregational Church as its first and only pastor.

In the early years the ladies of Ruso organized a park club. They planted trees and also held bake sales to raise money to purchase benches and tables for the park.

The first post offices were in the Burgess General Store and Hanson's Drug Store. Two rural routes were established to serve the surrounding area, later the routes were merged into one. The route now has an intermediate office at Benedict where the rural carrier picks up mail. It is now 133 miles long.

The first fire in Ruso, in 1910, was a major town disaster. Wilson's Harness Shop, Roulier's Meat Market, the barbershop, and the real estate office all were destroyed.

Business was brisk during the early days. For example, during the 1910 Christmas season Ed Burgess's general store was so busy nine clerks were employed to serve the shoppers. Looking back, prices on some items seemed very cheap. In 1917 a hay rack bed, sixteen feet long, with all the coal you could pile on it cost 90 cents.

Ordinarily the lumber used for construction in Ruso was hauled on sleighs from Velva during the winter.

Most of the older people in the community remember the prairie fire of 1914 which burned from Benedict to Long Lake, about eight miles south of Ruso. The fire was about three miles wide.

Isolation was another problem faced by many of the early settlers. Some of the older women of the community tell of not going to town for five years because the men usually went for supplies.

A comment was made in Ruso one time that the Dirty Thirties made everyone equal. They were all poor, and all friends.

Today, Ruso's only business is the post office. Children are bussed to Butte, Max, or Velva to attend school. The original jail still stands and services are still held at First Lutheran Church.

Ruso, North Dakota was once a bustling community - 1909

A Little Town

"A little town is where you don't have to guess who your enemies are. Your friends will tell you."

"A little town is the only place on earth where people past middle age are called by their first names when they saunter down the street."

"A little town is where everybody knows everybody else's car by sight and also where and when it goes."

"A little town is where few people can get away with lying about the year they were born. Too many people can remember."

"A little town is where people with various ailments can air them properly to sympathetic ears."

"A little town is where, when you get the wrong number, you can talk for 15 minutes anyhow."

"A little town is where the ratio of good people to bad people is something like 100 to one. That's nice to remember."

"A little town is where it is hard for anybody to walk to work for exercise because it takes too long to stop and explain to people in cars who stop, honk, and offer a ride."

"A little town is where city folks say there is nothing to do, but those who live there don't have enough nights in the week to make all the meetings and social functions."

"A little town is where businessmen struggle for survival against city stores and shopping centers."

"A little town is where everyone becomes a neighbor in time of need."

"A little town is where those same businessmen dig deep many times to help with countless fund-raising projects."
"A little town is where it's nice to be when rearing a family."
"A little town is where you don' have to lock your door every time you leave the house."

"A little town is where many teenagers say there's nothing to do and they are surprised to learn that their big-city peers are saying the same thing."

"A little town, when all is said and done, is a nice place to live."
Anonymous
Sentinel Butte Bicentennial Committee,
Golden Valley County Pioneers, 1976

Main Street Ruso, North Dakota - 1976
(DPDP - Ken Jorgenson)

In 1903 a rural post office was established a few miles south of the present location of Ryder. It was first referred to as Centerville, the name requested by Austin Gray, its first postmaster, who seemingly had plans to start a town by that name. The postal department, however, informed the community that there was already a town by that name.

The following story tells how Ryder got its name. The weather was very cold when a postal inspector was sent to the site. He had to come by team and sled from Minot where he had borrowed a buffalo coat from Arthur F. Ryder, a partner in a Minot hardware store. Ryder refused to accept payment for the use of his coat so the postal representative, in gratitude, named the rural post office after him.

The town struggled for three years without a railroad. In the spring of 1906 Ed Fredeen, acting as agent for the Minneapolis, St. Paul & Sault Ste Marie Railroad (Soo Line), purchased the present townsite. Tracks were laid, a station was established, and on July 19, 1906 town lots were sold to the highest bidder. The amount of the sales price, over the appraised value of the lot, was put into a park fund for the town. Some $3,600 was received.

The Ryder post office was moved and opened in the new railroad town on October 12, 1906 with Ole J. Bye as postmaster.

Many of the business places were moved from the old townsite to the new town and new business places also sprang up. The town became a thriving little community. There were three banks, four hardware stores, six general stores, three livery barns, five hotels, five restaurants, six elevators, a photograph gallery, a blacksmith shop, furniture store, barbershop, drug store, three doctors, a dentist, two lawyers, and three churches. There were over a thousand people in the community who would support a newspaper so an entire printing plant was also set up.

Ed Fredeen established the Fredeen Hotel which became well known throughout the state. It was heated by steam, had a fine lobby, dining room, and kitchen, and could accommodate forty-four diners at one time. There were twenty-seven bedrooms and not a better equipped hotel could be found in the state except in Fargo or Grand Forks.

In 1957 a municipal sewer system was installed and in 1962 bids for a water system were opened. In 1968 the Village of Ryder became the City of Ryder.

The present businesses are: Ryder Exchange, Sandy's Place, Ryder Cafe, Ryder Co-op Credit Union, Farmers Union Oil Company, Farmers Union Elevator, Ryder Lumber, Ryder Food Market, Ryder Post Office, Ted's Garage and Implement, and Barb Folden Tax Service. Calvary Presbyterian Church, St. John's Lutheran Church, and St. Charles Catholic Church presently serve the community. The focal point for many community activities is the City Park; the original band stand is still being used.

In 1978 a museum was established to preserve and display Ryder area artifacts, documents, and structures of historical value. It is open to the public on specified dates or by appointment.

Many groups in the Ryder community have organized throughout the years. Those that are still active and the year they organized are: Ryder Community Club, 1906; Home Economics Club, 1910; American Legion L. C. Jensen Post No. 99, 1919; Independent Order of Odd Fellows Lodge No. 116, 1908; Banner Rebekah Lodge No. 75, 1910; Busy Bee Homemakers, 1948; Happy Hour Senior Citizens Club, 1973; Friends, Incor-

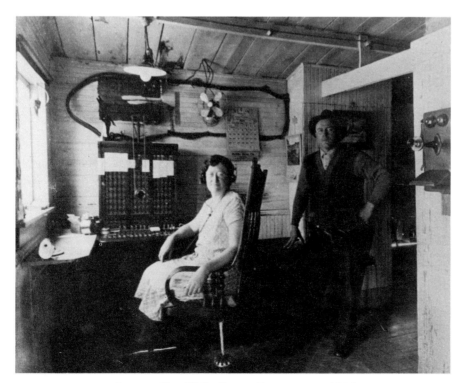

Queen City Telephone Company - 1928
Hannah Cronin, operator & Blaine Officer, manager

Bird's-eye view of Ryder, North Dakota - 1907

porated, 1985; and the Ryder Community Club II, 1987.

The Ryder Fire Department was organized in 1909 and in 1954 the Ryder Fire District was organized. Since then the two communities of Ryder and Makoti have merged several of their services. The two school districts reorganized in 1969 to form the North Shore schools. North Shore School is a member of the Missouri Hills Consortium along with the schools of Parshall, Plaza, Garrison, and Max. Elementary students from both towns are taught at Ryder; junior and senior high school students are taught in Makoti. The fire departments and districts merged in 1970 to form the Ryder-Makoti District. And a Ryder-Makoti ambulance service was organized in 1980.

The Ryder School Reunion was held in 1974 and the city celebrated its Diamond Jubilee in 1981. Both celebrations were attended by several hundred people and were successful. A two-day celebration, July 15-16, 1989 combined three special occasions, the State Centennial, the Ryder School 80th Anniversary, and the 85th Anniversary of St. John's Lutheran Church. Ryder was also named a North Dakota Centennial Community.

This is a brief history of the Ryder community, of the people who built the farms and of the town and the organizations that make the Ryder area one of the better rural communities in North Dakota.

Farmers worry only during the growing season, but town people worry all the year 'round.

Edgar Watson Howe,
Country Town Sayings, 1911

Second Anniversary Celebration of Ryder, North Dakota - 1908

S*anish

by Bernice Houser

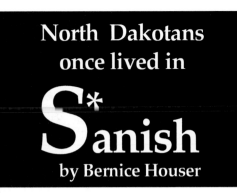

Sanish (Sah-nish) was located on the east bank of the Missouri River in southern Mountrail County. It lay in a valley with hills to the north and south. Elm Creek wound through the townsite which had been known as "Old Crossing" by the Indians. It was one of the places most used by the great herds of buffalo crossing the Missouri River. Charles W. Hoffman, Superintendent of the Fort Berthold Indian Reservation named it when he surveyed and located the Reservation towns in 1910. The name was taken from the Arikara Indians who called themselves "Sanish—Real People."

The land was opened to settlers in 1915; however, squatters arrived a year earlier. W.F. Thompson from Blaisdell, Dave Gibb from Ross, Charlie Gardner from Makoti, and Wilbur and Otis Mummert from York had all come in the fall of 1914 and spent the winter there with the intention of going into business as soon as lots were for sale. Early 1915 saw more activity and buildings were erected along a street of sorts running north from the base of "Crow High." By July there were fifty-four businesses including eleven restaurants. A post office opened with mail coming by team from Brookbank post office on the Gibb Ranch north of town. A ferry service accommodated ranchers from the west until 1927.

A new townsite was surveyed and platted in the summer of 1916 a half mile east of the original location and the first auction of lots was held on November 11 of that year. The town's first election was held in April 1917. In the spring of that year many of the buildings were moved to the new location.

The first train arrived in Sanish on July 24, 1915. A branch line of the Minneapolis, St. Paul and Sault Ste Marie Railroad (Soo Line) ended here and after the Verendrye Bridge over the Missouri was completed in 1927 Sanish became one of the great livestock shipping centers in the northwest.

The first school was built in 1916; in 1928 construction was begun on a new brick building and in 1937 an $18,000 addition, including a gymnasium, was erected. The first senior class graduated in 1930; the last in 1953.

A small park near the river was practically abandoned after the bridge was built; a new park was established across the river in the big cottonwoods. It was the scene of much activity during the 1940s when the "famous" Sanish Rodeos were held nearby.

The *Sanish Pilot*, published by J. S. Patterson and edited by Robert Norris, was the town's first newspaper; however, the best known was the *Sanish Sentinel*, published by Charlie Pickering from 1915 to March 1951.

The golf course, situated in the rolling hills north of the town overlooking the river, was considered one of the best in the state during the 1930s.

Crow Flies High Butte, towering above the river on the south side of the town, was the site of Verendrye National Monument which honored Pierre Gaultier de Varennes, Sieur de La Verendrye, the first white man to visit the state.

Although few realized it at the time Sanish was doomed as early as 1931 when a proposal to build a bridge across the Missouri at Elbowoods, downstream from Sanish, was made and the Corps of Engineers announced that it had drafted a plan for a dam on the river to divert water to Devil's Lake. The dam would back water up to Williston. The plan was not adopted at that time, but the bridge was built. When the proposal became a reality years later both the Elbowoods (Four Bears) and the Sanish (Verendrye) bridges were torn down. The Sanish bridge was sold for scrap; the one at Elbowoods was reassembled for the "new" Four Bears bridge near New Town. The buildings at Sanish, Van Hook, and Elbowoods were moved to new locations, the largest of which became New Town, and the old townsites all became part of huge Lake Sakakawea.

Sanish's government came to an end officially on April 29, 1953. On April 30, 1953 some $13,619.77 was transferred to the City of New Town. The old townsite is now under water; it is known as Sanish Bay.

Bird's-eye view of Sanish, North Dakota
(SHSND)

The second town to bear the name Sanish came into being because of controversy over moving the original town. The majority of Sanish citizens chose to move to a townsite east of their present village to establish a larger community by joining with people from Van Hook whose town was being partially flooded by the dam and who were losing a good portion of their trade territory.

A few, however, did not like the way the plan was being carried out. They wanted a town that would retain the name Sanish and wanted to protect their interests. They chose a new site on the hills south of Crow Flies High Butte. Since funds were transferred by popular vote to the east site, New Town, they began with very little.

One leader, Bigelow Neal, had come from Garrison to help landowners try to get a better deal in their acquisition dealings with the Corps of Engineers. He became secretary of the "New" Sanish Townsite Company which was promoting the townsite at the "Bridgehead." Other officers were Herman Jahnke, president; Fred LaRocque, vice-president; Ted Bangen, treasurer; Allen Hinsverk, director; and Esther Krueger, assistant secretary. They proceeded to sell stock and buy a 240 acre tract of land from A. A. Ellingboe. The townsite plat was filed in November 1950 and an addition on the west was filed in June 1951.

The group had its problems. First, no provision had been made for an approach off the rebuilt portion of North Dakota 23 for access to the site and it took many meetings with federal, state, and county officials before this goal was achieved. Second, the campaign carried out by both townsite promoters was filled with unpleasantries regarding the opposition. Third, many people who were sympathetic to "New" Sanish's cause were retired or nearing retirement and decided to move to other localities. Lastly, with the Corps of Engineers promising replacement of all public improvements for the east townsite it was difficult to entice buyers to a town where these things could not be offered.

However, by 1955 at least 70 lots had been sold and the population was large enough to warrant incorporation. A census showed 120 persons living in the town. Electors voted 45 to 0 for incorporation. On May 3, 1955 Sanish was reborn.

John W. Schneider, the town's first mayor, resigned before finishing his term; he was succeeded by John White Body who died while in office. Jack Lacey became mayor and upon his death Elmer Rambel filled the office until the town was dissolved.

The Sanish post office had been threatened with closure several times. A half hour before its "final" closing on April 30, 1954 it was announced that it would remain open in "New" Sanish. Mrs. David (Mary) Dinwoodie was appointed postmaster; she continued in that capacity during the life of the village and beyond, until May 1980 when the "Sanish, N.D." postmark was finally retired.

Crow Flies High Butte and Sanish, North Dakota
(SHSND)

The old line of the Sanish Farmer's Telephone Company served the new village until March 1954. In October of that year Reservation Mutual Aid Telephone Cooperative brought in dial service.

Few businesses ever operated in the new town. Besides the post office there was the Royal Garage, Dinwoodie Manufacturing, Hinsverk's Store, with the only lunch counter in town, and Four Bears Bar, known as the "Snakepit," probably the town's most famous business place. It actually housed a live bear or two for a time, and stories are still told of some of the "wild and wooly west" type of activities that took place there.

The village of Sanish was dissolved June 28, 1974 and became part of Unorganized Township 152N, R93W.

In October 1976 the Four Bears Bar caught fire and was destroyed along with the old Hinsverk Store nearby.

In August 1985 an oil drilling permit was issued to EP Operating Company to drill a wildcat well, called the Sanish 1-23. A site was cleared in the southern portion of the townsite; a well was drilled 14,262 feet into the Red River formation and in July 1986 was plugged as a dry hole.

Sanish began in a little protected valley on the banks of the Missouri River and wound up on a high, windy hill overlooking Lake Sakakawea. Today, it doesn't exist, even on highway maps; however, a few residents remain "up on the hill." The site continues to be called Sanish and the highway department maintains a sign at the approach on North Dakota 23 that says "Sanish 1," but for all practical purposes, Sanish is gone.

Sanish, North Dakota overlooked the Missouri
(SHSND)

Home Town of 319 North Dakotans

S*awyer

by Bob & Delores Booth

The Souris River, also known as the Mouse, is located in north central North Dakota and has its source in Saskatchewan. It twists and turns southeast and makes a loop flowing back north into Canada. Near the southwest loop of the river the first pioneers of record, John Francis Booth, his brother Edwin, and the James Wilson family, all from South Dakota, came to settle in the beautiful valley in 1882. Elmer Francis and his family, along with the families of Joe Tennai and Perry Johnson, settled a few miles upstream. A number of other families from Minnesota, Iowa, and South Dakota came a short time later.

The valley offered food, fuel, and shelter. Black Butte, a high hill rising from the plain, was located north of the valley. It served as a lookout for Indians and proved to be a source for gravel. Rich, flat farmland was found north of the butte, and deep coulees with spring water and lignite coal deposits were found south of the valley.

Just south of Black Butte the area's first post office was established in 1886 in Nathan D. Terrel's country store. Terrell was named postmaster; the facility was named for the Black brothers who were local ranchers. Terrell's daughter, Amy, became postmaster and when she married William H. Wilson it was moved to the Wilson home and renamed Echo. When the Soo Line Railroad built through the area in 1893 and established the townsite of Sawyer the post office was finally moved to the new town in April 1898 and named Sawyer. Fred L. Hartlieb was the postmaster. The origin of the town's name is uncertain. Some claim it was named after an official of the railroad, others claim it was named for one Colonel Sawyer, a horse racing expert.

The railroad company offered many incentives to the pioneers and the new town grew rapidly. The village incorporated in 1908.

The first school, a two-room wooden structure, was built in 1904, and a four-room brick building was erected in 1910. The high school graduated its first class in 1919.

Religious groups first met in local homes and later in the schoolhouse. Congregational, Nazarene, and Baptist churches were established between 1905 and 1910. South of Sawyer pioneer German-Russians established their rural churches. About 1938 the Congregational Church was sold to the Lutherans. In 1957 the Mennonites built a new edifice in Sawyer. Congregations are still active today, but membership has declined and churches have difficulty keeping resident pastors.

Between 1905 and 1915 Sawyer had two banks, two hotels, three lumberyards, three livery stables, four grain elevators, a feed mill, three blacksmith shops, a newspaper the *Clipper*, later the *Sawyer Telegraph*, a drug store, resident doctor, a grocery and clothing store, and a meat market. The town had telephone service, a plant provided electric lighting, and the railroad scheduled four passenger trains a day. The community also supported the Royal Neighbors and the Woodman Lodge.

Bird's-eye view of Sawyer, North Dakota - 1909

The little town with business places on both sides of a two-block area began to decline for many reasons: the advent of the automobile, World War I, the growing city of Minot only sixteen miles northwest, buildings lost by fire, the Dirty Thirties, bank closures, and failed businesses.

World War II brought a minor revival. The war effort resulted in the movement of some of the younger generations to available employment and the older ones retired and moved into town. A new post office was built in 1966.

Population has remained quite stable because of a good school system. Improvements have been made and in 1950 Sawyer was one of the first communities to get involved in school reorganization, expanding its school district from 36 to 194 sections of taxable land. Reorganization has resulted in added classrooms, another gymnasium, and the development of one of the finest small school systems in this part of the state.

During the devastating flood of 1969 townsfolk cooperated to save homes and property. During that same year the community's dream of a city water and sewer system came true. And although the new US 52 bypassed the town, the community was confident enough in the future to build a new fire hall and a most efficient adjoining City Hall. It is used for many group meetings. In 1985 Main Street to the bridge and many side streets were paved.

When the Soo Line Railroad abandoned passenger rail service the depot was moved to Pioneer Village in Minot, located on the State Fair Grounds.

Today, just two grain elevators remain; much grain raised in the coun-

Bank robber caught in the act at Sawyer, North Dakota - 1910

tryside is hauled to distant markets by large trucks. A small grocery store, located in the first brick post office, and Renee's Corner, an excellent eating place located in one of the old bank buildings, serve the general public. A small machine shop on the west edge of town also serves the community. These are the surviving businesses of a once thriving little settlement.

Two active organizations in Sawyer today are the Senior Citizens and the Lions Club.

Sawyer's population is still over 300. It is located in a lovely valley and with its friendly people it is an excellent place to raise a family and to retire to.

Sawyer Grocery in Sawyer, North Dakota - 1988

There is such a lack of conversational opportunities here. It is the real limitation to country town life.

Sherwood Anderson
Letters of Sherwood Anderson

In 1910 the Chicago, Milwaukee and St. Paul Railroad built across the Standing Rock Indian Reservation and established a station named Selfridge. Its townsite subsidiary, the Milwaukee Land Company of Chicago, Illinois, platted a 12-block townsite there in May 1911. Located in the south central part of North Dakota in the middle of Sioux County the town lies in the northern section of the reservation.

It became an incorporated village in March 1919. No one knows exactly how the town got its name.

242 North Dakotans live in Selfridge
by Judith J. Walker
*

The town began to grow only when the reservation lands were opened for settlement and Sioux County was organized in 1914, although a post office was established there in May 1912 with Eben W. Philput as postmaster. One of the first business places to open after the first town lots were sold in 1911 was a general store operated by B. L. Smestad and the Sioux Lumber Company opened soon after Smestad began selling groceries. On August 12, 1918 G. E. Langbein was appointed the first depot agent in Selfridge. That same year the *Selfridge Journal* published its first edition; James Fulton was its editor. Considered a pillar of the community in the early years the paper succumbed to adverse economic conditions and ceased publication in May 1979.

With the opening of the lumber company fine new homes were built to replace the original crude shanties. Several attractive homes first built by J. K. Wead and B. L. Smestad during the early 1900s are still being lived in today. In 1925 the village of Selfridge boasted of 51 homes and 63 business places. Today, there are only 8 businesses left and about 60 homes.

Agriculture has always been the mainstay of the town's economy. The farmer-owned elevator which was established in 1919 still serves the community, but it is now privately owned. The Selfridge Cheese Company began operations in 1960 and continues to provide employment and a market for milk produced by local dairy farmers.

The Selfridge Public School has played one of the biggest roles in keeping the town alive. It has fought hard to keep its doors open and operating in the best interest of its young people. Peak enrollments were reached during the boom years of the 1940s; however, during recent years the school population has decreased to 90 students taught by 12 teachers.

One of the major events in the town's history occurred on March 31, 1983 when the Milwaukee road ran its last train through Selfridge. Shortly thereafter the road pulled up its tracks and the railroad land was sold.

The town began to lose people in the 1970s. During recent years it has maintained a population of about 240. The majority of its residents are descendants of German-Russians and Native Americans. Small groups of Irish and Norwegians also live in town. Pioneer families whose descendants make Selfridge their home today include: HisChase, Gayton, Walker, Morgen, Engel, Schneider, Hinton, Vollmuth, McCay, Sandland, Lund, Umber, Feist, and Oster.

The town's oldest living resident is Rose Black Tongue HisChase; she was born in 1902. Her father was Frank Black Tongue, a Sioux Indian. She later married Pius HisChase. During the town's Diamond Jubilee celebration in 1986 she was chosen Jubilee Queen. In conjunction with that event the town published a 75th Jubilee Book.

Main Street Selfridge, North Dakota - 1984
(SHSND)

March, 1918, showing oldest building in Selfridge, The Sioux Lumber Company. This building
has been moved West of the railroad track and is now occupied by the Oscar Wuitschick family.

(SHSND)

A new town was only the same town in a different place.

Susan Glaspell,
"His Smile," *The Pictorial Review,* **1921**

Grasshopper spreaders for poison
Used in the 1930s a mixture of saw dust, molasses and a poison mixture (SHSND)

In 1904 the Great Northern Railroad Company extended its line northwest from Mohall and established a station named Sherwood as the terminus of its Granville branch. The station was named for Sherwood H. Sleeper, a Mohall banker and right-of-way agent for the railroad. The townsite was owned by Sleeper who had purchased it from a homesteader. It grew rapidly and was incorporated September 1904.

Sherwood's population has fluctuated through the years. One time, during the period 1904 to 1910, the population was thought to be between 700 and 1,000 people. The early boom was short-lived and by 1910 the population stood at 328. It increased to 455 by 1930 and since then has declined to its present population of 286.

Grain raising was the chief industry in the new territory and to store and market the crops a number of grain elevators were built. At one time there were seven different companies purchasing grain; however, through the years fire claimed most of the elevators and now only the Farmers Union elevators remain. It was claimed that in 1906 Sherwood marketed more wheat than any other town of its size in the state.

At one time there were three hotels in the town. The Metropolitan was

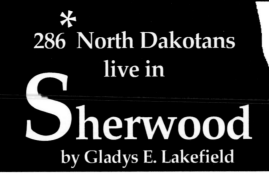

286 North Dakotans live in Sherwood

by Gladys E. Lakefield

built in 1904 and demolished in 1978. The Victoria Hotel, built in 1906, operated until 1941 and then was converted to a garage. The third, The Norman, was never completed and was later razed.

Over the years, many restaurants and cafes have served the city. Once there were seven in operation at the same time. In the early days the main course was beans and bacon. General stores and food stores have also been numerous and when the town's population was larger and farmers lived on almost every quarter section of land they were all busy.

Sherwood has had many businesses come and go including barbershops, photo shops, bowling alleys, drug stores, hardware stores, TV and radio shops, a Gamble Store, tin shop, harness shops, livery barns, dray services, and service stations. Probably the oldest continuing business in Sherwood was the K. R. Flem

Company, an International Harvester Implement dealership which operated from 1904 until 1986. One time there were three banks in operation. The first issue of the *Sherwood Tribune* was published on November 3, 1904 when Sherwood was only eight weeks old. Telephone service was established in 1905.

Sherwood's post office originated in 1902 as a rural facility named Bolaker. It was moved to a different location the next year when Minnie Alexander became postmaster and was moved again, later, to the new railroad town. In January 1905 it was renamed Sherwood.

Schools were begun before the town was incorporated. One-room schools first served the area. A high school program began in 1908. In 1922 a new two-story brick school was built and it is still in full operation today. A new grade school addition and a new gymnasium were added in 1965 and 1966.

Churches have also been an important part of the community. Today, there are three active churches: the Catholic Church erected a large brick structure in 1916; the Lutheran Church was built in 1961; and the Methodist Church in 1909.

Main Street Sherwood, North Dakota - early 1900s
(SHSND)

The first wedding in Sherwood took place in the Victoria Hotel on December 1, 1904. The first death occurred on July 10, 1910. Since the city was without a cemetery at that time it purchased ten acres of land southwest of the city and platted a burial ground.

Sherwood has suffered from various disasters, tornadoes, high winds, fires, and accidents. One large fire in the 1930s destroyed many of the original wooden structures; in 1980 a fire consumed the rest of the old buildings on Main Street. A tornado in 1911 killed three people and wounded fifty others.

Today, Sherwood is still a thriving community, although train service was discontinued in 1980. It is neat and orderly, the streets are paved, and it has an excellent water supply. The community depends on agriculture and oil production for its main sources of revenue. There are three service stations, one bank, a hardware store, a lumberyard, a Jack and Jill Food Store, two bars, welding and oil field services, two trucking firms, an elevator, and a restaurant.

The majority of residents are of German, Norwegian, Swedish, and French backgrounds. Most of the early settlers came here by wagon or train during the period 1902 to 1910.

Probably the biggest event in Sherwood is its annual observance of Memorial Day, commemorated for over fifty years. Many communities from Canada participate in this event. Ceremonies begin with Canadian Legionnaires and American Legion members exchanging flags at the Canadian border two miles north of Sherwood. A program at the school, a parade, and cemetery services complete the program. Almost every year there are baseball games, rodeos, or carnivals in the afternoon. This may be the only place in the United States where foreign Legionnaires participate in Memorial Day Services.

Sherwood has produced its share of doctors, lawyers, dentists, corporation managers, and successful business people. The community's social centers are school, the cafe, the bars, and the Senior Citizen Center.

Sherwood's greatest claim to sports fame came in 1982 when the high school football team won the state championship in nine-man football with an undefeated season. At that time Sherwood had the smallest school in the state with a football program.

Sherwood is neat and the residents are proud of it.

First snowmobile built in Sherwood at the Sherwood Auto Co.
(SHSND)

A load of lumber for the Imperial Lumber Co. - early 1900s
(SHSND)

Shields has been in existence for a long time, longer than most Grant County towns. You can find Shields on the antique stage coach line map that hangs in the Marquis de Mores Chateau in Medora. It was used by the Marquis in 1885.

The village was named for an early day contractor, Nathaniel Shields, his wife Mary, and their children Mark, Arthur, Maude, and Laura. Mary nursed the sick and delivered babies in the area, both white and Indian. Shields built St. James Catholic Church in 1896; Indians and whites have shared services in the facility each week ever since.

The name was first given to the post office which was established in September 1896 in the sod house on the Shields's homestead. Shields was named postmaster. In 1898 the post office was moved to the "Spud" Murphy store on the Cannonball River, just opposite of the Indian subagency, Porcupine. Murphy had come to Fort Rice in 1867 as a soldier and after discharge came to the Shields area and married Sagy Win, a member of Sitting Bull's band. Later in life he married a Sioux maiden, Frances White Buffalo. Murphy ran the store and post office until 1909 when H. E. Fleming bought the store and took over the post office.

Early mail carriers were rancher Billy Owens and Denny Hallahan who loaded the mail on a horse at the Old Stevenson Ranch on the Cannonball (Timmer) and following the river delivered it to the Wade post office, some thirteen miles southwest of Shields. From there mail was delivered to another rural post office, Janesburg, located eight miles south of Leith.

William V. Wade came to Fort Rice, Dakota Territory in 1872 by wagon train. He helped build the Standing Rock Indian Agency. In 1884 he was appointed a deputy United States Marshall and in 1888 he came to the Shields area and established a ranch on the Cannonball River where the family operated a small store in their log cabin. In 1893 Wade post office was established, it closed in 1920 and the mail was sent to Shields.

When the Chicago, Milwaukee and St. Paul Railroad constructed its Cannonball branch line near the Murphy land in 1910 it established a townsite named Shields on Secs. 24 and 25, T132N, R84W and Secs. 19 and 30, T132N, R83W. The railroad was forced to stop and open and close gates when it went through McLaughlin's and Parkin's pastures. Major William Belden, a member of the House of Representatives in the first session of the state legislature, platted the seventeen-block townsite of Shields and on July 26, 1910 approximately $22,000 worth of lots were sold.

At one time the approximately 300 people living in Shields enjoyed a hotel, drugstore, newspaper, elevators, rooming-house, schools, churches, railroad doctor, livery barn, garages, barbershop, tailor, harnessmaker, bulk gas station, Independent Order of Odd Fellows Lodge, Commercial Club, cream stations, grocery stores, blacksmith shop, restaurants, implement, butcher shop, dance halls, block and stone companies, train service, drayline, dairy, ice cream parlor, stockyards, and hardware store. None of these businesses are operating today. The city plant was replaced by REA (Rural Electrification Administration) and the one town phone was replaced by a city-wide system by the RTA (Rural Telephone Administration).

Today, Shields has a branch post office. Its 1912 schoolhouse has been converted to a tavern and its owners,

Main Street Shields, North Dakota - early 1900s
(SHSND)

First Anniversary Celebration in Shields - early 1900s
(SHSND)

Elmer and Van Imhoff, have provided a community center for public use. The 1910 depot houses the Weinhandl Museum. By 1989 the community planned to open two other museums to help celebrate the state's Centennial. In the 1880s Indian Agent Major James McLaughlin established his Circle M Ranch and constructed a log house on his daughter's allotment at Shields. Plans are to move it onto the Grant County Historical Society lot beside the 1917 St. Gabriel Catholic Church Museum. McLaughlin is a local hero, a friend of the American Indian. He married a Sioux maiden, Marie Buisson, and many of their descendants live in the area today.

Shields has experienced four murders during its history; the most notable being the killing of Guy Bolten by Turkey Track Bill.

Enduring events which the American Indian and whites share include the annual Pow Wow and Shields Celebrations each June and the baseball games that have been played in the community since 1911. The community continues to honor its professional Indian pitcher, Joe Day, who became famous in the 1920s.

The community is also proud of Mary Louise Defender Wilson, Miss Indian American II, and Lisa Ternes, a member of the North Dakota High School Centennial Band. Ternes participated in the 1989 Rose Bowl Parade as part of the state's Centennial celebration.

More about the history of the Shields community can be found in the Jubilee histories of Flasher, Selfridge, and Carson and Carrie Weinhandl's *Prairie Pioneers* and *My Book of Many Things*.

The first train going through Shields, North Dakota - 1910
(SHSND)

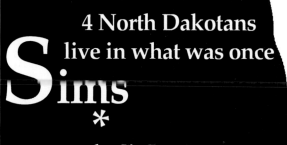

4 North Dakotans live in what was once Sims *

by Sig Peterson

Sims is the oldest town in North Dakota west of Mandan. It began in September 1879 when the Northern Pacific Railway's main line reached its location. At that time it was called Baby Mine because a coal mine had been opened there in the fall of 1873. The mine was abandoned but reopened on July 5, 1879.

The coal mines and an abundance of spring water at the site were very attractive to the railroad and a settlement sprang up almost immediately.

Colonel Eber H. Bly purchased Sec. 11, T138N, R86W from the Northern Pacific Railroad in February 1880. The name changed to Bly's Mine. In May 1883 the railway surveyed the townsite, laying out twenty-six blocks and twenty half-blocks. The site was renamed Sims in honor of George V. Sims, chief clerk of the Northern Pacific Railroad office in New York.

Thirty-six blocks and twenty-four half blocks were later added and named the Newell Addition. The Terra Cotta Addition came later, including the area where the Lutheran church was eventually built.

By 1883 the Carbon Pressed Brick and Lime Company with investments of about $30,000 was in full operation. The cornerstone for the

first North Dakota Capitol building was made in Sims and some Sims bricks were used in its construction. The first Morton County Courthouse was made of Sims brick, as were several buildings in Bismarck and Mandan.

The brick company, which had employed about 125 men, went out of business in the late 1880s. The bricks were not durable because of lime deposits in the clay. The underground coal mines employed about 150 workers, but better quality lignite was found further west, causing a gradual shutdown.

The Oakes House, a $15,000 three-story hotel, was built in 1883. It housed offices for the brick company and the company coal mine. In 1884 a $5,000 community building was erected (it also served as a school). By this time Sims had three general stores, two real estate offices, several saloons, two boarding houses, the

Looking east in Sims in 1885

Northern Pacific depot, a post office, a lumberyard, banking service, a grain buyer, a number of coal mines, a brick yard, and the brick company hospital.

Estimates give Sims a population of about 1,000 in the mid-1880s. By 1906 the census reported 300 residents. At this time the neighboring town of Almont was founded. In 1906 there were three stores and several other services in Sims. By 1910 the population had dwindled to eighty-six. Most of the businesses had moved to Almont.

The first church denomination in town was English Presbyterian, whose parishioners held services in the community building and had a cemetery northwest of Sims. The Lutherans organized a congregation September 30, 1884 and met in homes until a parsonage was built. Services were then held on the second floor. Their cemetery was laid out in 1884 and a church was built and dedicated in 1900. Regular services still continue. The congregation's 100th Anniversary was held in July 1984 with about five hundred people attending.

On November 18, 1890 area residents were advised to fortify themselves against a Sioux Indian uprising. Government rifles and ammunition were issued and residents entrenched themselves atop Anderson Hill. Farmers and their families from as far away as the Heart River came for protection. The uprising never materialized, but nonetheless several anxious moments were had.

Sims was a cattle shipping center for a large area. Cattle were driven to Sims from as far away as the South Dakota state line, since it was the closest shipping point. If no empty cattle cars were available cattle were herded in the adjacent hills until, in some instances, a special train came from Mandan.

School enrollment in the 1880s peaked at eighty with a three-month fall term and a three-month term in the spring. A new two-room school was built in 1907. But by 1920 enrollment had decreased so much that only one teacher was hired. The school closed in 1945. In 1962 the building was moved to Almont and remodeled for a teacherage.

The Red Trail followed the railroad when possible, so all auto traffic came through Sims. In 1928 US 10 opened for traffic directly west from New Salem to Glen Ullin, bypassing Sims. A line change was also made on the Northern Pacific Railway in 1948, discontinuing service to Sims. Until this time a store and post office had been maintained, but there has been no service since.

A *Bismarck Tribune* clipping, April 9, 1884 reads: "The excursion to Sims was one of the largest ever passing over the Northern Pacific Railway. Eight coaches were filled in Bismarck and Mandan, making the excursionists 784. The tour of Sims presents a very solid and pleasing appearance. Its buildings are mostly of brick, which has given the town the name of 'Brick City'."

Currently Sims is home to a family of four. But memories and stories of the enterprising pioneer town still live.

Sims church in 1985

*The Sims school
Classes of 1911-1912*

Section crew at Sims depot about 1900

Home Town of 92 North Dakotans

Solen

by Margaret Hoffman

Solen was founded in 1910 along the Cannonball River on Sec. 30, T134N, R80W when the Northern Pacific Railroad built its branch line west along the river and located a station there. The town was named after Lucille Van Solen daughter of Honore Picotte, an early fur trader said to be of noble lineage who came to the area from France in 1825, and his wife Alma, a Santee Sioux from Montana. Lucille was educated in eastern schools and when the family moved to Standing Rock she was the first teacher in the first school on the reservation. She married John L. Van Solen, a partner in the Parkin Ranch, and there they ran cattle along the Cannonball River, wintering them near the present townsite.

The very earliest businesses that were started were a general merchandise store owned and operated by W. L. Clark and a grain elevator established by Winter Trusdale. In 1916 the first bank was established by Benno and Otto Schimansky and was managed by James Zelenka. By the end of 1930 there were many new businesses, among them were four general merchandise stores, a hotel, two lumberyards, two garages, a pool hall, a Standard Oil bulk station, a well-drilling business, a barbershop, and a butcher shop. Electricity for the town was furnished by a light plant located in Otto Schimansky's garage.

Dr. Paul F. Rice and his wife who was a nurse served the community. Both were veterans of World War I. Rice came to the Solen area around 1910. When the United States entered World War I in 1917 he volunteered for the Army Medical Corps. While in France he met an army nurse, Claire O. Jardins, whom he later married. The couple lived in Solen after their marriage until 1948 when he was killed in an auto accident in Michigan.

Hilda Higgins (Mrs. Walt) was the depot agent in Solen from 1914 to 1965 when the railroad tracks were removed after the Northern Pacific discontinued service to the town. Throughout the years businesses failed, many buildings were moved out, and people moved away.

The Catholic and Congregational churches (UCC) have been active in the community from Solen's early history to the present time. The first Sacred Heart Catholic Church building was a white frame structure built about 1915 and was replaced in the late 1970s with a modern structure. The UCC meets in a remodeled early school building. Sacred Heart Church operated a school for about fifteen years during the fifties and sixties.

Bingenheimer Mercantile Co. - late 1940s
Lumber and hardware store

Solen School District No. 3 resulted from a division of Cannonball River School District in 1925. A new red-brick structure built in 1922 served until a modern plant was finished in 1975. The district was reorganized in 1968 and includes territory from Sioux and Morton Counties.

The businesses that remain in operation today are the Solen post office which was established in February 1911, Hoffman's Garage, Big Foot Bar and Grocery, Dar's Hair Hut, and a management consulting firm, the Robert McLaughlin Company.

Although Solen has few residents today, each year in March former residents now living in the Bismarck-Mandan area gather in Bismarck for a dinner dance. Several hundred people attend this yearly re-union.

Solen Public School built in 1922

A little country town, with its inflexible social conditions, its petty sayings and jealousies, its obstinate mistrust of all that is strange and its crude gossip about all that it cannot comprehend . . . may be as complicated and as hard to live in as great Babylon itself.

Henry Van Dyke
The School of Life

School buses in front of Otto Schimansky's Garage - 1920s
Solen was one of the first districts to run buses

ouris which became a city in 1901 is located six miles from the Canadian border. In that year the Great Northern Railroad Company established a terminal station named Souris on its Bottineau branch line. The Souris post office was established at the site in July 1901, the townsite was platted in August 1901, and the next year Souris incorporated as a city and its school district was organized. There were, however, a number of businesses at the site long before the rails were laid to Souris. The first was Qually's Restaurant which fed its customers in a tent.

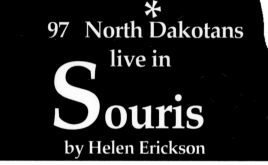

97 North Dakotans live in

Souris

by Helen Erickson

The name Souris, the French word for mouse, was taken from the Souris River which flows into North Dakota from Canada. Legend has it that some of the very first French explorers encountered many field mice while camping on its banks. Sometimes the river is called the Mouse River.

Souris grew by leaps and bounds in its early years. At one time the population was between 1,000 and 1,300 and there were about seventy thriving businesses. One of the original is still in operation today. The State Bank of Bottineau, Souris Branch, has operated continuously in the same location for ninety years. The Cenex station, better known as the Farmers Union Oil Company, a mini-mall which includes a grocery, hardware, cafe, and post office, a tavern, and the Bottineau Elevator, Souris Branch, are the other businesses which are operating today.

The city has suffered from floods and fires over the years. The most recent fires were the burning of a Farmer's Union tanker in 1970, Monkman's Cafe on February 6, 1972, and a grocery store in 1979.

The first school was built in 1904 and the first senior class graduated in 1923. The old familiar structure at the north end of town was replaced by the present school in 1957.

The Methodist Congregation built a church in 1902; later on they merged with the Presbyterians and sold their building to the Lutherans. The first Catholic Mass was held in a private home. A church was built in 1904, but it was sold later when the population decreased. The only church in Souris today is Trinity Lutheran Church which was organized in 1925. The congregation erected a new brick church in 1950 and an entry addition was completed in 1976.

There were gas lights on the street corners until 1925 when the Frykman brothers installed an electrical generating power plant and operated it until 1929. In that year it was purchased by Otter Tail Power Company. The water and sewage system was installed in 1956.

Oil was discovered in the area in 1951. Recently oil drilling activity has been on the increase in the area northeast of Souris. There are several producing wells in the area.

Agriculture has always been an important industry in the Souris area. At one time there were many diversified farms, but now there are mostly grain farms. Farm size has increased steadily in the area, many abandoned farmsteads dot the landscape, and there has been an increase in the number of "sidewalk" farmers.

There have been no passenger trains through Souris for many years and the freight train service has declined.

The Souris Community Club was organized in 1974. It purchased the former John Deere Implement building in 1975, but it was later converted into a mini-mall and the club purchased the Redekkan Lodge building for its present community gatherings.

Entertainment in Souris centers on church, school, and Community Club activities. Cenex sponsors an annual spring oil sale and provides a dinner for its patrons. A community fund raiser is held each spring; activities include a Fun Night and a dinner served at the school.

Probably the biggest day in the history of Souris was the 4th of July celebration in 1905. Between 4,000 and 5,000 people attended a baseball game between Westhope and Souris.

Monkman's Cafe burning to the ground in 1972

Main Street Souris, North Dakota - 1990s

Souris City Park and Playground

The railroad has played an important part in the community's history by bringing in settlers, mail, machinery, and consumer goods and by transporting shipments of wheat, grain, coal, and cattle to distant markets.

In the spring of 1881 the Northern Pacific Railroad established a station at the mouth of the south fork of the Heart River. Later a small town located south of the river began to grow and was named South Heart. The South Heart post office was established October 18, 1883 with Bernard O. Finger as postmaster. In May 1908 a new townsite was platted by William Kennedy a short distance east of the original site.

In 1909 the Holland Dakota Land Company was organized to bring families from the Netherlands to North Dakota. Many of the early settlers were Dutch, Polish, and German immigrants who were persuaded to immigrate because of cheap land. They were primarily farmers and ranchers.

At first South Heart was a Catholic mission with masses being held in private homes. Father Dignam who directed the construction of St. Mary's Catholic Church in 1911 served as pastor until 1924 when he was succeeded by Father Schmitt who served until 1926. Father Rossler, 1927 to 1937 acquired a temporary rectory for the church. In

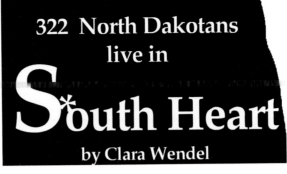

322 North Dakotans live in S*outh Heart
by Clara Wendel

1937 Father Andrews became the first resident pastor; he was succeeded by Father Brandner who succeeded him in 1944. Brandner served until 1976. During his tenure the old church was torn down and a new church and rectory were built in 1950 and dedicated in October 1961. Since 1976 the parish has been served by Monsignor Golowitch, 1976-1981; Father Chamber, 1981-1985; and Father Schumacker 1985 to the present.

Youngsters in grades one through eight attended South Heart Public School which was completed in 1916. The school consisted of five small classrooms and a gymnasium. After completing the eighth grade students often attended high school in Dickinson. In the fall of 1933 the local school included curricula for students in grades nine through twelve.

Two orders of nuns taught classes at South Heart, the Franciscan Order from 1939 to 1947 and the Sisters of the Holy Family of Nazareth from 1947 to 1959. The sisters' house is

now part of the present day teacherage. There are thirty teachers employed full-time to educate approximately 060 students.

Throughout the years the South Heart School District has consolidated with other rural school districts in Stark County.

Growing enrollments made it necessary to build additional classrooms, a stage, a larger gymnasium, an industrial shop, and administrative offices.

Many years ago the South Heart community consisted of a blacksmith shop, three grain elevators, the Powers, Occident, and Farmers, grocery stores, the Palace Hotel, a bank, a post office, church, community hall, railroad depot, public school, and Heidt's Bar. Many of these buildings were either torn down, burned, or closed because of financial difficulties.

Recently many modern facilities have been constructed to meet the town's needs: the Senior Citizen Center, the South Heart City Hall built in 1974, St. Mary's Catholic Church, Farmers Union Oil Company, Farmers Coop Elevator, South Heart Fire Hall, First National Bank of Belfield-South Heart Branch, Bear's Den Bar, the Triple D Apartments, South Heart Apartments, a low income housing complex, and the post office.

At the Adamski Park adults get together to play couples' softball and volleyball. Youngsters participate in T-ball and little league baseball. The South Heart City Park is another popular place where children like to play. Each year the Womens' Fire Auxiliary Department has been in charge of power pulls, including modified pickups and tractors pulling a weight, and masquerade dances as fund-raising activities.

South Heart held its 75th Jubilee celebration on June 17-19, 1983. "After 75 years we're still all heart" was a popular saying.

W.J. Kennedy's General Merchandise Store - late 1800s

The Senior Citizen Center in South Heart, North Dakota

A hick town is one where there is no place to go where you shouldn't be.

Robert Quillen

Northern Pacific Railroad depot of South Heart

Home Town of
444 North Dakotans ✻

St. Thomas
by Duane Littlejohn

The first settlers arrived in the area in 1879. Two years later the St. Paul, Minneapolis and Manitoba Railroad (later the Great Northern) began building a branch line north through Pembina County. A station was located on Sec. 3, T159N, R53W and a post office, Saint Thomas, was established there in July 1881. Thomas J. Lemon who was appointed postmaster suggested the town's name for his former home, Saint Thomas West which was the capital of Elgin County, Ontario.

Townsites along this line were controlled by Solomon G. Comstock and Almond A. White of Moorhead, Minnesota who platted a 56-block site in 1882. It incorporated with a town government four years later.

The first general store was built by Thomas and George Lemon; their first residence, considered a very fine home, remains occupied today.

The railroad arrived in 1882, establishing the town as the largest grain shipping point in the world; the town boasted of fourteen elevators. That same year the *St. Thomas Times* began publication and the public school began operation.

In 1887 the Bank of St. Thomas was established and during the next few years an opera house, fourteen saloons, an indoor skating and curling facility, the fastest horse racing track in North Dakota, gas lights, dial phones, and many other businesses were added to the town.

Hi-tech farming methods and the addition of several crops such as dry edible beans, soybeans, corn, sugar beets, and potatoes for the nation's fast food restaurants, along with specialty crops used in food preparation have changed this agricultural town, previously noted as the largest grain shipping point, to a "Garden of Eden" sometimes referred to as the "Nile of the North." The varied crops have added to the stability of the area's economy. The evening straw-stack fires of years ago have been replaced by the lights of potato and sugar beet harvesters and the hum of an edible bean processing plant.

Since 1980 the city lost about 16 percent of its population. The continued presence of four local churches are monuments to the varied ethnic and religious backgrounds of the local population which includes English, Irish, Germans, and Scandinavians. This diversity of backgrounds comes together as a common community spirit when cooperation is needed to improve the quality of life with the undertaking of a community project.

Ambition has always been a virtue admired by local residents and is evidenced by the well-maintained residences and businesses in the town

Caesar, when he first went into Gaul, made no scruple to profess 'That he had rather be first in a village than second in Rome.'

Francis Bacon
Advancement of Learning
II, XXiii, 36

and on the area farmsteads. A United States ambassador and editor-in-chief of *Life Magazine* a r e counted as two of the prominent citizens who were born and raised here.

The town's school has always been a center of community participation as witnessed by several bond issues for school expansion that have passed by overwhelming majority votes. In the fall of 1990 the elementary school enrolled 106 students, 40 were enrolled in high school. During the summer of 1987 the seating capacity of the school gymnasium was increased to seven hundred seats to accommodate expected increases in attendance at basketball games.

St. Thomas has a full complement of facilities including paved streets, central water, sanitary sewer, cable television, a seventeen-acre park and recreational complex, paved municipal airport, and an elderly housing complex.

The local Booster Club created a Community Development Corporation which has built a community restaurant and post office by raising contributions and managing the building for the common good. The recent addition of mobile home lots by the city is an effort to attract more residents to the town. Twenty-two homes in the city were substantially improved by a special housing project in 1985 under the sponsorship of city government.

The town celebrated its centennial in 1980 with a three-day event that will long be remembered. An estimated 4,000 people viewed the parade which had 167 entries. A 200-page centennial book, *A Century of St. Thomas Times* was published to commemorate the event. The Fire Department celebrated its centennial in 1986 as one of the oldest organized fire departments in the state.

St. Thomas built a Centennial Park on Main Street in 1987, to commemorate its history and the state's centennial.

Aerial view of present day St. Thomas, North Dakota

Main Street St. Thomas, North Dakota - 1976

Stanley, the county seat of Mountrail County, is located in the north central portion of one of the largest counties in North Dakota. It is located in the northwestern part of the state with the smoky waters of the Missouri River forming its southern and southwestern boundary. North Dakota 8 and US 2 pass through the city.

In 1887 the St. Paul, Minnesota and Manitoba Railroad (Great Northern) laid tracks through this area during construction of its line west from Minot towards Great Falls, Montana.

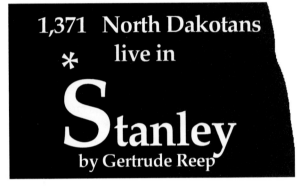

1,371 North Dakotans
* live in
# Stanley
by Gertrude Reep

In all probability it was responsible for first making the decision to locate a town at the site. The United States Government Survey plat filed in District Court in June 1894 shows the railroad tracks and the "Stanley" site located in the NW1/4SW1/4 of Sec. 21, T156N, R91W, now Idaho Township.

While there have been several explanations for the selection of the name, the facts appear to be lost in the mists of time. It is likely that the railroad's survey and construction crews, well aware of the topography, were influenced by the land when selecting names of the various sidings and water tank stops. So it is not unlikely that the name Stanley with an English meaning of "dweller of the rocky meadow" was chosen as the rails were laid in the Coteau du Missouri or "little hills of the Missouri." Some, however, say the site was named for Colonel King Stanley, an early pioneer, and others claim it was named for a Fort Berthold commander, David Sloane Stanley.

The Stanley site coexisted with the homestead of George W. Wilson who is considered the founder and promoter of the city. He filed homestead papers in 1901 and received his patent for the land in 1904. He and his family lived at Minot where he was connected with newspaper work. While living there he came to Stanley often enough to comply with the homesteading laws and in 1902 he had the townsite platted, built a home, and started a newspaper, the *Stanley Sun*. In 1908 he established a hotel and the next year opened a telephone exchange. The hotel remained in operation by the Wilson family until 1969 when it closed its doors.

Settlers began arriving in the early spring of 1902 with the first business place to open being The Pioneer Store. Other business establishments included a lumberyard, a pool hall, a livery barn, a department store, a bank, a lunch hall, and the office of a lawyer and land commissioner.

By 1906 the townsite was booming. Great Northern records reveal that during the spring months prior to July of that year, over 125 carloads of immigrants' effects were unloaded at

Stanley. The town had forty-two business establishments, two churches, and not a "blind pig" in sight. That year four grain elevators were built, making a total of five with a combined grain capacity of 150,000 bushels.

In December 1909 the city incorporated. At that time it was engaged in intense competition with four other communities to become the county seat. It succeeded in the general election of 1910. Four years later the construction of a courthouse styled in French Renaissance architecture was begun. It was the only structure built north of the railroad tracks for many years.

Perhaps the very first settlers in the community could be termed "Old American" with roots in the eastern part of the United States but very soon thereafter came the Scandinavians and other northern Europeans. Syrians settled in a community to the west as did a large group of Bohemians, and a Finnish settlement was established about fifteen miles to the south, all of whom visited the town for various reasons throughout the years. In 1911 the census of Stanley was listed as 518.

The first church structures built were Roman Catholic and Presbyterian with Evangelical Lutherans and Baptists soon to follow. At present those religions still maintain parishes along with Seventh-day Adven-

Community gathering on Main Street in Stanley - early period

Stanley's Community Hospital

tist, Maranatha Fellowship, and Free Lutheran parishes.

With the organization of the city in 1902, a school district was also formed and a two-room frame building was erected. Two years later a two-story brick building containing four classrooms and a basement was in use. This building was expanded in 1913 when the first high school graduation took place.

The school system continued to grow with a substantial structure built in 1927. In 1953 an elementary school building was erected and in 1961 a separate high school unit was built with additions several years later. By this time the original 1904 structure was demolished and the 1927 building was replaced with an additional elementary school in 1985. School reorganization and the discovery of oil created the need for the expansive building program.

An important milestone in the city's history is June 12, 1952. Local residents not only celebrated its 50th Jubilee, but they also conducted dedication ceremonies for a new Community Hospital. Stanley had expanded from a few tar paper shacks in 1902 to a thriving county seat of 1,486 folks.

Twenty-five years and one month later, in spite of a tornado that skipped along the southeastern edge of the city, local residents again paraded and celebrated their 75th Jubilee. The years between had seen a swell in the population to nearly 1,800 souls during the peak of oil activity, but with the leveling off in that industry, the head count dropped back to slightly more than 1,600. While never experiencing "boom or bust" activity, the city has always experienced a steady and sure growth.

The two highways still pass through the city and the Empire Builder of Amtrack stops daily at the train depot. The city has an airstrip of 50 by 3,400 feet, pavement overlay with a 300 by 300 foot parking ramp. The hospital has expanded and it as well as medical, dental, and optometry clinics continue to serve the area. A beautiful retirement home serving fifty-seven patients began operating in 1960 and is considered superior in nursing home care. A housing development program has eliminated any "slum" areas and the city continues to serve the area with over seventy business establishments and service outlets in addition to over twenty civic organizations. And Main Street has five business operations that are in the third generation.

It is a good city to live in. And even the city's fire hydrants are painted to depict patriotic characters held in esteem by the residents.

The Court House in Stanley, North Dakota

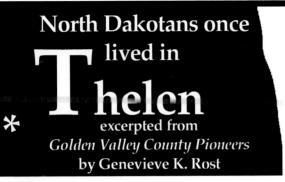
excerpted from
Golden Valley County Pioneers
by Genevieve K. Rost

Thelen, located approximately seven miles southeast of Beach, North Dakota, was named after John M. Thelen, original owner of the townsite. The Northern Pacific Railroad Company's branch line, built from Beach to Ollie, Montana, crossed his land and the railroad established a station there in 1915. Thelen laid out a small townsite east of the tracks in August 1916 and lots went on sale September 25, 1916. Among the first purchasers were J. F. Boyer, F. J. Hill, August Brockmeyer, T. E. Hayward, C. B. Bollum, A. J. Beiers, the Occident Elevator Company, Thompson Yards, Inc., Edward Honuson, and the Rocky Butte Church.

The town never grew to any size. Water was provided to all Thelen residents from a city well, dug in the center of town. For most of its history it consisted of: a general store; two grain elevators, the Farmers Elevator and the Occident which burned to the ground in the early 1920s. They then bought the Farmers Elevator; Thompson Lumber Yards which was operational for only about two years; and the Rocky Butte Church.

The Rocky Butte Church was built on land donated by Mary Telford and dedicated in 1910. Cora Beier and a Mrs. Haugen started a Sunday School. In 1919 it was moved to the town from its original site three miles south of Thelen. The basement of the church was used for all types of meetings. After the town's popu-

lation dwindled the church was sold and moved to Trotters.

The history of Thelen is really the history of a few families.

The August Brockmeyer family moved to Thelen in April 1917. Brockmeyer had grown up in Iowa, moved to Carrington, then homesteaded near Alpha. He started a blacksmith shop in Thelen and after about a year he moved a mile east and lived there for fifteen years. He ran a threshing rig and cook car, traveling from one neighbor to another threshing crops. The rig was powered by a Hart Parr engine. Brockmeyer also owned one of the first Rambler automobiles in the area.

Josepheus Boyer homesteaded in 1903 when he arrived with four of his children, Cora, Mata, Lawrence, and Ervie. Boyer was a carpenter. He had been foreman for a large construction company and had worked at Klondike, Alaska during the gold rush days. Boyer built his own farm buildings and those of many homesteaders as well. He built the Congregational

If you would be known, and not know, vegetate in a village; if you would know, and not be known, live in a city.

Charles Caleb Colton,
Lacon, Vol. i, no. 334, 1820

Church in Sentinel Butte which is still a sound, rigid building. Boyer's house still stands near Thelen.

Boyer's daughter, Cora, filed on a homestead in 1904. In 1909 she married another early homesteader, Abraham Beier. The next year they built a fine brick house. Beier hauled Hebron bricks from Sentinel Butte when it was more than -30 degrees F. Both were active in church work.

Abraham Beier had the first grain binder in Billings County. His wife, Cora, was leader of the first girls' 4-H Club in the county. Beier served on both the rural school board and the county welfare board for several years. Cora, her mother and sisters, and Mrs. Helen Brockmeyer were members of the Worthwhile Women's Club, the first homemaker's club in Golden Valley County.

Mata Boyer Bolum and Goldie Boyer Crouse ran the general merchandise store for about two years. It was next operated by the Troy Beach family and later managed by the Bert Palmer family. Mrs. Palmer was Lillie Boyer.

The Oscar Clarin family settled two and a half miles south of Thelen. He served on the local township board, the school board, the Agricultural Adjustment Administration (AAA) county committee, and was a member of the state AAA committee for seven years.

Ernest L. Walker, Martha Smith Walker, and Nancy Smith Hollenbeck filed homesteads near Thelen. Martha worked in the dining room of the Sentinel Butte hotel, and in Glendive for twelve dollars per month. She earned enough money to put siding and a gable roof on her house, and bought wallpaper for it.

The Thelen post office operated for only a short time, from July 21, 1920 until July 30, 1921. It reported a population of 15 in 1920; ten years later the population was only 4.

**Evelyn Cook, Herman Dietz,
Paul C. Popiel, Alma Waldahl,
Muriel Waldahl**

Thelen Congregational Church
(SHSND)

About Small Towns Along The Alaska Highway:

The isolation inevitably impels people to turn to one another, and what all these tiny settlements add up to is one very strung-out small town. "You live life under a microscope," said the waitress at the Mountain View Motor Inn. Wherever I stopped, at this roadhouse or that general store, the news was bound to be fresh - either gleaned from CNN via satellite dish (newspapers are scarce) or, even better, the latest gossip, rumors, updates on the daily dramas of life.

"The smaller communities are anything but simple," Father Marcel [Vogel] remarked as we sped down the icy, twilit road toward his home base at Our Lady of the Way in Haines Junction. "The inner workings are complex, and a lot of it's unwritten." And it can take a surprisingly long time to fit in. "A quarter to a third of the people move every two years," he said. "So one of the first questions they ask you is, 'How long are you going to be up here?' That is, 'Is it worth making an investment in you?' And the first year, of course, it's simply 'Are you tough enough to stay here?' "

And despite the romantic myth, this small-town scrutiny makes it pretty hard for fugitives from the law to lose themselves in the frozen north. "They're usually caught," shrugs Marvin Taylor. "People can detect them very quickly." Or, as a Mountie put it, "People still believe that we don't have faxes and satellite communications and that they can disappear. We know everyone who comes up here."

Richard Olsenius,
"Alaska Highway," National Geographic,
November, 1991, pp. 76-77

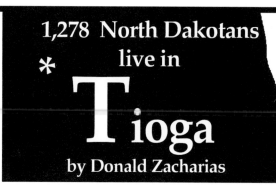
In 1887 a sidetrack and telegraph station named Tioga were established in eastern Williams County on the main line of the St. Paul, Minneapolis & Manitoba Railroad. *Tioga*, an Iroquois Indian name for "Peaceful Valley" probably refers to Tioga County in New York State; it apparently has no local significance.

Nicholas Comford, a townsite agent for the railroad, purchased the homestead of Joseph Jones in 1902 and platted a four-block townsite bordering the station. In that same year Nels W. Simon was appointed postmaster. He, along with U. H. Dixon and others, purchased lots from Comford.

The section house was one of the first buildings constructed in town. Interestingly enough, the first section laborers were nearly all Japanese. John McMahon, probably one of the first white people to work on the section crew, is responsible for planting the trees which beautify downtown Tioga today.

The first store was built in 1902 by Simon. A two-story structure, it housed a general merchandise and grocery store, the post office, and a barbershop; one section of the top floor was used for living quarters for Simon and his family. The other section served as a community hall. Many events were held there: religious services, suppers, programs, lodge meetings, dances, lectures, shows, and political gatherings.

The town's mercantile section expanded in 1905-1906 with the opening of various commercial enterprises: blacksmith shop, meat market, pool hall, hardware store, harness shop, hotel, tailor shop, tavern, drugstore, printing shop, and livery barns. At one time the town had three livery barns.

Dr. Robert Stobie, the town's first doctor, arrived in 1906. He served the entire area, treating patients in his home and travelling the countryside to care for the ill.

Fire destroyed the west side of town in 1907; however, most of the business places were rebuilt.

Early homes and business places were heated mostly by lignite coal, hauled from local mines. That changed with the discovery of oil in the region; now little coal is mined locally. Montana-Dakota Utilities Company provides natural gas for heating today. Tioga was the first city to receive North Dakota natural gas from the Signal Oil and Gas Plant, located just east of the city. The plant is now owned by Amerada Hess.

At one time the town was the largest primary grain market in the world, much of it coming across the Missouri River from McKenzie County. Farmers crossed on the Walters Ferry, reached Tioga the second day, unloaded their grain, and left for home the following day. Incorporated as a village in August 1909 it changed to a commission form of government in 1952.

Tioga became a boom town when on April 4, 1951 Amerada Petroleum Corporation found oil in the Nessen Anticline, a geological formation that is part of the Williston Basin. The discovery at Clarence Iverson No. 1 opened a new era for the state and for the community.

Oilmen, speculators, brokers, and laborers flooded into town, crowding into available living quarters, overloading schools and community facilities, and creating a host of new businesses. Drilling peaked in 1966 when 27,000,000 barrels were pumped from 1,965 producing wells.

The oil boom dramatically affected Tioga. Before oil was discovered the town had a population of about 500; by 1959 the population had soared to 2,700.

Today, Tioga has a population of about 1,300 with a clinic, hospital, nursing home, large park, swimming pool, radio station, newspaper, theater, bowling alley, funeral home, airport, four new churches, three schools, modern stores, many beautiful homes, and a very efficient fire department with a city and rural division. The town also has an ambulance crew and a large number of volunteer EMTs.

Although oil has played an important part in the development of Tioga, now known as the Oil Capital of North Dakota, ranching and grain farming continue to be the key factors in the economy of this area, and make Tioga the great city it is today.

Clarence Iverson Monument

Tioga Public School bus - 1919

Main Street Tioga, North Dakota - 1910-1912

T*owner

Home Town of 669 North Dakotans

by Nordis E. Wanberg

Towner was named for Colonel Oscar M. Towner, an early rancher, promoter, and speculator. A man of boundless energy filled with innovative ideas he helped promote the land boom in Dakota Territory, specifically, the Mouse River country and the area around Towner, the county seat of McHenry County. He established a ranch on the Mouse (Souris) River four miles south of the city.

Between August 14th and 17th, 1886 the St. Paul, Minneapolis and Manitoba Railroad (commonly called the Manitoba) laid the first tracks in the Towner area while constructing its line between Devils Lake and Minot. Two years before a town named Newport, located about four miles southwest of present day Towner had been established and had grown to include a post office, stores, and a newspaper, but when the railroad established its station at Towner the site was quickly abandoned. P. Kelly was named the first depot agent at Towner and the first depot was a 24 by 60 foot frame building constructed in 1886. On October 11, 1886 the railroad supplement timetable shows an extension to Minot.

Realizing the possibilities of the area S. G. Comstock and A. A. White, owners of the Northwest Land Company of Moorhead, Minnesota which handled townsites for the railroad in the area, purchased Towner's original townsite. They had the town surveyed and platted in August 1886,

the next year in May the plat was filed. The owners then began selling lots.

Comstock and White donated the lot for the first building in Towner to Philip Frisby and his wife in 1886. Lumber was hauled from Devils Lake and the Frisby's built a one-story, two-room shack with a tar paper roof. Then followed a hotel, hardware store, restaurant, general stores, rooming house, saloon, meat market, blacksmith shop, livery stable, and a meeting hall for dances and other entertainment. The post office was established on December 11, 1886 with Robert McCombs as the first postmaster. Andrew Gilbertson built the Towner Merchant's Bank which opened on March 24, 1893. It was the first bank on the Great Northern line from Grand Forks to Cut Bank, Montana. In 1915 Hagen Thompson started the Pioneer State Bank which today is the State Bank of Towner.

Towner was incorporated on May 4, 1892. The first census of 1892 recorded 40 heads of families and a total population of 152. On May 2, 1904 the Village of Towner became the City of Towner.

During its history the city has had nine newspapers. The first issue of *News and Stockman* edited by Robert McComb and C. D. Rice appeared in May 1887. Only one newspaper operates today, the *Mouse River Farmers Press*.

Churches and school were always important institutions in new settlements. Towner's first school was a wooden structure erected in 1887, the next, a two-story brick building was constructed in 1909 and the present grade and high school was built in 1952.

Circuit rider laymen, pastors, and

priests first served the territory. Reverend T. S. Reishus, the first regular Lutheran pastor called to Towner arrived in 1885. He served a big area, from Burlington to Towner, Round Lake, and later Rugby Junction. The first church building built in 1908 for Zion Lutheran Church had its cornerstone laid on November 22; it was dedicated July 4, 1909. The first funeral was that of Mrs. Gustave Johnson, the first woman buried in the Union Cemetery and the third burial there.

The pioneer pastor, Reverend R. T. Wanberg, and his bride came to Towner in August 1919. For more than forty-five years he served the Towner Parish, Berwick and Upham churches in the Rugby area, Norway on the river, Denbigh, and he also established the congregation at Granville. Wanberg's wife, an accomplished pianist, pipe organist, and speech and drama teacher, taught and shared her talents with the Towner area until her death in May 1960. Wanberg died in January 1988 having seen 100 Christmases and New Years.

The Episcopal Church, although active for many years was dissolved in the 1930s. The Presbyterian Church was incorporated on June 3, 1894. The congregation presently owns the first church building erected in the city. It was dedicated September 2, 1894 with the understanding from banker Andrew Gilbertson that the building be used jointly by the Lutherans and the Presbyterians.

The first Catholic Mass was held in a railroad section house in 1888. The first Catholic Church wasn't built until 1905.

McHenry County was organized in 1884 and was named after the Honorable James McHenry, a member of the Territorial Legislature from Clay County, then a part of Dakota Territory. There were no white settlers in the county until 1882 when they began to arrive in substantial numbers. The census of 1885 revealed that in four years time the population had grown to 800. Towner became the county seat on December

Main Street Towner, North Dakota - ca. 1890

Dedication of McHenry County Court House - 1908

18, 1886.

Some homesteaders filed claims around Towner, but most of the land fell into the hands of large ranchers who took advantage of luxurious prairie grasses, the Mouse River which provided water, and an open range policy to raise large herds of beef cattle. Early ranchers other than Towner whose spreads were south and west of Towner were Ed Hackett, Hans Kopperdal, Theodore Rom, Ole and Andrew Gilbertson, Ulrich and Ole Thorson, Martin Bredalen, Jacob Nelson, James Pendroy, J.B. Laton, Jim Reed, Coutts Majoribanks, Edmund E. Thursby, and George Stevens. John Ely, Tom Forsythe, Robert and Tom Fox, Joe Elliot, Oscar Lynburner, and Hans Oium ranched north and west of Towner.

Edwin B. Payne, who came in 1886, was the first doctor in Towner and in the county. A Civil War veteran and widower, he married Abbie W. Walrath in 1887 in the first marriage ceremony performed in the town. Another doctor, O. S. Craise a Canadian and graduate of McGill University, came to the area in 1910. He retired in 1954. His two nurses, Mrs. Elizabeth (Fox) Shipman who died at age 102 and Dorothy (McDonald) Lunde, who were known as "Angels of Mercy," traveled with him throughout the county making house calls. Homer Hill who operated the drug store for over forty years was the young people's silent benefactor, revered for his wisdom and philosophy.

The first meeting of the Towner Historical Society, now the McHenry County Historical Society, Museum, Incorporated, was held on August 10, 1962. Mrs. R. T. Wanberg was elected its first president. The society is housed in the old Zion Lutheran Church building which was built in 1908.

Towner, The Cattle Capitol of North Dakota and County Seat of McHenry County, had a population of 669 in 1990. Businesses which supply products and services throughout the United States include the Towner Nursery, Gunter Honey, Winger Cheese, Incorporated, and Hutton Contracting Company.

Towner is also the administrative center for several government programs: Headstart, Child Development Center, Agriculture Stabilization and Conservation Service (ASCS), Soil Conservation Service (SCS), and Farmers Home Administration (FHA).

Although the depot was sold and moved away the Great Northern Railroad, now the Burlington Northern Railroad, still runs through the city and provides service. Passenger service is provided by Amtrack, although to board one must either travel twenty miles east to Rugby or fifty miles west to Minot. Freight trains are also scheduled along the line.

Annual

events which are celebrated in the city include The All Faith Service held at the McHenry County Historical Society Museum in June, the annual rodeo and 4th of July parade, Kiddie Parade, Crazy Days, The Harvest Inn, Flower and Art Show, Thanksgiving Give Away Turkeys by the merchants, Christmas Bonus Bucks, Visit of Santa Claus, and high school graduation.

The community has many clubs including: Future Farmers of America, 4-H, Homemakers, Craft, Painting, Jaycees, Women's Club, Darners (Women), Democrat, Republican, Veterans of Foreign Wars, American Legion, American Legion Auxiliary, Chamber of Commerce, Girl and Boy Scouts, Towner Senior Citizens VIP (Very Important Persons to the Children and Grandchildren), Order of the Eastern Star, Rainbow Girls, Mouse River Lodge No. 43, and the Towner Golf Club.

The city park includes playground equipment, tennis courts, a softball field, a picnic area and campgrounds free to all.

As one enters the Union Cemetery through the stone archway gates given by the Pioneer Daughters and wends one's way around the many beautiful trees and shrubbery one comes to the Memorial which is dedicated to all McHenry County veterans who died fighting for their country. The brick edifice houses an enclosed large plaque with the engraved names of all who died, from World War I through the Viet Nam conflict.

Citizens of Towner, North Dakota - 1895

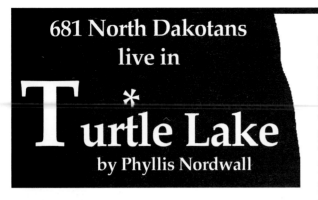

681 North Dakotans live in

T*urtle Lake

by Phyllis Nordwall

O ur town, Turtle Lake, will observe its centennial in 2005, but the area was settled several decades before.

In 1884 two Hansons established farms which are Centennial Farms. The earliest homesteader on the south side of Turtle Lake, (the lake takes its name from its shape) was Peter Miller in whose farmhouse the Turtle Lake post office was established in January 1886. During the next several years business establishments opened up nearby, and a townsite called Miller was promoted, but the Northern Pacific Railroad

Company in its push westward from Denhoff bypassed that site and purchased land owned by George R. Wannemacher of Dickinson, North Dakota. Wannemacher and F.D. Haevener, anticipating a boom, platted a townsite called Wanamaker in July 1903. The probability that the new town would prosper caused the Turtle Lake post office to be moved there in April 1904.

The Denhoff extension, built in 1905, stopped several miles east of Wanamaker. The railroad built a station there, calling it Turtle Lake. In July 1905 the McLean County Townsite Company platted the Turtle Lake townsite and the Turtle Lake post office along with every other building in Wanamaker was moved to the new town. Locally known as the "twin cities," the townsites Miller and Wanamaker were abandoned along with Arvidson, a townsite platted by J. W. Arvidson on land he owned.

By 1922 a row of grain elevators by the railroad tracks testified to the industry of the area. Lightning struck one of the tall structures, and all but one burned down in a spectacular blaze. They were soon rebuilt. Another disastrous fire occurred in 1966 when the Memorial Hall which housed the fire trucks burned.

The train depot was remodeled in 1969 and serves as a meeting place for the senior citizens, who call their organization the Sixty-Niners. The track is still maintained and a lonesome train whistle can be heard occasionally.

In the 1960s when Turtle Lake adopted the slogan "The Hub City of the Lake Region," the numerous lakes were alkali, supporting many water birds but no fish. With the partial completion of the Garrison Diversion Canal, fresh water was pumped into a chain of lakes close to town and a whole new recreation area was developed. The lakes are stocked with fish, and a large park

Main Street Turtle Lake about 1912

complex built in the middle 1980s provides softball diamonds and picnic areas. Looking toward the future the city dedicated a municipal airport with a 3,200-foot turf runway in 1986.

Even before the town incorporated, Methodist, Baptist,and Roman Catholic Churches organized. The farming community was settled by people of Scandinavian and German heritage and many of their churches and schools dotted the countryside. With the coming of automobiles and better roads those churches combined and built in town. In observing the 1987 World Day of Prayer, eight churches joined in the worship service, signifying the unity and harmony that exists in our community.

Although Turtle Lake School District No. 11 was organized as early as October 1892, it did not serve the town for over a half century. Reorganized in 1900, its boundaries were changed; further reorganization in the area took place in September 1902 with the creation of Crooked Lake School District No. 26. In August 1913 land was shifted from that district to Lake Williams School District No. 72 which served the town. That district was reduced in size in July 1922; eventually, citizens through reorganization and consolidation of local districts created Lake Williams School District No. 72 in

The elevators of Turtle Lake - 1912

June 1959.

School was held in a variety of buildings before a two-story frame building was constructed in 1907; it was replaced with a brick structure in 1923. Classrooms were added in 1939, but enrollment outgrew capacity; and after extensive planning and reorganizing, a new Junior-Senior High building was dedicated in 1961. In 1972 the Turtle Lake-Mercer School District No. 72 was formed.

In 1907 G. E. Heinzeroth came to town as a young medical doctor. He had only his small office building on Main Street, but he touched the lives of every family, near and far, as he

tended to the sick in their homes. A 32-bed community hospital was constructed in the early 1950s; it was staffed by Dr. Harold Kuplis and competent nurses. After Kuplis' retirement in January 1984 the hospital went through a trying period because of changes in government policies and a succession of doctors who stayed for only short periods of time. Under the leadership of a dedicated Board of Directors and the concern of everyone in the community the facility is still operating and expectations are for steady progress in the near future.

Turtle Lake has had a public library since 1923. In spite of some difficult years the library is now thriving and serving the reading public, especially the children.

The Commercial Club is an organization of business people whose purpose is to promote the welfare of the community. They can point with pride to many improvements and developments. Almost every person in town is a member of one or more of the numerous civic, service, volunteer, or social organizations that meet regularly.

Aerial view of Turtle Lake in 1986

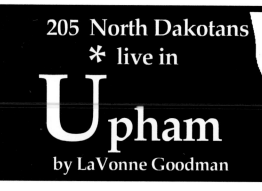

205 North Dakotans
* live in
Upham

by LaVonne Goodman

The Towner-Maxbass branch line of the Great Northern Railroad was built in 1905, facilitating the establishment of Upham in the summer of that year. Located in Meadow Township in north central McHenry County the town lies two miles from the Mouse (Souris) River Valley, a site chosen by the first pioneers who began homesteading in and along the valley in 1887. Upham's townsite was platted in June 1905 on property owned by the Dakota Development Company of Willmar, Minnesota.

Not everyone agrees on the naming of the town. Some say it was named after Dr. Warren Upham, a long-time superintendent of the Minnesota Historical Society. Others suggest it was probably named for Henry Pratt Upham, a close personal friend of James J. Hill and president of the First National Bank of St. Paul.

The village prospered as immigrants came to claim free land. By 1915 Upham boasted three lumberyards, two hotels, three general stores, a butcher shop, several hardware and machinery businesses, two livery stables, a small hospital staffed by two doctors, a newspaper, the *Upham Star*, a drug store, three banks, five independent elevators, and several other enterprises necessary for a prospering community.

A three-story, ten-room brick school was built in 1906 to serve Upham's educational needs. Three additions to the school have since been built, the latest in 1967. The school still serves the community.

Each ethnic group quickly formed church congregations using their native languages. The Icelandic Melankton congregation was incorporated in 1897, the Norwegian Bloomfield congregation in 1900, and the German Peace Reformed in 1907. The Methodists briefly had a congregation; they built a church which was purchased by Melankton in 1923.

Upham served a diverse clientele. To the east, along the Mouse River Valley, was the Icelandic settlement. The Norwegian settlements lay north and west, and the Germans and German-Russians to the southwest. The area to the south and east was mostly inhabited by Americans who came from the states along the Ohio and Mississippi Rivers. These settlers formed a nucleus the foreign immigrants built upon in learning to become Americans.

This seems to have been an auspicious mix, for the community and the town prospered.

Progress seems to be measured by material things. Upham acquired wooden sidewalks and three gas street lamps in 1912. A municipal light plant was built in 1925.

In 1947 the village reorganized as a city, with a mayor-council form of government.

In the early 1960s the principal streets were paved. A sewer and water system were also completed.

Through the years Upham has been supported by several civic-minded organizations such as the Commercial Club, the American Legion and Auxiliary, the Upham Betterment Club, GALA women's group, and various church auxiliaries. The Women's Christian Temperance Union purchased and developed a square block park which has been faithfully tended and is still used today.

In the past two decades Upham has suffered a decline common to most rural cities due to the exodus from the farms. While it once grew and prospered because it filled a need in the area, Upham now reflects diminished demand for a local business center. Progress is now measured by survival. Upham still has a school, post office, hardware store, repair shop, grocery, dry goods store, cafe, two bank stations, two bars, a bulk station, three churches, a construction company, a substantial grain elevator complex, and a fine community of people who love to call Upham home.

Main Street Upham, North Dakota - late 1970s
(DPDP - Todd Strand)

Upham State Bank, Upham, North Dakota
(SHSND)

Original public school in Upham, North Dakota
(SHSND)

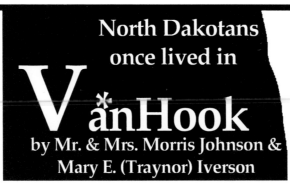

VänHook

by Mr. & Mrs. Morris Johnson &
Mary E. (Traynor) Iverson

Van Hook has the distinction of having moved twice during its history. People squatted for sometime near the townsite while it was being platted. They moved to the site in 1914. The town moved again in 1953 when the federal government purchased land for the Garrison Reservoir; many people moved to New Town.

The federal government opened land on both sides of the Fort Berthold Indian Reservation for settlement in 1912. In anticipation of the planned construction of a Minneapolis, St. Paul & Sault Ste Marie Railroad (Soo Line) branch line to the Missouri River the Van Hook townsite was platted in June 1912. Rail service to Van Hook was provided when track was laid two years later and a station established. The town served as railhead until early 1915 when the line was completed to Sanish on the Missouri. The completion of the line assured that the town would become an established, progressive city. It was named for Fred Van Hook, an early surveyor and area homesteader.

In 1915 the town's growth was so rapid it was nicknamed "The City of Speed." Signs were erected at the city limits which read: "The City of Speed—speed limit 75 mph—beat it if you can!"

At that time the city included the Soo Line depot, two banks, two lumber companies, an undertaker, a doctor, two lawyers, an opera house, two newspapers, and two hotels. The post office was established January 19, 1915 with John W. George as postmaster. These and several business offices were among the forty-four registered businesses.

In 1953 the site was determined to become partially inundated by the lake created by the construction of the Garrison Dam. The land was sold to the federal government. In 1987 some of this land was declared excess and was repurchased by Mountrail County. The area is now being developed into one of the finest recreational areas in North Dakota, the Van Hook-Traynor Park.

It is located on the shore of Lake Sakakawea, the lake created by Garrison Dam. One of the large bays of the lake is called Van Hook Arm and is known world-wide for its excellent walleye fishing.

Van Hook should be given the name "The City that Would Not Die." It is no longer an incorporated village or city, but the area still carries the name. It now hosts more summer campers than it had residents in 1953.

The desire to continue Van Hook is so strong that its former residents have held a reunion every five years since 1967. Plans are already underway for the next reunion in 1992.

Traynor Satermo Hardware Store - ca. 1936

West side Main Street VanHook, North Dakota - winter of 1914

Though he be a fool, yet he keeps much company, and will tell all he sees or hears, so a man may understand what the common talk of the town is.

Samuel Pepys,
Diary,
September 2, 1661

Main Street VanHook, North Dakota
(SHSND)

Home Town of 63 North Dakotans

V * oltaire

by Pamela Seibel & Inez Bradshaw

Voltaire Township, T152N, R79W, was organized in 1903. In 1900 the Soo Line Railroad established a station named Voltaire in the NE1/4 sec. 1, T152N, R80W in Brown Township and the NW1/4 sec. 6, T152N, R79W in Voltaire Township. It was probably named by railroad officials to honor the French philosopher Francois Voltaire; some, however, suggest it was named after an early settler. Some of the first settlers in the area were the Castles, the Hunters, the Henrys, and the Colters.

Voltaire was a small town. In addition to the station there was a store owned by Weise and Thompson, a hardware store operated by H. G. Bundy, and a hotel managed by a Mrs. Anderson. Banking services were provided by Ole Engebretson and two elevators, the Farmers Elevator and another owned by one Sparks served the farmers. A few years later the Farmers Elevator burned. The post office was established January 21, 1901 with Ole Ranum as postmaster.

The first schoolhouse was located in the northeast part of town, but in 1918-1919 a consolidated school was built in the western part of town.

Voltaire was incorporated in 1929 for the purpose of bringing in electricity. The board of trustees at that time was composed of C.P. Byers, Lawrence Williams, and Milton Schmidt with Con Solvberg acting as clerk and treasurer.

Like all towns Voltaire has experienced many changes. For example, the store originally owned by Weise was bought and managed by Con Solvberg. About 1929 it burned and Solvberg moved his business into the town hall. Later he and his nephew, Magnus Solvberg, formed a partnership and established The Voltaire Mercantile which operated until the uncle and his family moved to Marysville, Washington. Melvin Frantsen was the next operator of the store; later it was Wayne Odegard. Eventually the building was unoccupied and it was sold to one Lienhart of Velva where it became part of Erv Anderson's Star City Motor.

The Voltaire bank was later used as a restaurant, operated first by the Carl Olsons and later by Bertha and Bob Colter. Christ Roebuck eventually purchased the building, disassembled it, and took it to Velva where he used it to build his first home.

Another historical building, Meyer's Restaurant, has been remodeled several times, first by M.P. Bonine who used it as a rooming house and then by the Martin Knutsons who used it as their home. Later it was remodeled again and, with a post office added, it became the home of Bob and Millie Latimer.

The first school building was purchased and remodeled into a home for the Con Solvberg family. It has had several occupants since.

In 1960 the Voltaire School District No. 26 was reorganized with the Velva School District. The school in Voltaire continued to operate until 1966 when it closed because of declining enrollments. Students now are bussed to the Velva school. The building was bought by Delbert Krumwiede who demolished it and constructed a new home.

The most enduring institution in the community has served it for over eighty years. On March 24, 1909 five families met at the Christ Roebuck home to organize The Hjerdal Congregation. Present were the M. A. Holte, Gunder Setran, Ed Holte, Peter Thoreson, and Christ Roebuck families. The group agreed to organize under the name of Hjordal Norwegian Evangelical Lutheran Congregation of McHenry County.

Thoreson offered a piece of land on which to build a church and locate a cemetery. M.A. Holte, Roebuck, and Setran along with Thoreson were appointed as a committee to survey the land and were asked to report at the next meeting which was held on March 30. The congregation also contacted Pastor Olaf Rossing and hoped to meet with him at their next meeting. At the next meeting which was held again in the Roebuck home the committee reported that they had surveyed the land and had selected an acre and a half on which to build their church.

The first officers elected were: Reverend Olaf Rossing, president; Peter Thoreson, Ed Holte, and Gunder Setran, trustees; Johannes Roebuck, treasurer; and M. A. Holte, secretary. The group decided they couldn't offer the pastor a fixed salary; he was supported the first year by a free will offering. The annual meeting was set for the first Monday in December every year.

On March 29, 1916 the congregation voted to build a church next to the cemetery. Funds for the building were obtained by donations from members and friends of the congregation, from the Ladies Aid, and by securing a small loan from the bank. The cost of the new building was $2,065. Still an active congregation Hjerdal Lutheran offers Sunday School classes and has an active women's organization. The church celebrated its 75th Anniversary in 1984.

Today a younger, active, and hardworking generation lives in and loves the community and continues to keep the town clean, neat, and presentable with well-kept yards, gardens, and trees.

Under the spreading chestnut tree
The village smithy stands;
The smith a mighty man is he
With large and sinewy hands.
And the muscle of his brawny arms
Are strong as iron bands.

Henry Wadsworth Longfellow,
The Village Blacksmith, st. 1,
1842

Main Street Voltaire, North Dakota - 1976
(DPDP - Todd Strand)

Walcott was founded in 1880 when the St. Paul, Minneapolis and Manitoba Railroad, later the Great Northern, established a station by that name on land belonging to Frank E. Walcott. He had purchased it from the railroad the year before and when the station was established he platted the Walcott townsite in December 1880.

The earliest settlers and businessmen came from eastern states, but many subsequent arrivals were immigrant Norwegians, with some Germans settling southwest of the town. Many of the Norwegians had emigrated from Hallingdal, Norway, and so Walcott became the birthplace of "Hallinglag of America," which in 1982 celebrated its 75th Anniversary there. A city park monument commemorates this occasion.

The post office was established January 6, 1881 with Walcott as the first postmaster. The post office originally had three routes; two still remain after consolidation. He also started a general store, and many other businesses opened during the next several decades including: cafes, saloons, hardware, blacksmith, elevators, harness shop, druggist, hotel, doctor, livery, millinery shop, lumberyard, undertaker, stockyards, banks, jeweler, barbershop, butcher shop, creamery, photographer, newspaper, auto dealer, machinery dealer, garages, theater, oil dealer, opera house, recreation parlor, real estate office, and others. Otter Tail Power Company brought electricity

in the 1920s, replacing the town's thirty-two volt light plant.

With the coming of the Great Depression and World War II, Walcott's heyday passed, but the town still endures with guarded optimism for the future.

A Norwegian Lutheran Congregation was established in 1889. The church building, completed ten years later, is still used today. An Evangelical United Brethren Church was located in Walcott for twenty-five years, but was moved to Kindred in 1954.

A grade school, built in the 1880s, was relocated and enlarged about 1912 to accommodate high school classes. About 1930 the wooden structure was torn down and a gymnasium built with the lumber. A new brick schoolhouse was also constructed. This served until 1971 when it was razed, after the school merged with Kindred. The gymnasium serves as a community center today.

Walcott still has rail service to its elevator. Once three elevators existed,

75th Ann. of Hallinglag of America - 1982

however, all burned, and the present one was rebuilt in 1972. The first parsonage burned in 1905 and the church steeple burned in 1948. Walcott has escaped major fires and tornadoes, but in 1955 a tornado devastated many farms southwest of town.

Current businesses include: Harvest States Elevator and Fertilizer, welding shop, cafe, tavern, post office, grocery, barbershop and beauty shop, and a service station.

Walcott has an active volunteer fire department, a Senior Citizens organization, and an American Legion Post and Auxiliary. The Legion annually holds Memorial Day services and a dinner.

The Lutheran Church is a community focal point, and annually serves a lutefisk supper to over 800 people. The Park Board maintains a good park and playground equipment and the city has installed modern water and sewer systems.

Walcott has maintained a stable population; it is only a half hour drive on Interstate 29 to Fargo where many residents are employed. There have been efforts in recent years to upgrade older houses and several new houses and two four-plex apartments have been built. The main street has been blacktopped and the town enjoys access to excellent hard-surfaced roads in several directions. A short bus ride brings children to the Kindred school. Prospects are favorable for retaining population and the essential services for the town and surrounding area.

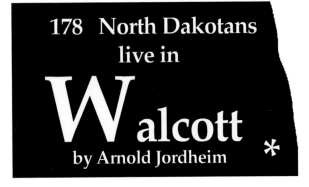

178 North Dakotans live in **W**alcott *

by Arnold Jordheim

A village is a hive of glass,

Where nothing unobserved can pass.

C.H. Spurgeon,
Salt Cellars,
1885

Business district of Walcott, North Dakota - 1895

Steamer pulling eight wagons of potatoes - late 1800s

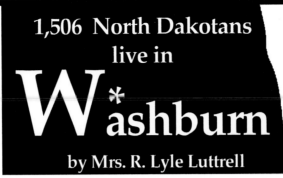

1,506 North Dakotans live in W*ashburn

by Mrs. R. Lyle Luttrell

The City of Washburn was established in 1882 as a riverboat landing and way-station for stage coaches. It was named for a one-time governor of Wisconsin, Cadwallader Colden Washburn, who was admired by its two founders, John Satterlund and John S. Veeder.

"King John" Satterlund was a Swedish immigrant, land promoter, and railroad contractor who had come from Port Arthur, Canada in 1878 and had set up a farming and stock-raising operation some fifteen miles north of Bismarck, Dakota Territory. Veeder had brought his family from Wisconsin to Bismarck in 1881, and in the spring of 1882 homesteaded on land forty miles north of Bismarck. Both men became partners in the townsite venture.

The first business in Washburn was a store established by Satterlund and Veeder. The first building in the new town served as the depot for the stages and as the post office which was originally located on George G. Rhude's ranch along the Turtle Creek. When the town was established the Turtle Valley post office was moved to the new site and re-named Washburn.

Early settlers in the area included many Scandinavians, Germans, German-Russian, and a Jewish colony, emigrants from southern Russia who returned to the eastern states after a brief attempt to adapt to the rugged conditions faced by the settlers. The homesteaders were quick to establish churches and schools. As the younger generation adapted to "American" ways church services, originally conducted in their parents' tongue, gave way to English. Washburn's first school, built in 1884, also served as a community church. Presently there are Baptist, Catholic, Lutheran, Methodist, and Bible congregations active in the city.

Washburn was officially founded on November 1, 1882. When McLean County was organized and named one year later it was designated as the county seat. The first courthouse, erected in 1884, was completely destroyed by fire in 1905. A second frame building, now used as a museum, served from 1905 to 1915 when a brick structure was erected. It is still used, although it has been remodeled and expanded.

Washburn was an important river port during its early days, with steamboats en route from St. Louis to Montana landing daily. It depended on the river for transportation until 1901 when the Bismarck, Washburn and Great Falls Railroad extended its line from Wilton. The company was owned by Cadwallader Washburn's older brother, William Drew Washburn. By 1901 riverboat traffic had dwindled to little or nothing. Plans for the Northern Pacific Railroad to reach Washburn never did materialize. The Soo Line now serves the area.

Early businesses in Washburn included two hotels, a flour mill, a livery stable, and several saloons. A printing press purchased by Satterlund and Veeder was housed in a building on Main Street and the first edition of the Washburn Times was printed on May 10, 1883. Since that time there has always been a weekly newspaper in the city.

The main industries of the area have always been farming and stock-raising. Coal has long been and continues to be an important resource, with coal-powered generating plants in the county, and nearby on the west side of the Missouri River. They generate huge amounts of electrical power that is transmitted many miles to adjoining states. The manpower needed for the construction and operation of these several plants and coal mines, has brought numerous new families to the area, a welcome addition to the city.

Many active local organizations contribute their time and talent to serve the community in various ways. Some of them are the American Legion and its Auxiliary, the Jaycees and the Lions Club, the Knights of Columbus, two women's clubs, the Masonic Order and the Order of the Eastern Star, various church organizations and homemakers clubs, Boy and Girl Scouts, and booster clubs associated with the school. The Washburn Civic Club is active as a Chamber of Commerce and civic booster organization.

Present day public school in Washburn, North Dakota

Since the first observance of Memorial Day in 1884 it has been a special holiday in Washburn, with a band concert, parade, and a program honoring the war dead.

Riverboat Days in June is an annual celebration that attracts crowds to enjoy games, races, a carnival, shows, and other activities. An annual Art Show each fall is another high point of the year. It provides a showcase for the talents of area artists.

Fort Mandan, three miles west of the city, is an authentic replica of Lewis and Clark's 1804-1805 winter quarters. It was built by the McLean County Historical Society which also operates two museum buildings in downtown Washburn. The Joe Taylor cabin, now located on East Main Street, was the home of an early Painted Woods settler, a printer from Pennsylvania who came west with Sully's Army in 1863-1864. From 1869 until his death in 1908 he trapped and hunted, wrote books on frontier life, and also edited the *Washburn Leader* which was printed until recent years.

The Sioux Ferry, the last sternwheeler on the Missouri River, is preserved in Riverside Park. A boat ramp is also available there; a great spot for walleye fishing.

Washburn boat landing along the Missouri River - early 1900s

Western North Dakota 4-H Camp, a beautiful wooded camp along the Missouri River, is located two miles west of the city on a county road. Painted Woods Golf Course, one of the finest, most beautiful nine-hole grass green courses in the state, is lo-cated five miles southeast along US 83.

Historic, beautiful, friendly, and nestled along the banks of the Missouri River, Washburn is proud of its past and is looking forward to the future.

Main Street Washburn, North Dakota - 1902

When the Northern Pacific Railroad extended its branch line west from Golden Valley into Dunn County in 1914 it intended to establish a station named Werner. In May of that year the Tuttle Land Company of Dawson, North Dakota platted the Werner townsite alongside the railroad's partially-completed grade. Later that same year the railroad was completed and the Werner station established.

The town was named after John Steinman Werner, a successful busi-

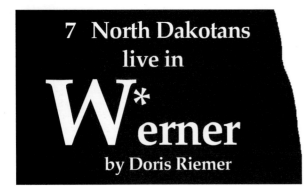

7 North Dakotans live in

W*erner

by Doris Riemer

nessman in Dawson who was also a relative of Lee Pettibone, the president of the townsite company. Werner, born in New York City in September 1862, later worked for the Remington Repeating Arms Company, traveling throughout the country as an exhibition marksman. Finding Dakota to his liking he homesteaded near Dawson in 1883 and later moved to the town and entered business. He invested in property and opened a bank in Werner after it was established. Many people would have preferred the town to have been named Three Springs, where the first store, destroyed by fire, had been built.

The town's first settler was T. L. Quill, a Norseman. In 1914 he had driven his Ford automobile along Spring Creek and had observed the fine grass and the prosperous farmers in the area. He bought a town lot, purchased the Renville store and post office, and had it moved on wheels pulled by a threshing engine into Werner. This structure was the

town's first business and house. The building later became a drug store and housed the office of Dr. I. M. Law. Quill, a dentist, built another store across the street.

In 1915 Olai Williams, an exceptionally active town booster, built a model hardware store. Two years later the town was incorporated. By this time many businesses had been established: the Hutchinson Lumber Company, managed by Grant Talcott, John Hanks built a pool hall, a restaurant was managed by Sten Williams, the Equity Elevator and Trading Company, the Star Elevator, Werner Hotel, Hulett Brothers and Implements, J. L. Bessaw Barber Shop, Robinson and Darwin Blacksmith Shop, Traxel Butcher Shop, the William and Johnson Hardware, Miller and Christensen's General Store, Ableman and Pulver's Feed Barn, and the Farmers Elevator which was destroyed by fire in 1921. At one time the town supported two banks, the Merchants State Bank whose cashier was L. A. Winters and the First State Bank of Werner whose cashier was F. W. Leete. At this time the only cooperative in Dunn County was the Farmers Cooperative Creamery.

In 1915 the *Werner Record* began publication under the editorship of Alex McDonald. Four years later it was sold to Hugh Black who changed its name to the *Werner Spotlight*. By 1930 the town had grown to over 300 residents and 25 profitable businesses.

At one time the town was served by three churches: Roman Catholic, Presbyterian, and Lutheran. In its early days a Lutheran pastor, Horneland, from Dunn Center, was asked to hold services in the Quill Grocery store in the Norwegian tongue. In 1919 the Lutherans purchased the Leete lots and built a church. A Reverend Taylor was called from Taylor; he served five towns.

Saturday nights and the Fourth of July were major occasions for the surrounding community. Shopping and visiting were enjoyed by everyone and Werner was said to have had the best dances in Dunn County.

People began to leave Werner during the Great Depression; in 1970 town government was dissolved. In 1975 a tornado nearly demolished the last elevator in Werner.

If an experiment started by state government had continued and had been successful Werner's population would be considerably larger than what it is today. People who wanted to persuade farmers to diversify the state's agriculture began to promote the dairy industry and when the Nonpartisan League gained complete control of the state government in the election of 1918 some Leaguers were inspired to promote the cause. In March 1919 Governor Lynn Frazier signed into law legislation which directed the Commissioner of Agriculture and Labor to establish a State Experimental Creamery. Sponsored by Leaguers from Morton, Mercer, and Dunn counties Senator A. A. Liederbach of Dunn County was instrumental in solving the problem of the creamery's location.

A farmers co-operative creamery which had fallen on bad times was available in Werner. The Werner creamery had a few advantages to recommend it: its availability with much of its equipment intact, a dependable supply of pure water from an artesian well, most of the area's newspapers supported the idea of a state creamery, and access to the Chicago market over Northern Pacific Railroad lines.

The experiment was short-lived, however. The creamery operated only for about seven months; it opened about June 1, 1920 and closed in January 1921. The experiment ended for various reasons. Although innovative methods were used to gather cream to insure a quality product the supply was not sufficient to justify the operation. Though encouraged by local newspapers and the Better Farming Association area farmers did not practice dairy farming in a big way. Furthermore, the creamery had to compete with Wisconsin processors who were closer to the Chicago market and many communities in the state had their own creameries. The creamery also got caught in the stormy politics of the 1920s.

The seven people who still live on the old Werner townsite love the quiet, clean, and beautiful spot and there are many more who cherish fond memories.

To say the least, a town life makes one more tolerant and liberal in one's judgment of others.

Henry Wadsworth Longfellow
Hyperion, 2.10, 1839

Grain elevators in Werner, North Dakota - 1976
(DPDP - Ken Jorgensen)

North Dakota's Experimental Creamery at Werner - 1920
(SHSND)

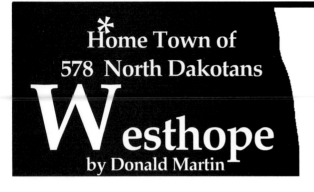
Westhope was founded in the fall of 1903 when the St. Paul, Minneapolis and Manitoba Railroad Company (Great Northern) decided to extend a branch line west from Souris across the Mouse River; but its origins began when an inland, rural post office named Richburg was established in January 1900. Some five months later the postmaster, Jules Beaudoin, moved his store and post office several miles southeast of that original location. Two years later, in June 1902, Conant E. Nelson acquired title to that land and in August, he and his silent partner, Grant S. Trimble, platted the Richburg townsite.

That same year Fred H. Stoltze of St. Paul, Minnesota purchased 160 acres of land about one and one-half miles east of Richburg, obviously working in collusion with the railroad officials. The following year the railroad de-cided to extend its branch west from Souris across the Mouse River. Stoltze told the people of the community that his townsite would be as far as the much desired would go. In July 1903 Stoltze announced that the new town would be called Westhope, and in August he platted the townsite. On December 10, 1903 the *Westhope Standard* headlined that the "Trains Are Running." Westhope had two post offices for several months: the Scotia office was moved to the town in the fall of 1903 and in December was renamed Westhope; the Richburg office was also moved there, but discontinued in February 1904.

Bottineau, the nearest rail connection prior to 1902, had meant a three-day wagon trip for Westhope community citizens for supplies and other amenities. Now, Westhope became the center for a major grain and livestock marketing area. In its early years Westhope had eight elevators; at present two modern facilities have more storage capacity and serve the farming community well.

Significant changes occurred in the community in 1920: US 83 was routed through town; a modern hotel, The Gateway, was constructed; and a Customs and Immigration Station was built on the United States-Canadian border. Other commercial enterprises and services were also established to support the area.

Westhope is blessed with three strong church denominations: Roman Catholic, Lutheran, and Presbyterian. The latter two have built new sanctuaries recently.

Today, streets are paved with curb and gutter, and this combined with well-tended yards and homes give the town a very attractive appearance. A good fire department and an ambulance service add to the assets of the community.

The school system is outstanding, the physical facilities having been completely rebuilt since the fire destroyed the old structure on December 25, 1949.

In 1952 the first oil well was developed in the area, providing employment and adding a rich source of income for the community.

The business district has suffered fires. In 1969 Main Street lost four buildings and in 1982 a new Gateway Motel, Cafe, and Lounge opened after an old structure burned.

Medical and dental needs are met by a satellite clinic which adjoins a 59-bed nursing home facility, opened in 1957 and administered and supported by the Lutheran churches in the surrounding area.

Recreation facilities include a fully modern Country Club with a fine club house and a challenging eighteen-hole golf course which overlooks the Souris River. The community also maintains a swimming pool, tennis courts, a baseball complex, play grounds, and a lighted football field for evening game enjoyment.

Westhope citizens are hard-working, dedicated, and always willing to help in any way to better their community. After all, Westhope's motto for years has been: "We make progress a practice, not a promise."

Present day Public School in Westhope, North Dakota

Homes and the Westhope Public School - 1908

The town of Westhope, North Dakota - 1910

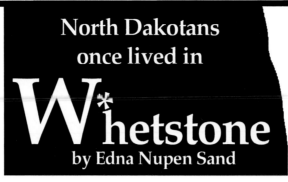

North Dakotans once lived in W*hetstone
by Edna Nupen Sand

This town was constructed about ten and one-half miles west of Killdeer, along the Killdeer to Grassy Butte wagon trail and mail route about one-fourth mile west of Mountain Creek. Old North Dakota 25 was later constructed along this route. It is now designated North Dakota 200.

The origin of the town's name is unclear. One version suggests that it was named for Jack F. Whetstone, the mayor of Killdeer who in partnership with Henry Schwartz and his wife had built a store. Another version suggests it was named for Whetstone Buttes, a range of hills topped by a peculiar sandstone formation hard enough that Indians and early settlers used it for sharpening tools and weapons.

A general store, lodging-house-restaurant, livery barn, and blacksmith shop were built during the late fall and winter of 1915-1916 and opened for business in the spring. A mail delivery point was also established.

Henry Schwartz and his wife operated the store which they had built in partnership with Jack F. Whetstone; they eventually purchased his interest. Besides selling merchandise the store bought cream, butter, eggs, furs, and hides and during the winter put up ice from Mountain Creek and Spring Creek. Ole Klevegard and his wife operated the lodging-house-restaurant and the livery barn which was destroyed by a prairie fire in 1917. They promptly rebuilt and continued to provide meals and lodging for travellers and feed and shelter for their horses until the early 1920s when it became evident that motor vehicles would replace horse transportation. A man remembered only as "Fritz" and his unknown partner operated the blacksmith shop until they both joined the armed forces during World War I. The shop was last operated by Oscar Johnson of Grassy Butte; he quit in 1922 and sold the building.

In 1916 Whetstone celebrated the Fourth of July with a rodeo, sports events, an evening fireworks display which included roman candles, sparklers, rockets, and hot-air balloons and a dance on a floor specifically built for that purpose. Called a "bowery" it had a roof overlaced with brush.

Locals formed a Home Guard Company and conducted drills and practices during 1917 and 1918. The July 4, 1918 celebration, attended by a large crowd, included patriotic speeches given by local men and an evening dance. Thunderstorms kept most of the activities indoors.

Met in Killdeer by a local delegation and conducted to Whetstone, Lynn J. Frazier, the state's first Nonpartisan League governor, was the featured speaker at the 1921 Fourth of July celebration. The day's festivities concluded with a barn dance at the Johnny Johnson farm.

Throughout its history Whetstone was a favorite place for meetings, for people of the community to get together to visit, play cards and even to hold church services in the store when it was too cold to hold them in the little church on the hill.

A baseball team was organized in the late 1920s and was active until the early 1930s. It played such teams as Oakdale, Grassy Butte, Little Knife, and Werner.

In the fall of 1927 the general store was sold to Herman and Christina Nupen who together with their five daughters operated it until July 1942. Nupen dismantled the building and used the materials to construct a home at the foot of the Killdeer Mountains, near the South Gap.

The Whetstone Cemetery and Chapel are located a couple of hundred yards west-southwest of the original Whetstone townsite and are carefully maintained by local folk, many of them descendants of the original settlers.

One always believes one's own town to be more stupid than any other.

George Elliot,
Middlemarch, Book II, XVI, 1872

Whetstone, North Dakota - early 1920s

Salute to Selfridge

Our home town is a small town,
As most folks would define small.
But to us it will always be,
The Number One Town of all.

I was born and raised here,
My sons were too, you see.
So if I sound partial to it,
That was intended to be.

Small town folks are friendly,
They all know each other by name.
About our city cousins,
We could never say the same.

When I die and go to heaven,
As someday, I trust I will do.
I hope if there are any small towns,
I will live in one up there too.

by Eva Kelsch
Selfridge Jubilee, 1911-1961, p. 141

Willow City was one of many towns established as a result of the state's expanding railroad system. During 1886-1887 the St. Paul, Minneapolis and Manitoba Railroad Company (Great Northern) extended its system by building a branch line northwest to Bottineau from its main line at Rugby Junction. It established a station in the early summer of 1887, near where the line crossed the Willow Creek, and named it Willow City, after the creek and its abundance of willow saplings which lined its banks.

281 North Dakotans live in W*illow City

by Diana Sanderson

One of the oldest towns in Bottineau County it was originally named McRae when an inland post office was established there in November 1886 and Roderick McRae was named postmaster. In November 1889 the name was changed to Willow City. Rural free delivery was established in the early 1920s.

The townsite itself was platted by the Northwest Land Company of Moorhead, Minnesota in January 1889. In April 1890 Willow City was organized as a village and held its first election. In 1906 it was incorporated as a city; Angus Crites was elected its first mayor. The same year a city hall was built; it housed the council chambers, jail, and fire department and served as a schoolhouse when a fire destroyed the school.

Notre Dame Academy, a Roman Catholic boarding school, opened its doors in 1907, the same year Willow City Public School held its first high school graduation exercise for a class of one. Notre Dame Academy remained in operation for sixty-two years closing its doors in 1968. The Willow City public school district was reorganized in the fifties; the Overly school district and surrounding rural districts became part of the local school system.

In June 1907 a fire swept through main street and destroyed many business establishments: lost were two hotels, four general stores, two drug stores, and many other businesses. After this disaster the city fathers joined forces to replace the last wooden structures with brick buildings. There have been other fires throughout the years but they have been confined to isolated buildings.

The city has had an active fire department through the years and in 1956 the Willow City Rural Fire Department was organized. It purchased the Diepolder implement building which houses three fire trucks and an ambulance in part of the structure. The other part has been converted to a Community Hall and is used by every organization in town. The city is blessed with an abundance of good water and in the 1950s a city-wide water system was installed with a water tower, sewage system, and a lagoon.

Five churches serve the city: the First Lutheran, St. Paul Lutheran, Roman Catholic, Presbyterian, and the Church of God.

The city's population has fluctuated through the years. Today, it is a thriving, bustling, active, and caring community; a community where everyone knows everyone else. It's a great place to work and raise a family.

Main Street Willow City, North Dakota

Main Street Willow City, North Dakota - ca. 1905

There's more mischief in the village than comes to one's ears.

Cervantes
Don Quixote, Pt. i, Ch. 46

Wilton, a melting pot of Ukrainians, Germans, Scandinavians, and other nationalities, has one asset that has influenced its growth since its beginning: a favorable location. In early days it sat on the rim of one of the largest lignite deposits in the world; now it is situated on US 83, near Bismarck which makes medical assistance, shopping opportunities, and employment readily available.

In 1898 General William D. Washburn, former United States Senator from Minnesota and flour industrialist from Minneapolis, purchased 40,000 acres of Northern Pacific grant lands for the purpose of developing its resources and promoting settlement.

In May 1899 he selected a town site — four blocks in Burleigh and eleven blocks in McLean County — which he named Wilton for his former home in Maine. The first post office was established on June 20, 1899 with Philip K. Eastman as postmaster.

Washburn realized that if he wanted to populate the area and develop coal mines it would be advantageous to construct a railroad to his land. He organized the Washburn, Bismarck and Fort Buford Railroad in May 1899 and sold it to the Soo Line in 1904. F. M. Pettigrove was the first station master. The depot (which is on the National Register of Historic Places) has drawn attention because of its unusual architecture: its upper story, shaped like an oriental pagoda, is thought to be influenced by Washburn's wife, who was interested in the Orient.

In 1901 the mine opened which became by 1907 the largest lignite mine in North Dakota with as many as 900 Ukrainian, Austrian, and Hungarian miners and a payroll of $90,000 per month. A brick factory producing 20,000 bricks daily was also operating.

Because of the mines Wilton had two suburbs, Chapin and Langhorne. Chapin had the large loading tipple and a large hotel, called the Beanery. With its forty-eight rooms for single men it provided house cleaning employment for many local women. It was also the site for dances, home talent plays, and card parties. Langhorne was the home of many miners who built larger homes than those in Chapin.

Truax-Traer began open pit stripmining, using huge machines, when they purchased the mine in 1930. The consequent loss of jobs forced many miners to move their houses from Chapin and Langhorne two miles east to Macomber, named after Washburn's associate, W. P. Macomber, who came in 1899 to sell land, bring in settlers, and explore the rumored lignite deposits. He was called the Father of Wilton. In the mid-1940s the company moved to Hazen, leaving behind huge ridges of spill piles as evidence of their existence here.

The first building to be erected in Wilton was Michelson's Store, the second was Robert Cotton's Livery Barn. A grain elevator was built that summer of 1899. A number of tents housed people in the process of building the town. The Jacob Killians were already on their farm at Wilton's south edge in 1887. It was a stopping place for settlers, supplying them with food and shelter while they sought land and built their homes.

Wilton has five established churches

Wilton in 1908

St. Peter and Paul Ukrainian Catholic Church

within its city limits and one in the rural area outside town. In 1903 the First Presbyterians built a chapel and in 1929 they built their present church. It has had a great Christian influence on the lives of its young people; many have entered the service of their church.

The Ukrainian Greek Orthodox Church, another Wilton landmark, is on the National Register of Historic Places. Built by Ukrainians who fled Russia in search of freedom long before the Communist Revolution it is no longer in use, but it is well kept.

The Sacred Heart Church was built in 1906; it was replaced by a new brick structure in 1959. The St. Peter and Paul Ukrainian Catholic Church was constructed in 1890 northeast of town but was moved into the city to better accommodate the many miners who lived there.

The Mission Evangelical Free Church had its beginning as a Swedish Mission Church in 1895 east of Wilton. It affiliated with the Evangelical Free Church of America in 1952 and built a new structure within the city in 1978. Organized by Swedish settlers in 1893 Sunne Lutheran Church remains rural, but serves many Wilton residents.

Wilton had two doctors, Dr. Thompson and Dr. Thelan. Thompson,

came in 1901 as the mine doctor; delivered the town's first baby, Edwin Aune on February 14, 1902; and lived in Wilton the remainder of his life. Aune, too, lived in the community until his death in 1982. Thelan came as the Northern Pacific Railroad physician and retired many years later because of ill health.

The first school, with one teacher, was built in town in 1901. In 1911 a large brick structure was erected and in 1952 a gymnasium, shower rooms, and some classrooms were added. In 1966 a new high school was constructed and in 1978 a new elementary school. To date the school has issued 1,433 high school diplomas. The school is the community's focal point with its basketball, football,

dramas, concerts, proms, and other programs.

Wilton has two outstanding volunteer services, the ambulance and the fire department which are on call at all times. It has two stores, two bars, two garages, two retirement homes, a bank, drugstore, cafe, and laundromat.

It has an energetic Senior Citizen Club with about 125 members. Other clubs are the American Legion and Auxiliary, Lions, Homemakers, and Scouts.

Wilton has had an interesting and colorful history: good times and bad times. But it is a good place to live and enjoy the great outdoors. It is a place where neighbor knows neighbor.

The 1924 Wilton High Girls' Basketball Team
(left to right, front to back: Ella Gilmore, Minnie Flinn,
Victoria Hefta, Violet Larson,
Nellie Livergood, Erma Armstrong, Bonnie Drewer, Matilda Spitzer)

Home Town of 1,171 North Dakotans
Wishek

by Howard Breitling &
Lillian W. Dempsey ✳

Established in 1898, Wishek stands at the site where the Missouri River Division of the Minneapolis, St. Paul and Sault Ste Marie Railroad (now Soo Line) (built west from Kulm that year) met with the Aberdeen, Bismarck & Northwestern tracks. The townsite platted there in September was named for John H. Wishek, a pioneer entrepreneur, banker, politician, and builder who was responsible for securing the right-of-way between Kulm and the junction. Wishek, later known as "Father Wishek," located some ten thousand settlers on lands in the region.

Many of the settlers were German-Russian immigrants from South Dakota; the area settled by German people has remained predominantly German.

After the Soo Line built the Pollock branch south out of Wishek in 1901,

the town became a freight division point and an important railroad center. For years it maintained an eight-stall roundhouse and extensive car repair yards there. As many as twelve train crews worked out of the town at one time, but use of the roundhouse discontinued and the repair yards were moved to Enderlin in the 1930s.

The First State Bank, the first in McIntosh County, was chartered in 1898 by its founder John H. Wishek; it continued to operate until 1940. The Security State Bank organized by John J. Doyle in 1909 has functioned without interruption since its inception. Both banks gave support to early businesses such as the Doyle grain flat house, 1898; Bailey's Livery and Feed; Nickisch's Implement and Blacksmith Shop; the Hill House and the Sheridan House, two large hotel-restaurants operated by Mrs. Jenny Hill and Mrs. Carrie Sheridan in 1898; lumberyards; the Herr and Ackerman groceries; Krien fuel and coal; railroad crews; teamsters; and land buyers.

In 1918 E. P. Pfeifle began selling Chevrolet automobiles. Eventually,

competitors Ackerman and Preszler began selling Fords.

School was held as early as 1898 in the Palm building on main street. Two years later the Youngstown School District purchased block seven in the center of Wishek and erected a temporary school. In 1908 a six-room, two-story white frame building was completed and three years later the first eighth grade class was graduated. Two-year high school courses were offered until 1919 when the district completed a two-story brick high school building with a basement auditorium and offered a full four year curriculum. The first senior class graduated in 1921.

A Works Progress Administration (WPA) project, sponsored by the city which leased the site from the school district, resulted in the construction of an unusual native-stone and concrete auditorium with additional rooms on the second story designed for the use of the Home Economics Department. Completed in 1942, it now houses the Wishek Civic Center.

In 1960, under a state re-organization law, Wishek School District No. 19 began serving former districts in Logan and McIntosh counties. Enrollments increased by over sixty percent and school patrons purchased a ten-acre site on Wishek's east side and built an elementary and junior high school complex which was ready for occupancy in 1962. In 1964-1965 a National Guard Armory was erected on the school site and an agreement was reached which enabled the district to use the facility for physical education and classroom activities.

A senior high school building was completed in 1972. That summer the National Guard constructed a parking lot and an athletic field, marking the completion of an ideal complex to educate Wishek's youth.

Early church services in the community were non-denominational services conducted by pastors-at-large in the Palm building. As individual denominations organized and built churches, lots were provided by Wishek. The first, Grace Presbyte-

Main Street Wishek, North Dakota - 1914

rian, organized and built in 1904, but gave up its charter in the 1950s after a decline in membership. In subsequent years various churches organized, grew, prospered and built facilities: Saint Luke's Lutheran Church in 1905; First Baptist Church in 1908; Saint John's Congregational Church in 1912 (through a series of merges now the United Church of Christ); Wishek Reformed Church in 1917 (later merged with the United Church of Christ); the Evangelical United Brethren in 1918; and Saint Patrick's Catholic Church in 1925.

Several citizens joined forces with the Association of Commerce in 1925 to plan a park in an unplatted area on the southern edge of town, donated by the Wishek Investment Company. Trees and shrubs were planted and later shelter houses, fireplaces, and tennis courts were built. A swimming pool and bathhouse were completed in 1940 and a baseball and football field along with camping facilities were provided in later years.

The town's isolation prompted the community to develop an airport; runways were laid out in 1947 and an airport commission was appointed in October 1969. Subsequent improvements were made: three hangers are on the site; the commission has purchased an additional eighty-acre tract to realign the runway; an additional 2,000 feet has been added to the runway; and runway lights have been installed.

As early as 1949 plans were laid to build a community hospital; it began operation in April 1954. Ten years later an addition was dedicated. To comply with recent state requirements an extensive remodeling project and a new addition was completed in November 1987. The community also boasts of its Retirement and Nursing Home which had its inception in 1958. A ninety-five bed skilled care facility was completed and dedicated in October 1964. Thirty apartments for the elderly were added in 1978.

Wishek has many active clubs and organizations, some since the 1920s and earlier: Independent Order of Odd Fellows, the town's first fraternal organization chartered in 1906;

Wishek Round House - 1901-1903

Wishek City Auditorium

Fred Kelle Post of the American Legion; Wishek Volunteer Fire Department; GFWC Wishek Civic League; Boy and Girl Scouts; Tri-County Fair Association; Wishek Wildlife Club; Lions Club; Eagles Club; Jaycees and Jaycee Women; and several Extension 4-H and Homemakers groups.

Women have played an important role in the community's history. Mrs. Jennie Hill and Mrs. Carrie Sheridan contributed to the town's founding. In later years Mrs. Esther Herr served as the first woman school board member in this century, serving from

1959 to 1962; Mrs. Lillian Dempsey served as the first city magistrate from 1977 to 1984; and Mrs. Jonna Hochhalter serves as mayor from 1986 to 1990.

Wishek is known statewide for its annual fall festival, Sauerkraut Day, which has been sponsored by the community for over fifty years. The Tri-County Fair — McIntosh, Logan, and Emmons — dates from 1926 and has functioned continually except for several years during World War II.

Wyndmere, a neat little city in the eastern part of North Dakota, is located at the junction of North Dakota 13 and 18.

There is no record of who named the town, but legend has it that the name is of English origin, composed of two words: *Wynd*, a narrow land and *Mere*, a pool or lake. A narrow lane of pools or lakes apparently described the topography in early days before the land was dredged and ditched.

The town originated in 1883 when the Wyndmere station was estab-

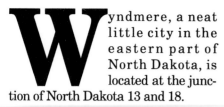

501 North Dakotans live in

Wyndmere

by Thelma Snyder ✳

lished on the Northern Pacific branch line between Wahpeton and Milnor, about a mile west of the present townsite. Joseph L. Meyer platted a 4-block townsite there in late 1883. What later became the main line of the Minneapolis, St. Paul and Sault Ste Marie Railroad (Soo Line) was constructed through the area in 1891; that line passed about a mile east of the Wyndmere station. Cyrus A. Campbell, a Soo Line townsite agent, decided to plat a new townsite where the two railroads crossed. He did so in 1899 and called it East Wyndmere. The new town soon drew many residents from Old Wyndmere and people from the small settlement of Moselle were also attracted to it. The latter had been established as a Soo Line station to serve a bonanza wheat farm known as the Cleveland Farm. The depots from Moselle and Old Wyndmere were brought to their new location and joined to make a "union depot." Other buildings moved to the new town were the Hilliard Store and the Methodist Church.

By 1900 four general stores were operating in the new town: the Hilliard Store, later known as the Odd Fellow Building, and now Paul's Electric; the George Otis Store built in 1900, now Johnson's Department Store; the Klenzing Store, since razed, on the present site of the post office; and the H. H. Berg supply house, since razed and now a parking lot for the school buses.

Churches have played a dominant role in the community's life since its beginning. The Methodist Church, moved by a rig pulled by eight horses, was first placed on the wrong site and was moved to its present location in 1900. In 1948 the building was remodeled and enlarged.

In 1901 a group of Lutheran ladies organized a Ladies Aid Society and began meeting in the homes of its members. They served monthly suppers, held bake sales, and in other ways earned money to buy the furnishings and the two lots for the Wyndmere Lutheran Church which was organized in 1904. The church building was erected in 1913-1914. From 1904 to 1913 services in the Norwegian language were held in homes, the City Hall, and the schoolhouse. Confirmation services and fu-

nerals were held in the Methodist Church. Although many changes and additions have been made over the years, the traditional white board church, with its high steeple, continues to offer a sight of spiritual inspiration.

St. John the Baptist Catholic Church was established as a mission in 1913 and was served by a priest from Lidgerwood. John Melenovsky donated three lots and the church was built at a cost of $2,648.50. In 1945 Wyndmere was raised to parish status; in 1966 the parish undertook a most important project, that of building a new church. It was erected in 1968-1969. St. John's Guild and Christian Mothers is the ladies' organization and they continue to be very active in the parish. The Catholic Youth Organization is also very active.

Wyndmere Special School District was created in 1903. The Earl School was built at that time for $7,300.00. In 1916 the first class of seven members graduated from Wyndmere High School. In 1958 school district reorganization occurred and adjacent townships and parts of townships were brought into the district. In 1962 a new Junior-Senior High School building was completed. The Earl School and the old High School were razed in 1984 and an addition to the Junior-Senior High School was built to care for the elementary grades. The Wyndmere Schools have

Early business places in Wyndmere, North Dakota

been the center of much community activity. The "Warriors" have excelled in many sports. In 1957 they were the State Class B Champs in baseball and in 1971 State Class B Champs in basketball.

Wyndmere hosted the Annual State Corn Show from 1933 until some twenty years later. In 1963 the Wyndmere Community Club organized the first Crop Show which continues today and has developed into one of the finest informative and educational shows in the state.

Located near the center of town is a recreational area called the "Rock Garden." Originally owned by "Doc" Olson it covers a half city block and is surrounded by a fortress like wall with a corner turret, all constructed of native stone. When cash was hard to come by in the 1930s clients worked off their bill by helping build the wall. Once this area was a beautiful garden with hundreds of varieties of flowers; it now provides a nice setting for picnics and youth activities.

Present day Wyndmere Public School

Today, the leading business places in Wyndmere include: Anderson Cafe and Service, C & J Cafe, Dotzenrod Implement Company, Farmers Union Oil Company, Garden State Bean Company, Haugen Farm Equipment, Hendricks Incorporated, Kelly Incorporated, Ken's Super Valu, Larson Processing and Lockers, Lincoln State Bank, Masheks Tastee Freeze, Midwest Sales and Construction, Paul's Electric, Schmit Incorporated, Siesta Motel, Tamlyn Insurance Agency, Wittenburg Enterprises, Wyndmere Custom Homes, Wyndmere Farmers Elevator, and Wyndmere Grain and Fertilizer Company Incorporated.

In 1985 Wyndmere celebrated its 100th birthday.

Rock Garden Park in Wyndmere, North Dakota

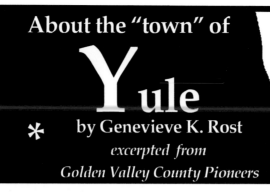
London financier Sir John Pender and his partners formed the Little Missouri Land and Stock Company in 1884. In the spring of 1883 Pender had sent Gregor Lang, a Scotsman, to explore the potential for making money in cattle ranching in the Badlands of western North Dakota. He established a ranch for Pender and managed the operation until disaster struck in the winter of 1886-1887 when most of the stock was lost. The Lang family eventually established a ranch near the Fort Keogh Crossing of the Little Missouri River, about thirteen miles northwest of Amidon.

A post office named Yule was established at the ranch in 1891 in a large store building that had been erected. Gregor's daughter, Sophia C. Lang, served as postmaster. Lincoln A. Lang, whose wedding dance was held in the building, Janet Lang, and William G. Lang also held that position. Mail was carried twice a month from Little Missouri by a pony rider.

The origin of the name is unclear. One explanation suggests that postal authorities studied the two names, Langrange and Julie, which had been requested on the petition seeking the post office, and decided to name the office Yule. Another suggests that it referred to the Christmas season.

Another early settler in the locality was Hilda Timm LaSotta Putney who came to the area with her parents in 1902, before it was surveyed. In 1905 the family filed on a homestead. There were no school houses so Hilda attended classes in the living room at the Tetly ranch for two years. Later she and her brothers and sisters walked many miles to a school which was located near what is now the Karnes Johnson ranch. Later a school was opened closer to the Timm home at the Westgaard place. She remembers riding to the Yule post office to get the mail when she was a young girl.

In 1905 Joseph K. Toft rode the freight wagon from Sentinel Butte to check out his claim at Yule. A few years later he told of many trips he made to Sentinel Butte in the winter with his team and sled, to haul in grain and haul out lumber. He said it was so cold he walked behind the sled to keep warm.

Oscar Odman came to his homestead in the area in 1906. He did his trading at Yule which was six miles south of his place. The trail past Odman's place had been used for a long time; its ruts were worn deep. A telegraph line was also built from Sentinel Butte to Yule, but when the Milwaukee Railroad reached Marmarth both the trail through Odman's yard and the telegraph line were abandoned.

It was a big day when the Northern Pacific's branch line from Beach to Ollie, Montana was completed in 1915. The Odman family drove their horses and springboard buggy sixteen miles to Ollie to watch the train come chugging in.

The Lang family built a spacious new log house at Yule. It had several bedrooms, a large kitchen, and a comfortable living and dining room. Billy, the Lang's youngest son, moved with his mother to Baker, Montana in 1908 where he built a new store, now known as Russell's Clothing Store.

After he and his mother moved to Baker, Alf Benson managed the post office until it was closed in March 1910. Benson had come from England and in 1908 his wife joined him. She was educated and talented and gave piano lessons on the grand piano at the Lang house to Hilda Timm whose father, William, cut ice to pay for them. The Lang family left the piano behind when they moved.

The Stevens family moved to the Lang ranch from Cash Township in 1926. The grand piano was still there. When the house burned to the ground in 1934 the remains of the piano were found in the basement. The Stevens family stayed at the site for several years in a bunkhouse.

In 1936 Alex LaSotta bought the Yule Ranch for taxes and added it to his holdings. After his death in 1937, his widow sold it to Nels Langdon and Andrew Johnston. They renamed it the VVV (3 V's) after a ranch Jo Johnston had owned near Watford City. John Rouzie and Dilse bought the ranch in 1960. They sold it to Russell Kiker who owned and operated it until 1974. The Kikers began remodeling the old store building to be their home. The job was completed by the Lloyd Weinreis family when they bought the ranch in 1975. They made a lovely home of the old building; members of their family are still living there.

In the dry places . . . towns, like weeds, spring up when it rains, dry up when it stops. But in a dry climate the husk of the plant remains. The stranger might find, as if preserved in amber, something of the green life that was once lived here, and the ghosts of men who have gone on to a better place. The withered towns are empty, but not uninhabited.

Wright Morris
The Works of Love, Chapter 1, 1952

The Original Yule Ranch House occupied by the Lang Family
This burned when the Stevens lived there.

(SHSND)

The phrase "small town" has come itself to carry a double layer
of meaning, at once sentimental and condescending. There is
still a belief that democracy is more idyllic at the "grass roots,"
that the business spirit is purer, that the middle class is more in-
tensely middling. There is also a feeling that by the fact of being
small the small town somehow escapes the corruptions of life in
the city and the dominant contagions that infest the more glit-
tering places. History, geography, and economics gave each
American town some distinctive traits of style that are embed-
ded in the mind, and the memory of this style is all the more
marked because of the nostalgia felt, in a largely urban America, for what seems the lost serenity of small-town childhoods.

Max Lerner
America as a Civilization, Vol. I, 1957

Z_{ap} had its beginning

Zap had its beginning when the Northern Pacific Railroad located a station named Zap along its new Knife River/Spring Creek Branch line which reached the area on November 26, 1913. The first townsite was laid out that same year on the original homestead of Jacob Kraft by L. C. Pettibone of Dawson, North Dakota, but it proved unsatisfactory.

The Tuttle Land Company, which had townsite rights on this branch and had planned to plat its Zap townsite in 1914, was outmaneuvered by a group of businessmen from the small community of Kasmer. The Zap Townsite Company, organized by J. B. Field, R. M. Stroup, and Eli Gunderson, was incorporated in December 1913 and was able to survey and plat the townsite in April 1914, thereby besting the Tuttle group. The company's property, however, was a half mile west of the Zap station and sidetrack and the railroad was reluctant to move the station to the new townsite. Company officials eventually took the problem to the State Board of Railroad Commissioners which solved it on May 31, 1915 by ordering the station moved to the townsite.

Kasimir Mastel, a German-Russian immigrant, operated a blacksmith shop on his farm which was located

The flood of 1952

near the Missouri River north of present day Zap. In March 1908 a post office called Kasmer was located there and Mastel was appointed postmaster. The Kasmer community eventually grew to include a creamery, a bank, several stores, and a newspaper, the *German-American*. Following the coming of the railroad, however, Kasmer was abandoned and businessmen and residents moved south to the new town of Zap.

The first building to be erected in Zap was a store owned by Ole Viken and Eli Gunderson. Shortly thereafter the First State Bank of Zap, managed by J. B. Field and R. M. Stroup, opened for business. Other businesses soon followed.

The origin of the town's name is uncertain. One version suggests that Pettibone named it after a coal mining hamlet in Scotland. Another, probably more accurate, suggests that it was named by the businessmen in the Tuttle Land Company, for their friend and fellow banker, John Zapp of St. Cloud, Minnesota.

Della Thompson became the town's first postmaster when she was appointed to that post on June 20, 1914.

Churches dominated community life. Immanuel Lutheran Congregation erected a small church about a mile north of Zap; it served the people for about twenty-five years. The congregation built a new church on its present site in 1928. St. Luke Lutheran Church was moved to its present site in 1938; it was a daughter parish of a rural congregation, St. John's Lutheran. Peace Congregational Church (Freundens Gemeinde) met in the schoolhouse for two years. In 1926 it erected its present structure. Zap Baptist Church was served by

clergy from Beulah until membership declined to the point where the members decided to join the Beulah Baptist Church.

The first school building was a frame structure. In 1923 the first high school department was added. In 1936 the frame building was replaced by a brick structure, built as a Works Progress Administration (WPA) project. Energy development activities resulted in increased enrollment and in 1981 a new, brick addition was constructed, adding four classrooms, a library, special education facilities, and office space. Four years later a multi-purpose steel building was erected, adding physical education, music, and drama facilities. From 1970 to 1983 the city's population increased from 271 to 625.

In 1948 the city installed a city sewer system and in 1971 it began to install a water system. It remodeled both in 1977 and again in 1983 when it built a water treatment plant and a new lagoon. In 1977 an FHA approved eight-unit elderly housing apartment building was erected. During the period 1977 to 1983 the city paved its streets and installed curbs and gutters.

Beginning in the 1920s the citizens of Zap have celebrated local industry by hosting an annual Lignite Jamboree, celebrating with parades and a carnival.

In May 1969 some 2,500 young people converged on Zap for a weekend of "fun." When local law enforcement officials couldn't control the "Zap-In" the North Dakota National Guard was called in to restore order. Martial law was declared by the governor on May 10. Reports of the incident were published in newspapers around the world, one as far away as Lahore, Pakistan.

Fine arts have always been important in Zap. In 1987 the Zap School Band was selected as one of two school bands in North Dakota to represent the state at the 10th annual

Gunderson Store at Kasmer
Moved to Zap from Kasmer in 1914

World Invitational Music Awards festival in Florida. The community launched a fund-raising effort, raising over $16,000 to send the band to the event.

The city currently boasts a nationally recognized professional artist in residence, and a young professional actor working in California.

Town seems to sharpen a man's appetite. A man is hungry all day long. A man is perpetually eating.

Charles Dickens,
***David Copperfield*, XXIV,**
1849-1850

Parade down Main Street Zap, North Dakota - 1940

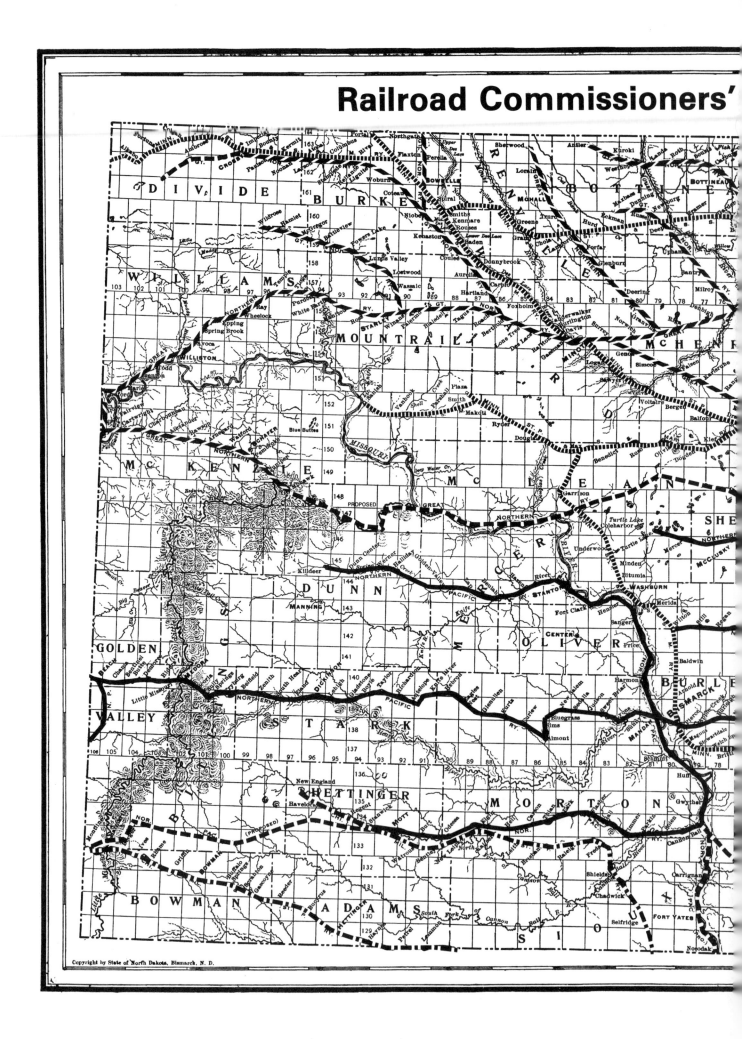

p of North Dakota - 1914

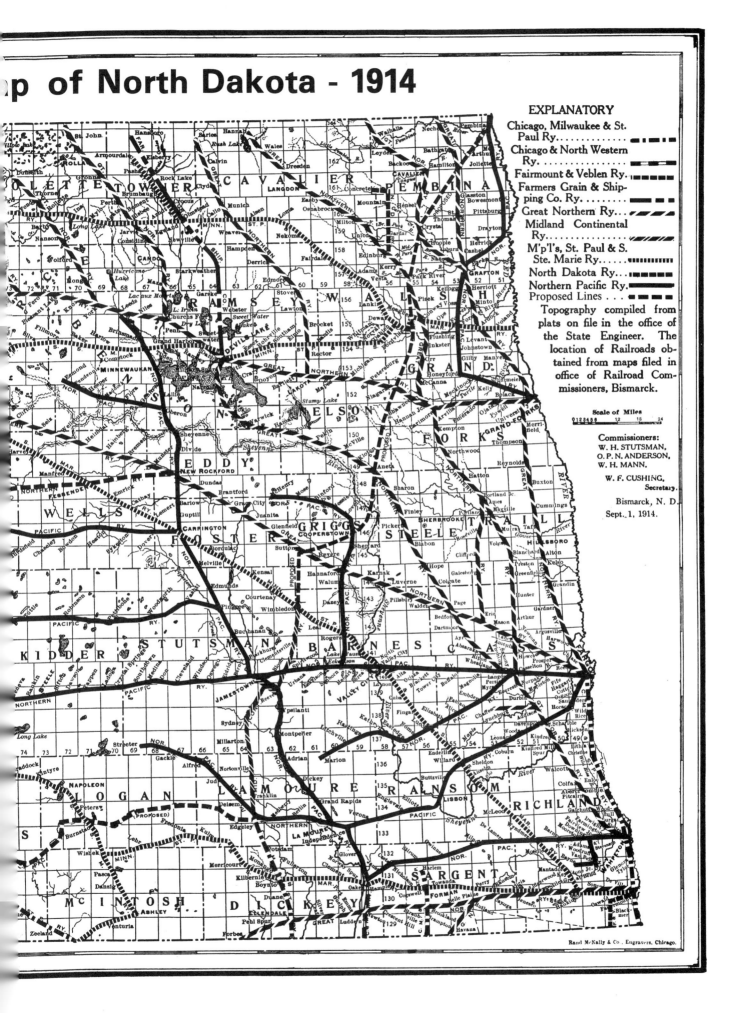

EXPLANATORY

Chicago, Milwaukee & St. Paul Ry.............
Chicago & North Western Ry. ....
Fairmount & Veblen Ry. ..
Farmers Grain & Shipping Co. Ry. ....
Great Northern Ry...
Midland Continental Ry.............
M'p'l's, St. Paul & S. Ste. Marie Ry...
North Dakota Ry...
Northern Pacific Ry.
Proposed Lines . . .

Topography compiled from plats on file in the office of the State Engineer. The location of Railroads obtained from maps filed in office of Railroad Commissioners, Bismarck.

Scale of Miles

Commissioners:
W. H. STUTSMAN,
O. P. N. ANDERSON,
W. H. MANN.

W. F. CUSHING,
Secretary.

Bismarck, N. D.
Sept. 1, 1914.

Rand McNally & Co., Engravers, Chicago.